The Ironic World of
EVELYN
WAUGH

Photograph by Felix H. Man, c. 1943 (courtesy of the National Portrait Gallery, London, used by permission of Mrs. Felix Man)

The Ironic World of
EVELYN WAUGH

A Study of Eight Novels

FREDERICK L. BEATY

assisted by Martha Ross Beaty

NORTHERN ILLINOIS UNIVERSITY PRESS

DeKalb   1992

© 1992 by Northern Illinois University Press
Published by the Northern Illinois University Press, DeKalb,
Illinois 60115
Manufactured in the United States using acid-free paper ∞
Design by Julia Fauci

Library of Congress Cataloging-in-Publication Data
Beaty, Frederick L. 1926-
    The ironic world of Evelyn Waugh : a study of eight
novels / Frederick L. Beaty.
      p. cm.
    Includes bibliographical references and index.
    ISBN 0-87580-171-4 (alk. paper)
    1. Waugh, Evelyn, 1903-1966—Criticism and
interpretation.   2. Irony in literature.   I. Title.
    PR6045.A97Z6165   1992
823'.912—dc20   92-1305
                    CIP

To

Zachary
Daniel
James
Andrea
Sarah

Contents

The Ironic World of
EVELYN
WAUGH

Introduction

THE IRONIC MODE looms very large in much of Evelyn Waugh's fiction; but despite passing references to it by Waugh scholars, its full significance has not been generally recognized. In the belief that irony is fundamentally interwoven into the fabric of his writing—much as modern ironologists have perceived it to be in the universal condition of humanity—I have undertaken to examine its nature and functions as Waugh applied them to theme, plot, and character. I believe that a careful study of his irony and his ironic perspective not only enhances an enjoyment of his work but is crucial to an understanding of his artistry.

Yet the analysis of irony, though fascinating, can be a precarious undertaking. When one approaches something essentially indirect and tentative in a straightforward manner, there is always some short-term risk of diluting its impact and diminishing its fragile charms. Irony's inherent characteristics—subtlety, obliquity, complexity, sophistication, through which it evokes in the reader a spontaneous awareness of its import—do not easily weather direct inspection. But these characteristics are precisely the ones that in the long run make close examination worthwhile. The ramifications of irony are so extensive and its place in both literature and life so important that whatever is temporarily lost through dissection should be far outweighed by the discovery of its inner workings.

Irony has been recognized as a literary concept since its beginnings in ancient Greece, but until the eighteenth century it was traditionally viewed, rather narrowly, as a rhetorical device. Since then, the term has been expanded to encompass not only human speech but human actions, philosophical speculations, and perspectives on art. Its scope and diversity have increased so enormously that there seems to be no succinct definition for the subject as a whole. The problem of capturing its essence is well summed up in Wayne Booth's assertion that "there is no agreement among critics about what irony is, and many would hold to the romantic claim . . . that its very spirit and value are violated by the effort to be clear about it."[1] Yet despite general recognition of the concept's slipperiness, almost every critic tries to encapsulate it. D. C. Muecke's statement "that the art of irony is the art of saying something without really saying it"[2] may be as specific and as flexible a characterization of this continuing explosion of ideas as is possible.

But even if irony defies complete crystallization, a breakdown of its essential elements and their interrelationship does help to bring it into clearer focus; and the endeavors of recent ironologists and literary scholars have been extremely valuable. Despite certain differences in semantics and methods of dissection, most critics seem to agree on irony's fundamental ingredients. According to this consensus, there must always be an element of contrast, ranging from a direct contradiction through various grades of incongruity, difference, or undermining to the slightest hint of diminution or retraction. The most frequently employed ironic discrepancies are between appearance and reality or between the expected and the unexpected. To be truly ironic, the disparity must also involve the element of innocence—either as confident unawareness on the part of a victim or as pretended naiveté on the part of an ironist. The ironist is frequently referred to as an *eiron;* the victim is often called an *alazon* when his victimization is stressed or a naïf when his innocence is emphasized. Moreover, the unexpected event happening to an *alazon* or naïf should be one that he expects *not* to occur; an event that he merely does not expect is not usually considered ironic. A third essential for irony is some degree of objective detachment on the part of the ironist, whether author, narrator, or character.

Ironies are ordinarily divided into two main categories—the rhetorical or verbal, in which the speaker is being ironical, and the situational or observable, in which occurrences are seen to be ironic. In the rhetorical variety the ironist, dissembling innocence or ignorance, plays his tricks by his choice and arrangement of words; and Waugh uses many verbal or rhetorical techniques, including understatement, overstatement, misrepresentation, ambiguity, double entendre, internal contradiction, innuendo, analogy, fallacious reasoning, caricature, parody, burlesque, and the mock-heroic. Waugh occasionally employs an unusual form of verbal irony known as *ingénu*, which occurs when the ironist, instead of speaking in his own voice of pretended innocence, utters the truth directly through a character who unknowingly speaks for him.

Situational irony in Waugh's writing occurs in plot, circumstance, theme, or in characters' reactions, attitudes, and motives. It can be displayed through action, symbol, or the substance (not the language) of a statement. This kind of irony frequently occurs as a sequence of events, in which the ironic incongruity is between the expectation and the outcome, or as a dramatic moment, in which the irony can be immediately grasped by an observer—the reader or a character—who is already aware of what the naïf is about to discover. Muecke explains the difference between the effects of these two kinds of irony as similar to that between "surprise" (in an irony of events) and "suspense" (in dramatic irony). Other types of situational irony prevalent in Waugh's fiction are simple incongruity (mere juxtaposition of contraries), dilemma (choices appearing equally bad or equally good), irrationality or misapprehension (either a misuse of logic or a use of logic leading to an illogical conclusion), deliberate deceit (the irony of a lie being in its very plausibility), foreshadowing (something taking on a different meaning in the light of subsequent events than was originally intended or interpreted), self-deception (holding to a belief that is known or proved to be false), and self-betrayal (revealing the opposite of what one intends or expects to reveal). In these cases, too, there should be at least a shade of belief or expectation that something will *not* happen.

Forming the chaotic background in much of Waugh's early fiction is a type of irony in which contrarieties assume universal proportions. Variously referred to as general, philosophical, metaphysical, world, or cosmic irony (though these terms are by no means used synonymously), it presents a view of the whole universe as made up of inherent contradictions and portrays all humanity as the innocently unaware victim of impossible situations. Waugh also incorporates some concepts and techniques associated with romantic irony, which, by approaching art as a duality existing in both the real world and the imagination, reveals the contradictions within the art itself. Examples from the novels include the breaking and remaking of the artistic illusion, in addition to frequent use of indeterminacy and unresolved paradox.

This brief overview of irony's basic characteristics is intended only to serve as a frame of reference for the following detailed analyses of individual Waugh novels, where concrete examples will further elucidate, and be elucidated by, specific types of ironies. The whole range of irony is far too complicated to be fully represented here. It has been the subject of many lengthy volumes covering virtually all of literature. It has been approached from differing points of view and been subjected to extraordinary analytical scrutiny. Since much of that work has little bearing on Waugh's practice, I have tried rather to extract what does illuminate his use of irony.

Especially helpful for my study have been Douglas C. Muecke's *The Compass of Irony* (1969), *Irony* (1970), and *Irony and the Ironic* (1982); Norman D. Knox's "Irony," in *Dictionary of the History of Ideas* (1973-74); Wayne C. Booth's *A Rhetoric of Irony* (1974); and Eleanor N. Hutchens's *Irony in "Tom Jones"* (1965). Muecke's three volumes, containing many pertinent examples, are invariably clear and incisive explorations into the nature and effects of irony. *The Compass of Irony* is particularly comprehensive and sophisticated, explaining the subject in great depth as well as breadth. Muecke not only pursues the applications, implications, and nuances of each type of irony but also examines its relationship to, and distinction from, other types of irony. Knox's classification of all ironies according to the victim's fate, the attitude toward the victim, and the concept of reality involved provides useful, if somewhat rigid, differentiations. Booth's outstanding contribution is his questioning method for detecting and interpreting an irony through rejection of its literal meaning and reconstruction of its intended meaning. Booth suggests possible clues and strategies to be employed but warns of the pitfalls involved in carrying the process too far (over-reading) or in not carrying it far enough (under-reading). Hutchens's admirable literary critique of Fielding's irony deals with all aspects of *Tom Jones*, including plot, theme, and character portrayal, but gives particular attention to verbal irony by showing in great detail how various subtle shifts in tone or meaning affect the text and the reader's interpretation of it.

In applying the insights of these and other critics to Waugh's art, I have striven to use as generic or self-explanatory a vocabulary as

possible, except when a manifestation of his irony is better elucidated through the phraseology of a particular critic. Although
those who deal with irony seem to be moving in the direction of a
more uniform system of reference, there is at present no one set of
definitive categorical terms common to all. Critics sometimes use
different labels when referring to identical kinds of irony or the
same label when indicating different varieties. Probably this situation is unavoidable because of the subject's inherent nature, since
the name chosen for a particular irony depends on the variables of
context and point of view. The difficulties involved in nomencla-
ture, as well as the complexities of interpretation, are clearly illustrated in a passage from Muecke. Concerning the irony of a
democracy having to defend its ideals against a hostile totalitarian
state by adopting totalitarian methods, he explains:

> If we look at this as something happening contrary to our expectations
> and intentions we call it an Irony of Events. If we see others confidently
> unaware that this has happened we call it Dramatic Irony. If we hear
> one of our leaders defending totalitarian measures as a bulwark against
> totalitarianism we might see it as Irony of Self-betrayal. If we see the
> situation as a dilemma we call it Irony of Dilemma. We could even iso-
> late and juxtapose exactly parallel incidents from the opposed camps
> and speak of Irony of Simple Incongruity.[3]

Although I have attached labels where they seemed most useful or
appropriate and have tried to employ those most commonly understood, I have intentionally avoided tagging every instance of irony.
My main purpose is to show how irony functions to add unstated
and often crucial meaning to Waugh's text.

Irony as Waugh's Perspective and Method

*E*velyn Waugh's consummate skill as an ironist is especially evident in his most highly acclaimed fiction, and one may reasonably assert that the appeal of particular works in his canon is closely related to their success in the ironic mode. Certainly his first five novels—*Decline and Fall, Vile Bodies, Black Mischief, A Handful of Dust,* and *Scoop*—display a distinctive art that depends upon their author's ability to remain emotionally disengaged from his characters and their wildly chaotic environments. As the ironic perspective that permits a nonjudgmental reveling in the world's absurdities and incongruities gradually wanes in these early novels, Waugh's tendency to stand back from his creations with seemingly cavalier detachment undergoes noticeable alteration. With the subsequent introduction of a first-person narrator in *Work Suspended* and a deepening concern for character development in both that fragment and *Put Out More Flags*, a more direct and seriously involved approach begins to take hold.

With *Brideshead Revisited*, the first of Waugh's novels to depict a Catholic rather than a neopagan environment, the change becomes profound. The enunciation of a positive spiritual norm, absolute and unequivocally expressed, offers an alternative to mundane disorder and obliges the author, through a highly subjective first-person narrator, to utter moral pronouncements that are irreconcilable with irony on a philosophical plane. On the technical level, however, the work is filled with a great deal of vibrant irony, notably in character presentation and sometimes even with regard to religion. In the increasingly somber development of Waugh's later fiction—owing possibly to advancing age, disillusionment with wartime experiences, and reliance on the certainties provided by Catholic faith—only *The Loved One* represents an anomalous reversion to his earliest mode, though modified by graveyard humor and underlying religious conviction. Thereafter the brilliant ironic light that suffuses the most celebrated of his works flickers only on rare occasions. This is not to suggest that Waugh's later novels do not show an increasing maturity in other respects—such as mastery of plot and structure, psychological understanding of humanity, and moral perception—but that the seriousness and directness required by these advances preclude the light touch, the obliquity, and the disengagement demanded by irony. Nor does Waugh completely abandon irony as a technical device. Traces of it surface periodically in the autobiographical *Ordeal of Gilbert Pinfold* and in such manifestly religious compositions as *Helena* and the war trilogy, *Sword of Honour*; but in these works the dominant world view is no longer ironic.

The purpose of this study is to focus on the novels of Evelyn Waugh that are predominantly ironic—works that evince irony both as a way of perceiving life and as an artistic device for representing its unresolved paradoxes. Certainly before Waugh reached middle age, an ironic perspective seems to have been his instinctive way of confronting life's irrational conflicts. Irony also characterized the world view—or *épistème*, as Michel Foucault has called it in *The Archaeology of Knowledge*—prevailing in the modernist age among intellectuals who challenged the validity of traditional art forms, discursive practices, institutions, human sciences, and ethical codes.[1] Therefore it became for Waugh a most congenial aesthetic means of depicting the existential dilemma of modern man. That such an approach was virtually ingrained in him can be established from comments by his friends, his own recollections of youthful development, and a variety of his literary endeavors.

Waugh's friends saw in him a tendency to enjoy and even devise incongruities. The description Harold Acton provided Christopher Sykes for the authorized biography asserts of him in those uproarious days at Oxford: "His vision was strongly tinged with irony and he revelled in the absurdities of our acquaintances, the crankiness of certain dons. Neither he nor I affected gravity, 'the joy of imbeciles,' as Montesquieu defined it, but we took our pleasures seriously."[2] Akin to his inclination to indulge in playful, sometimes deceptive, provocation was a penchant for teasing. Nancy Mitford referred to it and to the resultant pleasure derived from shocking people as "one of the clues to Evelyn's strange nature."[3] Another old friend, Anthony Powell, also observed that Waugh "always delighted in teasing."[4] With tongue in cheek, Waugh himself suggested to Cyril Connolly that an incongruous combination of *The Loved One* and an essay on Ronald Knox in the same issue of *Horizon* would provide "a good tease" for both his supporters and his detractors.[5] Inevitably the aspect of his personality that delighted in conflicting dualities spilled over into his writings; teasing on the personal level readily translated into ironic rhetoric on the literary plane. In much the same way that he sported with acquaintances, he played with his characters and readers, withholding information from these deceived "victims" until some revelation would open their eyes. Waugh's fictional use of this approach is especially obvious in the opening scenes of *The Loved One* and *Love Among the Ruins*, where he misleads the reader into making false deductions about the location, only to shatter the illusions he himself has created.

This interest in the contrarieties typical of irony seems to have arisen quite early, for Waugh admits in his unfinished autobiography, *A Little Learning*, that as an adolescent he held "mutually contradictory principles" without being bothered by logical conflicts.[6] Although at Oxford he would declare himself a Tory, at Lancing he sometimes "pretended to be a socialist" and at other times "advocated the restoration of the Stuarts, anarchism and the rule of a hereditary caste"—always with a desire to startle his audience. In debates at Lancing his disputations were equally slippery. It was apparently "the fad" in the school's debating society to speak against one's own views since it would not be challenging enough to argue for something in which one believed.[7] Assuming that any issue might be persuasively defended or attacked from a particular perspective if the argument were sufficiently impressive, speakers sought strikingly original, even eccentric, approaches. Such emphasis on rhetoric rather than conviction inevitably fostered a kind of suspended judgment.

It was natural that Waugh should subsequently have gravitated to the Oxford Union, famous for its brilliant debates in a style that Christopher Hollis has described as "a parody of Parliament."[8] Oxford debaters often treated serious topics in a half-jocular fashion and employed exaggerated solemnity for mockery. The most celebrated of them strove to convince listeners not through logic alone but through disarmingly clever parries against somber adversaries. Hollis, in his account of a 1921 Union debate between American and English teams, remarked that the visiting Americans seemed "deadly serious" while the Oxonians, by contrast, "appeared casual, flippant and inconsequent."[9] A wittily ironical approach was generally considered to be the distinguishing feature of a Union debater, and Waugh attributed Hollis's remarkable success as a Union speaker to the fact that he had "one particular audience" whom he could address with assurance "that every allusion and every turn of irony would be recognised."[10] While Waugh conceded that this stylized oratorical manner was deemed "frivolous" when carried over into the House of Commons,[11] he was clearly attracted to it, and his autobiography establishes how deeply engrossed in it he became. He not only participated eagerly in the debates but reported on them for two undergraduate publications; and though, by his own admission, he was not an impressive speaker at the Oxford Union, he skillfully adapted the distinctive characteristics of its oratory to his writing.

One of Waugh's earliest literary creations to show the ironical cast of his mind was a play entitled *Conversion: The Tragedy of Youth in Three Burlesques*, composed for production at Lancing in 1921, when he was only seventeen.[12] Its three acts, loosely connected by the theme of conversion, provide divergent views on public-school life, with each perspective offering only partial truth. For a complete picture, all the views, though seemingly in conflict (as frequently the case with Byronic irony), must be taken in conjunction. In the first act, which melodramatically represents an educational environment that maiden aunts might imagine, the power of goodness is so strong that it compels a bully to mend his ways and inspires his victim to forgive him. In the second act, which exaggerates school exposés such as Alec Waugh's *Loom of Youth*, the atmosphere is overwhelmingly corruptive. Here an athlete who denigrates scholarship, leads a profligate life, and steals repeatedly finds a kindred spirit in a master who encourages him to new depths of depravity.

The more subtle irony of the concluding act, which purports to represent public-school life "as we all know it is," drives a wedge between educational theory and the reality of its application. In this rosy depiction all conflicts are sensibly resolved. Even the rub between a bored, rebellious athlete, who has created a disturbance in chapel, and a prefect, who succeeds in gaining his cooperation, seems to be settled amid lofty talk about proper attitudes and respect for others' rights. But the "Bolshevism" is not eradicated; it is merely bought off. What really persuades the offending student to alter his behavior is the prefect's promise to recommend him for captain of the house cricket team. Idealism is thus undercut by the pragmatic self-interest of both characters.

Greater sophistication came with *The Balance* (1926), one of Waugh's most daringly original works.[13] Experimentation with silent film techniques helped him to resolve some of the problems inherent in objective narration and showed him how to become disengaged from characters, actions, and even emotions drawn from his own experiences. As Robert Murray Davis has shown, the cinematic devices adapted for this avant-garde story not only made Waugh an expert in detached tone by the time of his first novel but paved the way for subtler application of them in subsequent novels.[14]

The Balance is a strange mixture of narrative and dramatic modes. The main portion is a screenplay in which the descriptive, sometimes directive, scenario is intermingled with the actual theater-showing and the film's captions, further embellished by imagined dialogue inferred from the actors' gestures and by commentary from several spectators. Framing this central core are sections in which Waugh gives real-life status to the film characters: a preceding dialogue obliquely introducing them, a third-person narrative exploring the innermost thoughts of the male lead, Adam Doure, and a bit of concluding dialogue with an unexpected twist. Waugh's aim in all of this was to create something like a camera's-eye view. Having become acquainted with filmmaking as a reviewer, amateur actor, and even a scenario writer (for *The Scarlet Woman*, in 1924), he had discovered what the camera as an observing and recording instrument could achieve by capturing divergent points of view and offering them without judgmental bias. Hence he strove to translate into his fiction such differing angles of vision.

Film techniques proved highly advantageous to Waugh. Cinematic montage in particular offered him much creative flexibility. Just as a film editor, by selecting and splicing various frames, would mount one visual image immediately after another to achieve a desired impact, Waugh juxtaposed both related and unrelated scenes in order to point up comparisons, contrasts, and incongruities without ever intruding an authorial comment. This technique also enabled him to effect shifts in time and place with a minimum of explanation, control the distance, vary the tempo, delete the unessential, and superimpose an implicit coherence on seemingly discrete elements, as in the rapid succession of Oxford rooms in which Adam's acquaintances respond variously to his dinner invitation. In a different way the film scenario encouraged Waugh to adopt the camera's unvarying perspective of seeing everything from an external position. Therefore the melodrama of Adam and Imogen's frustrated love, as well as Ernest's fatal accident, could be presented with complete nonchalance—a tone especially well suited to the final irony of the plot, when Imogen insists on being introduced to Ernest, who, as the reader already knows, is quite dead.

By adapting innovations of expressionist filmmakers and dramatists, Waugh added an even more ingenious element to his burgeoning talents. He learned how to externalize his characters' mental states by portraying them graphically through skits liberated from sequential chronology, as in Adam's imaginings of three possible ways to die and in the debate that Adam carries on with his own reflection in the river. In such instances the central character is made to achieve a modicum of detachment by projecting an image that is distinct from his real self, much as the author has separated himself even from those of his characters who embody his sentiments.

The fiction of Ronald Firbank, whose methods Waugh imitated in his fledgling days, served as another model in the refinement of his objective style.[15] From a 1929 essay evaluating Firbank's contributions to contemporary literature, it becomes evident which goals Waugh himself was striving to achieve.[16] He very much admired Firbank for being the first of modern writers to develop "a new, balanced interrelation of subject and form" that freed narrative from the shackles of nineteenth-century conventions, especially from the necessity for a sequence of events framed by time and linked by cause and effect.[17] His material, thus liberated, could be offered to the reader in a number of new and usually indirect ways, including montage or counterpoint, whereby the most incompatible elements could be juxtaposed to create bizarre effects. A distinctive device was Firbank's manner of presenting ideas or advancing story lines through discrete segments. He might, for example, barely mention a bit of information, then let it drop from sight for many pages, bring it up again in a new context, and so on until its significance, often ironic, would finally emerge. Since the disconnected components would become so imbedded in other details as to seem inconsequential, this technique tended to downplay important concerns while emphasizing unimportant ones in an ironic reversal of values. Waugh cites two instances in which Firbank handled material in this way—the progressive references to fleas at the Ritz from *The Flower Beneath the Foot* (1923) and to the baptism of dogs in *Concerning the Eccentricities of Cardinal Pirelli* (1926)—both of which build up gradually to unexpected results. That Waugh himself became very adept at the technique is shown in *Decline and Fall*, where separate allusions to the increasing seriousness of Lord Tangent's wound and his eventual death are presented only as corollaries to statements about less momentous occasions.

Firbank in his later work, written with great economy of language and the barest minimum of description, particularly relied for development of his stories upon conversational innuendoes. Waugh described this subtle device, which he himself imitated most conspicuously in *Vile Bodies*, as the reverse of the silent film technique. Whereas the filmmaker superimposes coherence on a succession of visual images through a flashed caption, Firbank gives meaning to a flow of conversation through a sudden visual image. Illustrative of what Waugh meant is the following passage from *Cardinal Pirelli*, in which an odd assemblage of conversants, so insignificant as to make their identification irrelevant, hint through idle gossip about the sexual irregularities of the highly unorthodox prelate:

> "Does anyone call to mind a bit of a girl (from Bilbao she was) that came once to stop as his niece?"
> "Inclined to a moustache! Perfectly."
> "Phoebe Poco protests she wasn't."
> "Ah, well; a little *Don Juanism* is good."[18]

The essence of this oblique, objective dialogue is, of course, irony. The author has completely withdrawn his own involvement; one cannot be sure whether any of the female conversants understands the full implications of her own or others' reporting; and the reader, without ever being certain of the "facts," must conclude, rather indeterminately, more than the surface meaning of the words would denote.

The possibilities of ironic subtlety were very much in Waugh's thoughts when he was considering what to call the novel that would eventually become *Decline and Fall*. In a letter of 7 April 1928, he asked Anthony Powell whether the progress of the novel's hero could aptly be designated "Untoward Incidents" and subsequently explained: "The phrase, you remember, was used by the Duke of Wellington in commenting on the destruction of the Turkish Fleet in time of peace at Navarino. It seems to set the right tone of mildly censorious detachment."[19] Actually Wellington and the Tories were outraged that in 1827, while Britain was attempting to carry out a treaty for reconciling Turkey and Greece, the British Admiral Codrington sank the Turkish fleet in Navarino Bay. Yet for political reasons, Wellington called the occurrence merely "an untoward event," explaining that he meant "unexpected, unfortunate" with no aspersions intended for the "gallant admiral." In view of Wellington's true feelings, his public pronouncement was ironic understatement to the point of duplicity. In this historical context, therefore, Waugh's proposed title of "Untoward Incidents" advertises a casually disapproving but uninvolved attitude toward the contents of his novel. Although that title would have been insipid even for those who caught the allusion, it is significant in showing the authorial stance Waugh meant to convey. He evidently preferred not to attack the bastions of authority—whether academic, social, ecclesiastical, legal, or penal—in a head-on assault but rather to employ a flanking movement. The oblique approach of the ironist provided a subtler, and for him more compatible, means of challenging entrenched power.

The title ultimately chosen for that first published novel points to another influence on Waugh's ironical method—Edward Gibbon's *Decline and Fall of the Roman Empire*. Waugh had undoubtedly mastered this famous chronicle; at Lancing he concentrated on history and subsequently held a history scholarship at Oxford, where as late as 1924 anyone pursuing a degree in that discipline was required to read Gibbon's work.[20] In a 1938 review he complimented the writing of Romilly Fedden for being "enlivened with numerous Gibbonesque sentences."[21] In *Helena* he emphasized the importance of style to the art of persuasion while targeting the renowned historian in an ironic jest: the character Lactantius, a Christian apologist, nods toward a chained gibbon and postulates some future "false historian, with the mind of Cicero or Tacitus and the soul of an animal," whose powers of language will overwhelm the truth.[22] Though deploring Gibbon's undermining of Christianity, Waugh could not help admiring his prose, in which irony appears to be an intrinsic aspect. Indeed few English writers have more subtly manipulated inconsistency, illogicality, and Socratic naiveté to suggest the unstated or question the asserted than Gibbon; and he was never more devastating, as his account of early Christianity shows, than when he seemed to praise. It is instructive that Gibbon credited Pascal's *Provincial Letters*, which he repeatedly read, with teaching him how "to manage the weapon of grave and temperate irony."[23] Similarly Waugh, in studying Gibbon, could have assimilated much about how to expose, without necessarily indicting, the follies, crimes, and misfortunes of a disintegrating culture.

Waugh's exploration of history may also account for the sociohistorical dimension in his novels, for he was concerned with some of the social, economic, and political concepts that have subsequently interested new historicists. Like Nietzsche, Spengler, and Foucault, Waugh rejected the idea of history as melioristic or teleological. Like M. M. Bakhtin, he regarded literature as the logical outgrowth of particular cultural environments and therefore presented both discourse and behavioral patterns as social phenomena. Although his revival of the distant past in *Helena* is set in the matrix of legend and ecclesiastical history rather than purely temporal circumstances, most of his fiction realistically chronicles the period through which he lived, and his central characters are usually products of cultural milieux with which he was intimately acquainted. In many of his works, notably *Scoop, Work Suspended, Put Out More Flags*, and *Brideshead*, references to actual people and events evoke the flavor of the present or the recent past, anchoring imaginary situations in a definite time and place. Even the fantasy of *Black Mischief* is built upon historical facts; and predictions of the future, as in *Vile Bodies* and *Love Among the Ruins*, represent projections of present trends. Inevitably such grounding of fiction in reality provided Waugh with opportunities to exploit ironic contrasts or similarities. For example, an allusion in *Brideshead* to King Edward's difficulties about marrying the divorced Mrs. Simpson serves as a backdrop for the possible marriage of Charles and Julia. In *Decline and Fall* the efforts of the League of Nations to restrict the movement of prostitutes between countries prompt Paul's naive thoughts about the complications of international travel; and in *Black Mischief* the elaborate titles adopted by the Emperor Seth parody those used by Haile Selassie.

Not only did ironic characteristics infuse Waugh's imaginative creations; they were equally evident in his nonfictional prose. The ability to distance himself from his subject served him very well in his travel accounts, written during a journalistic career that spanned more than thirty years. It was his refusal to become more than casually involved, as well as his determination to be a spectator rather than a participant in the situations and dramas he witnessed, that made him a credible, informative, and entertaining reporter. To some extent this technique was defensive, for it saved him from the need to make definite commitments and, by providing a semblance of openmindedness, rendered him more acceptable to his readers. He could thereby present his accounts not as the whole truth but rather as one man's perceptions of reality.

Waugh repeatedly advertised his intention to offer an unbiased view of what he observed. In *Tourist in Africa* (1960) he asserted: "As happier men watch birds, I watch men. They are less attractive but more various."[24] Yet he strove to do more than transform impressions and experiences into interesting reading; he hoped to portray deviations from civilized norms not with the acid subjectivity that often characterizes their depiction in his diaries but from the viewpoint of a genial bystander.[25] In *Remote People* (1931) he had earlier expressed the need to suspend judgment: "It seems to me that a prig is someone who judges people by his own, rather than by their, standards; criticism only becomes useful when it can show people where their own principles are in conflict."[26] Admirable though that idea may have been, it was not always possible for an outsider to comprehend an alien culture well enough to interpret anomalies from an insider's viewpoint, as shown by his records of travel adventures in the world's barbarous places— whether Africa, Latin America, or the United States. Indeed there were instances—for example, his endorsement of the triumph by enlightened Italians over backward Ethiopians in *Waugh in Abyssinia* (1936)—when he felt so strongly about a course of events that he allowed tendentious beliefs, tastes, and even prejudices to override his vaunted impersonality.

But Waugh's detached stance was not merely a literary device or a public pose. It seems to have been as natural an inclination in his personality as the other ironically oriented characteristics to which it is related—his youthful tendency to champion conflicting ideas and his early fascination with incongruities. This trait is of considerable interest in Waugh's case because it informed not only his perspective on issues and events outside himself but also his rather idiosyncratic way of approaching his own nature. That he sometimes considered disengagement from his environment to be a personal necessity is substantiated by one of his diary entries in 1943. Having been convinced by army service that he was not a man of action, he reassured himself that withdrawal from external distractions was essential to his career as a man of letters: "I do not want any more experiences in life," he wrote. "I have quite enough bottled and carefully laid in the cellar. . . . I have succeeded, too, in dissociating myself very largely with the rest of the world. . . . I don't want to be of service to anyone or anything. I simply want to do my work as an artist."[27]

Waugh was also inclined to look at himself from a distance and to form self-concepts from diverse points of view. From the self-portraits that emerge in his diary accounts, he appears as a man of many faces, who preferred not to be categorized as only one type of person. Aware of both the variability of human nature and the inability of anyone to depict his own character with complete objectivity, he represented himself even in these private records as would an actor assuming a number of roles—none of them false but, when taken in the aggregate, hard to reconcile as unified. The diaries written soon after his Oxford days show Waugh posturing as both intellectual playboy and responsible schoolmaster. The diaries of his later years project even more discordant images—reclusive country squire, sociable man-about-town (on periodic visits to London), opinionated writer, affectionate family man, and intolerant curmudgeon. Indeed such a protean nature is in keeping with the assertions of Waugh's friends that, like his father, he often gave the impression of playing theatrical parts instead of expressing a consistent personality.[28] That he was conscious of this role-playing can be deduced from his own statement about the autobiographical character Gilbert Pinfold: "The part for which he cast himself was a combination of eccentric don and testy colonel and he acted it strenuously . . . until it came to dominate his whole outward personality."[29]

Waugh gives no clear indication as to what prompted him to present himself in such a detached manner, and the critics who have ventured to theorize on this phenomenon have attributed it to widely differing causes. Jeffrey Heath sees the varied personas as "designed to shield the diarist from the world's scrutiny" and possibly even "from his own."[30] Alan Pryce-Jones, in an article highly suggestive of class consciousness, argues that Waugh was obliged to assume "manifold masks" so that he might transcend his Golders Green origins to become a successful chronicler of the social milieu about which he chose to write.[31] It is also possible that Waugh simply delighted in being different people at different times. Whatever the reasons, his practice of viewing both himself and others from the outside enhanced his ability to create a great variety of fictional characters.

This ironic approach Waugh also used to good effect in an essay discrediting the socialism that he feared might eventually transform British society. In imitation of Jonathan Swift's oblique protests against the economic theory that people constitute a nation's wealth, he produced "What to Do with the Upper Classes: A Modest Proposal."[32] Whereas Swift, in the guise of humanitarianism, had proposed that children of the Irish poor might cease being burdens if they could be sold as food, Waugh recommends a means by which the upper classes, instead of being purged like useless drones from the workers' hive, could be converted into a financial asset—at least until the classless society should become a reality.

To this end he advances what on the surface appears to be a rational argument. Since foreigners attribute British culture to the upper classes and regard the English Gentleman as the nation's unique creation, the snob appeal of products associated with the aristocracy (men's tailoring, for example) would so aid exports that workers in the new society could then enjoy imported luxuries. Traditional British education, such as it was before the socialists tampered with it, would attract foreign students and their money into the country. The beauty of aristocratic buildings and landscapes would draw foreign travelers, who seek not superior plumbing, socialized medicine, or uninhabited castles but acquaintance with "native life," which as popularly conceived for Britain means the lifestyle of the aristocracy. Moreover, implementation of this plan would have humanitarian as well as economic value since the "present rulers" would designate "reservations"—such as affluent sections of London, historic estates, a university, areas of countryside—where the nobility and "unprogressive" members of the middle class would be allowed to live as do some natives in the United States and Africa. Within these enclaves "nothing should be done to disturb their simple beliefs and natural piety."[33] As "protected persons" they could continue their traditional way of life, carrying on their peculiar tribal customs to their own pleasure and the benefit of tourism. The clinching argument for establishing these reservations, however, is that, from the viewpoint of class-warfare extremists, such segregation would facilitate "the eventual massacre" (316).

The reasons and methods Waugh gives for temporarily preserving the upper classes are so preposterous and the justifications so trivial as to invalidate the premises of his argument. By mimicking the shortsighted, impractical schemes of socialist economists, he pulls the ground from under their theories. By proleptically offering, with seemingly deadpan seriousness, specious objections that might be lodged against his recommendations, he further emphasizes the ludicrousness of his proposals. Yet the essay's success is achieved not merely through ingenious rhetoric but also through artful manipulation of diction. By calling the Labour Party victory of 1945 "the grand climacteric" (312) and the Ascot Races a "great festival" of the upper classes (315) and by suggesting that "medical missions" be sent to aristocrats from "the Institute of Anthropology" (315), the author hints through verbal incongruity that he is not being absolutely straight with the reader. Moreover, the subtlety of Waugh's irony is such that, as the foregoing examples attest, it can operate in two directions—somewhat whimsically toward the doomed aristocracy and more astringently toward planners of the socialist state.

When Waugh, on the basis of changes already wrought by Britain's Labour Party, extrapolated his views of the future welfare state in *Love Among the Ruins* (1953), his bitter hostility toward socialist philosophy prevented the detachment and humor that might have leavened this grim fantasy. Even so, ironic perceptions, expressed in varying degrees of subtlety and sophistication, shape much of the novella's fabric. In Waugh's dystopian society, led by socialist politicians, administered by inept bureaucrats, and sustained by unproductive workers, nothing is what it claims to be. God has been replaced by the State, and human identity has been reduced to numbers and file cards. In contrast to Robert Browning's exaltation of romantic love in his poem bearing the same title, love among Waugh's fictional ruins has become little more than hormone calling to hormone. In this planned society of womb-to-tomb welfare, where all functions are performed in the name of Progress, one of the most popular services—and the only one offering real security—is euthanasia, which many citizens choose in order to relieve the boredom of a life virtually devoid of excitement or human interest.

To illustrate the absurdities of socialist theory and the abysmal failure of its application, Waugh focuses on the archetypal Modern Man, Miles Plastic, who has been molded by the State in one of its orphanages. His career lays bare the inversion of values in the State's "progressive" penal system, where no one is "held responsible for the consequences of his own acts," wrongdoers are considered "only the victims of inadequate social services," and "maladjusted" persons, no longer called criminals, receive better treatment than ordinary citizens.[34] Miles's advancement in this society is not through his own merit but by virtue of his one "antisocial" trait, pyromania, whereby he escapes from drabness, frustration, or pain by obliterating whatever he associates with unpleasantness. Through each arson, contrary to logic and without any intention on his part, he achieves an improved situation. His incineration of an airforce base, resulting in the deaths of many airmen, leads him from a job as an obscure dishwasher to one as an official in the ever-expanding Department of Euthanasia.

Miles's interim experience in a State prison is even more desirable, since in the interest of rehabilitation he is sentenced by a sympathetic court—despite objections from his victims' relatives, who are reprimanded for their sentimentality—to receive lavish cultural advantages in what was once an aristocratic mansion. One of the most appealing ironies in the story is the way in which the narrator introduces the reader to Mountjoy. His description of a splendid manor house and its magnificent gardens gives no hint of its being a place of incarceration until he explains that the best rooms, "along the garden front" (2), are given to murderers and sex offenders. That Miles has adjusted perfectly to the freedom of this environment is indicated by his sadness when he roams the gardens for the last time before being released as the new penology's first success. Though his desire to return is later fulfilled, his changed circumstances—not as happy inmate but as distraught lover—cause him to burn the house down. Thought to be the sole remaining proof of enlightened penology by government ministers unaware of his responsibility for the fire, he is assigned the important job, symbolized by briefcase and umbrella, of promoting the construction of a new, more modern Mountjoy.

In human relations Miles is a reflection of his State training until he falls in love. Having been prepared for sex as a means of reproduction in a society that considers marriage and children necessary to complete citizenship, he is totally unprepared for the romantic emotions he feels for Clara, a ballerina whose "great golden beard" (43) is the result of sterilization gone awry. But the happiness he enjoys in their relationship and the domestic future he envisions when she becomes pregnant are shattered by her own lack of human feeling. Regarding love as unimportant and preferring to resume her dancing career, she chooses to eliminate both her distinctive beard and their unborn child, thus indirectly prompting the destruction of Mountjoy. Although the conflagration expunges Miles's passion for Clara, his State-arranged marriage to the "gruesome" Miss Flower presents him with a new source of unhappiness and seems to arouse his pyromaniacal tendencies, for during the ceremony he plays with his cigarette lighter until it ignites. The narrator's description of the flame—"gemlike, hymeneal, auspicious" (51)—provides a titillating conclusion that leaves the exact fate of this union to the reader's imagination while suggesting Miles's paradigmatic way of dealing with his problems. Particularly ironic is the allusion to the god Hymen, whose torch symbolizes the kindling of matrimonial ardor; in contrast, Miles's flame will likely reduce his marriage to ashes. The ending also points up the novella's underlying irony—that someone who has reaped the State's benefits and is regarded as its outstanding success should remain an unregenerate criminal, whose only recourse against conformity is destruction.

In addition to what Waugh's creative compositions reveal about his own use of the ironic mode, what he had to say, as a professional reviewer, about irony in the works of other authors also proves informative. Commenting on Graham Greene's *The End of the Affair*, Waugh calls the title ironic because "the affair has not yet reached its climax when the record ceases."[35] In this instance the physical relationship is concluded even before the woman's death; the spiritual reclamation of her surviving lover begins, through her supernatural intervention, after her admission to heaven. Evidently irony here is associated with an initially misleading assertion about the obvious meaning (the physical termination of the affair) in order that the hidden meaning (its continuation on the spiritual plane) may, when detected, become more striking. Such irony Waugh considered enriching and impressive. An instance of probably inadvertent irony in Greene's book, however, he thought detracting: he lamented the use of "the term 'make love' to describe sexual intercourse." Here again is the sense of discrepancy between what the phrase says and what it means, but Waugh finds the incongruity objectionable only in the specific context of a work exalting spiritual love. In other circumstances the euphemism might be acceptable, but in a novel where love assumes a most exalted character, it unintentionally takes on an "ironical twist" that in Waugh's view undermines the author's serious purpose.

In a review of J. F. Powers's *Presence of Grace*, Waugh examined two short stories presented from the viewpoint of a cat serving as narrator. "The essence of the observing and recording animal," he wrote, "should be false conclusion, the irony established by the reader's knowledge of what the humans are really up to and the cat's erroneous explanations based upon cats' motives."[36] Waugh's comment not only identifies the basic irony as the discrepancy between two conflicting perspectives but also suggests the necessity of reader involvement in deciphering irony. However sincere the feline interpretation may be, the cat must be regarded as a biased, unreliable narrator, and the reader is therefore obliged to reject the interpretation offered by the text in order to deduce his own more plausible, though unstated, version.

Despite an obvious fascination and involvement with irony, Waugh has received much less attention as an ironist than as a satirist. His early novels in particular have been commonly called "satires"; and literary critics, variously weighing the satiric, comic, and ironic components in them, have frequently argued about the validity of that label. Complicating the issue is Waugh's own denial of satiric intent, expressed in his 1946 essay "Fan-Fare," written in response to questions from American readers. To the query of whether his books were "meant to be satirical," he replied with an emphatic, unequivocal "No."[37] "Satire," he argued, "is a matter of period. It flourishes in a stable society and presupposes homogeneous moral standards" such as existed in "the early Roman Empire and eighteenth-century Europe." Satirists in those times strove to attack "inconsistency and hypocrisy," to expose "polite cruelty and folly" through exaggeration, and to effect public shame for wrongdoing. The traditional justification for satire—to bring about social and moral improvement—could have little meaning, he felt, in the Century of the Common Man since the would-be satirist and his reading public no longer share a common standard of values. The modern writer, if he aspired to render any services to a heterogeneous society, could do so only by creating what Waugh termed his own "little independent systems of order." Placing himself therefore in the tradition not of satirists but rather of the early monks who kept Christian civilization alive amid barbarian threats, Waugh designated himself a concerned modern writer who felt obliged to preserve learning, morality, and faith even while the outside world was crumbling around him. Like the monks, he was conscious of an obligation to transmit to posterity the remnants of a civilization greater than the one of which he was making a detailed record.

These enigmatic comments are all the more puzzling because they were made soon after a crucial turning point in Waugh's literary career. *Brideshead Revisited* (1945) was the first of his fictional works to show a pervasive Catholicism in the lives of its principal characters; and his determination to include God in future writing, as expressed in "Fan-Fare," indicates an unambiguous commitment to a serious purpose. In this context, satire would seem a most appropriate means of earnestly condemning whatever ran counter to his beliefs—a negative parallel to positive convictions, like the reverse side of the same coin. Hence his disavowal of it appears to contradict his declarations of religious faith. Perhaps, in keeping with his narrow view of satire's aims and the rarified sociohistorical conditions under which he thought it could thrive, he believed that its practice would be, if not impossible, at least useless in the struggle for human improvement. Certainly other intellectuals of the day—Oswald Spengler, T. S. Eliot, W. B. Yeats, and Wyndham Lewis—concurred that the old world order had been shattered by the First World War and that the principles by which Western civilization had been guided were no longer operative. The postwar era, therefore, contained no system of common ideals on which satire, as traditionally defined, could be based.

In addition to his stated reasons, Waugh may have been eager to gloss over the reductive, negative approach of his earlier entertainments once his enunciation of a definite, positive ethic in *Brideshead* had proved so gratifying to him and his readers. Or he could have rejected the label of satire—that most dogmatic of literary modes—principally because he did not wish to appear judgmental. He may also have realized that a holier-than-thou attitude would be incompatible with his own youthful participation in the profane amusements of post-World War I society. Or possibly, in accord with his earlier pronouncement in the Firbank essay that "the novel should be directed for entertainment,"[38] he felt that the reading public of the twenties and thirties would prefer diversion to castigation. One might even interpret Waugh's remarks in "Fan-Fare" as a refusal to be pinned down by presumptuous interrogation, as calculated perversity, or as the facetiousness at which he was so adept. But his denial of intentional satire seems too strong to be dismissed lightly, especially since the reader's question, unlike the inquiries that impudent interviewers often badgered him to answer, was one he did not have to bring into his essay at all unless he wanted to set the record straight.

It is possible that comments by Msgr. Ronald Knox, whose judgments he highly respected, may help explain why Waugh refused to consider himself a satirist. Knox, in the introduction entitled "On Humour and Satire" for his *Essays in Satire* (1928), describes the satirist as an unpleasant, treacherous fellow with reformist zeal, someone who considers himself immune to the vices he ridicules.[39] Although the satirist pretends to be amusing, he actually preaches a sermon from a negative point of view, believing it his obligation to scourge the follies of humanity. By contrast, a true humorist such as P. G. Wodehouse does not feel or provoke hostility toward his subject but makes his reader empathize with it. Whereas "the laughter which satire provokes has malice in it always," humor, by Knox's definition, is satire purged of its vendettas.[40] "The humorist," he asserts, "runs with the hare; the satirist hunts with the hounds."[41] In view of this dichotomy, which emphasizes differences of motivation, goals, and authorial involvement, Waugh would understandably have disclaimed being primarily either a satirist or a humorist. His methodology, whereby characters reveal their true natures without overt authorial intrusion, seems closer to Knox's concept of irony as a manner of expression that "is content to describe men exactly as they are, to accept them professedly, at their own valuation, and then to laugh up its sleeve."[42]

What Waugh himself had to say about satire in the works of other authors may partially explain his stand in "Fan-Fare." Whether or not the twentieth century was generally conducive to the production of satire, he recognized that creditable examples of it did exist. In a 1928 review he asserted that Laurence Housman's *Life of H.R.H. the Duke of Flamborough* contained purposive satire and that in *South Wind* Norman Douglas had produced "the only great satirical novel of his generation."[43] A 1930 review by Waugh compliments Wyndam Lewis for "genuine prose satire"[44]; and there is no doubt that Lewis's devastating broadsides on the intelligentsia, especially in *The Apes of God* (1930), constitute frontal satiric attacks impelled by *saeva indignatio*. By contrasting the vitriolic diatribes of his contemporaries with his own style, Waugh likely concluded that no comparable animosity had motivated or pervaded his novels, which were marked by a tongue-in-cheek approach. Instead of making direct, systematic assaults, he resorted to tentative, glancing blows, overturning rather than demolishing false idols. A much later reference to satire implies a certain disapproval of its intense and combative style. In a 1947 introduction written for Saki's novel, *The Unbearable Bassington*, Waugh commended the author for having "achieved a *tour de force*" by, among other things, "eschewing . . . the strong passions which are foundations of satire."[45]

One difficulty with Waugh's reasoning in "Fan-Fare" is that his early novels are tinged with what ordinarily passes for satirical spirit, since the comedy is often reductive and sometimes charged with deducible moral judgment. Another complication is the lack of consensus as to what constitutes satire, so that acceptance or rejection of that label varies according to individual theories. It should then not be surprising that there have been differing critical responses to Waugh's disclaimer. Those who do not regard it as deliberate leg-pulling have had to grapple with it and, if they believe that satire must also enunciate a positive ethic, with the question of whether or not a clear moral position can be deduced from the early novels.

Frederick J. Stopp, who in the composition of an early critical study received much assistance from the novelist himself, has argued that Waugh is both serious and accurate in separating his works from traditional satire. While granting that the novelistic entertainments contain a mixture "of farce, satire, and the comedy of manners," Stopp asserts that they are not predominantly satirical because they are not impelled by "moral indignation" or "any consistent animus" on Waugh's part.[46] In a chapter entitled "Comedy from Chaos," Stopp distinguishes between traditional satire, which he terms "a rational, consciously directed, and corrective exercise," and Waugh's "comic extravaganzas," which provide "no correction, but only rejection."[47] Malcolm Bradbury has further undermined the possibility of satire by identifying the early novels with comedy and finding in them "an unredeemable and anarchistic universe

with no secure centres of value."[48] Indeed he claims that Waugh
wrote a mixture of "social chronicle and fantasy in a spirit of comic
delight that absolves him from consistent moral presentation."[49]

Those who take issue with Waugh's disclaimer do so for diverse
reasons. George McCartney, apparently seeing no shred of truth to
the denial of satire, considers it "best understood as Waugh's consummate satiric ploy."[50] Other critics approach the subject with
qualifications. James F. Carens, repudiating the concept of formal
satire enunciated in "Fan-Fare" as too restrictive and possibly even
unrealistic, justifies a designation of Waugh's art as satiric by defin-
ing modern satire not as "a genre but an attitude toward man and
society"—one that may receive different degrees of emphasis in
any literary form and that need not be expressive of a positive
ethic.[51] Jeffrey Heath, on the other hand, finding a moral framework even in the early novels, postulates that Waugh was declaring
himself a moralist though not "a militant moralist, or satirist."[52] As
Heath reasons, Waugh was "firmly within" the main satiric tradition but refused to admit it lest the label of satire destroy his somewhat disingenuous pose of indifference to the world.[53]

Denying that "Fan-Fare" was meant to be taken seriously, James
W. Nichols argues that the early novels were "intended to be satiric,
as well as comic," despite notable differences between Waugh and
more conventional satirists.[54] In Nichols's view the standard of values commonly thought essential to satire is established in these
works through their tone, which reveals the novelist's adverse attitude toward contemporary manners, morals, and society. But
Waugh, unlike satirists of bygone eras who seemed convinced that
adherence to their standards could eliminate the ills against which
they inveighed, offers only the hope that codes of civilized behavior might improve the world, while at the same time demonstrating
through characters such as Tony Last and Paul Pennyfeather that
inherited ideals are inadequate to counter modern savagery. Although Nichols nowhere uses the word "irony," he does recognize
the "tension" or conflict in Waugh's perspective between a realistic
depiction of our society and a romantic, probably hopeless, wish
that traditional values would triumph.

In the work of William J. Cook, Jr., and Daniel James Machon,
irony receives more than tangential treatment. Cook, drawing
upon Northrop Frye's archetypal criticism, especially "The Mythos
of Winter," has analyzed Waugh as a satirist working in the ironic
mode.[55] Hence he traces the evolution of Waugh's fiction through

Brideshead as a progression from objective detachment to subjective involvement, focusing particularly on the relationship between narrator-persona and character-persona as a key to theme and tone. While most critics have conceded that satiric spirit and ironic mode are variously blended in Waugh's fiction, few have gone so far as Machon, who in his unpublished dissertation has argued that Waugh was indeed no satirist in the strict sense but rather an ironist.[56] In Machon's opinion, Waugh employed an ironic mask as a means of presenting his view of an anarchical world until the time of *Brideshead*, when he acknowledged its inadequacy by turning to the stability of a transcendental order. Machon, however, is more concerned with general irony—essentially a philosophical resignation to a chaotic, paradoxical, and unpredictable world—than with ironic methodologies.

Studies by two recent critics who explore the substantial and often perplexing changes that occurred in Waugh's fiction have a curious bearing on the subject of his irony as well. Although their arguments do not address irony directly, they not only touch base with some of the ironic elements in the novels but identify certain trends that parallel, and even correlate with, the ironic currents therein. Ian Littlewood theorizes that Waugh sought to shield himself against the unpleasantness of reality by means of five escape strategies.[57] The earliest of these were detachment of tone and humor, followed more or less progressively by romanticism and nostalgia until religion ultimately became the strategy that not only diminished but subsumed all the previous ones in such a way as to alter quite radically the character of Waugh's writing. Robert R. Garnett postulates that the early novels were impelled and enlivened by their author's ebullient sense of the comic, and he emphasizes Waugh's penchant for the disordered, the eccentric, the irrational, the absurd, and the unpredictable.[58] In Garnett's view the retreat of these comic instincts, occasioned or at least accompanied by a less tolerant attitude and "imaginative withdrawal from the world of active experience," wrought a crucial change that had a "deadly" impact on all the novels after *Scoop*.[59] Whatever the causes or effects of the literary transformation traced by Littlewood and Garnett, I would certainly add that it was also marked by a very definite falling off in Waugh's sense of the ironic—that natural inclination which had earlier given rise to his unique talent.

Because of irony's pervasiveness in Waugh's most widely read novels, it is my conviction that these works deserve to be examined

not primarily from the viewpoint of satire, comedy, or religion—
though all these ingredients must be taken into account—but from
the perspective of irony. In so doing, it is crucial, especially in view
of Waugh's assertions in "Fan-Fare," to bear in mind some consistent distinction between irony and satire. Northrop Frye's succinct
differentiations are helpful. "Satire," he maintains, "is militant
irony: its moral norms are relatively clear, and it assumes standards
against which the grotesque and absurd are measured."[60] But, according to Frye, when the reader is uncertain about the author's
stance or precisely what the author expects the reader's to be, the
mode is ironic with no more than a modicum of satire. The ironic
writer is, like Socrates, self-deprecatory, pretending to know nothing: "Complete objectivity and suppression of all explicit moral
judgements are essential to his method. Thus pity and fear are not
raised in ironic art: they are reflected to the reader from the art."[61]

Another oft-quoted distinction is that of Morton Gurewitch:
"Irony, unlike satire, does not work in the interests of stability.
Irony entails hypersensitivity to a universe permanently out of
joint and unfailingly grotesque. The ironist does not pretend to
cure such a universe or to solve its mysteries."[62] Although
Gurewitch's ideas are based largely on the theory and practice of
the German Romantics, they are applicable to the irony of
twentieth-century writers, who are more closely akin to the Romantics than to the neoclassicists or the authors of antiquity. Especially the decade of the 1920s is remarkably similar to the age of
the Romantics in its awareness of having lost an older world view
and of not yet having replaced it with a stable new order. Uncertainties bordering on nihilism are endemic to such epochs. As
Wayne Booth expressed it: "Irony is usually seen as something that
undermines clarities, opens up vistas of chaos, and either liberates
by destroying all dogma or destroys by revealing the inescapable
canker of negation at the heart of every affirmation."[63]

These critical concepts illuminate the basic philosophical orientation of Waugh's novels prior to *Brideshead*. Negativism characterizes the world view; instability is the governing principle of fallen
man and his society; and the lack of fixed belief, or even common
standards, produces a chaotic environment in which true love, integrity, and steadfast purpose cannot survive. In a situation so unreliable and unpredictable, firm conclusions become less valid than
suspended judgment, absolutes less useful than relativistic valua-
tions. The perceptive man, however, comprehends the difference

between appearance and reality, as well as the disparity between what might exist and what must be suffered, and therefore resigns himself to the paradoxical nature of existence. To illustrate this general human predicament through the specifics of plot and character, Waugh has employed techniques of literary irony that disclose the uncertainty resulting from unresolved conflicts and reveal unstated thoughts through incongruities in tone or context. In the absence of guiding principles, an unexpected turn of events is made to seem plausible, while the seemingly logical motivations of a character are shown to be unforeseeably different from his own perceptions of them or from what the reader initially deduces. Only a naive character or reader accepts the façade as ultimate reality, and then, like the classic *alazon*, falls victim to deception. Often Waugh's subtlest irony results from the discrepancy between what the text says and what it implies. His ironic methodology thus creates a countermeaning, a subtext, or something other than what at first appears to be the case.

In many of the novels Waugh's narrator-persona stands apart from his creation virtually to the extent of being an amoral observer. He might, as Keats described the epitome of artistic objectivity in Shakespeare, seem to take "as much delight in conceiving an Iago as an Imogen."[64] Certainly there is no explicit censure of scapegraces such as Grimes, Margot Beste-Chetwynde, Youkoumian, Brenda Last, or Joyboy, for while Waugh undoubtedly uses some of the reductive techniques common to satire—notably burlesque, caricature, exaggeration, and parody—his approach is indirect and subtle. Possibly because of inherent ambivalences in Waugh himself, the reader often cannot determine precisely where the narrator-persona stands or what his ethical viewpoint is. In analyzing his attitude toward the Bright Young People or the British upper classes, for example, one becomes embroiled in a series of apparent contradictions. Yet it is this ambiguity that allows those members of society about whom Waugh is most unflattering—and who theoretically should detest him—to be his most ardent admirers; from among his antithetical statements about them they can accept the palatable and reject the distasteful. Conversely, Waugh's failure to commit himself unequivocally on serious moral concerns—for example, birth control, fornication, and cannibalism in *Black Mischief*—has sometimes led to the problem all ironists face: that of being radically misunderstood.[65]

Unlike the detached narrator, the critic is obliged to take a stand wherever possible. To substantiate my contention that Waugh should be viewed primarily as an ironist, the subsequent chapters of this book analyze eight of his novels in order to show not only how his fictional world reflects his philosophical orientation but also how ironic techniques contribute, in specific contexts, to the interpretation of meaning. Irony appears in a multiplicity of ways: it varies in form from the simplest twist of a thought by one strategically placed word to structures so complex that one irony is intertwined with or built upon another; it ranges in effect from a barely perceptible, inconsequential distortion to a wrenching so tremendous as to change, quite radically, the course of the plot. Irony is often the chief instrument through which many creative tasks are accomplished: by its agency, theme is revealed, action propelled, character delineated, society criticized, laughter stimulated, horror intensified, and the reader delighted by his own ability to detect obliquely presented ideas.

Decline and Fall

*F*or *Decline and Fall*, in manuscript subtitled "The Making of an Englishman," Waugh invents a complex of shocking disparities through which to demonstrate the reeducation of his central character, Paul Pennyfeather, whose initial beliefs about the world are shattered by his experiential discoveries of its actual nature. The series of riotous picaresque adventures that strip away Paul's illusions about honor, love, society, education, the church, the law, the prison system, and even human nature detail his fall from blissful naiveté to a painful awareness of evil. Although exposure to the chaos of modern life forces him to question the behavioral codes of his stable, upper middle-class background—precepts which he confidently assumed to be adequate and appropriate for coping with any difficulties—the conflict between idealism and disillusionment is never wholly resolved. Ultimately he comes to realize that since neither approach offers the complete truth about life each must, as in Hegelian dialectics, be used to temper the other. The novel as a whole may therefore be viewed as an ironic parody of the Bildungsroman—one which, neither debasing the genre nor treating it seriously, merely plays with it in unexpected ways.[1]

Contributing much to the success of irony in *Decline and Fall* is the positioning of a detached narrator between author and central character. The novel's apparent cynicism toward suffering and death is therefore not necessarily the sentiment of the author, who has distanced himself from the work, but rather of an indifferent storyteller who represents the usual callousness of humanity. The disinterested pose of the narrator serves negatively, however, to stimulate the increased emotional involvement of the reader, who might consider obtrusive condemnation of evil as preachy or, especially in this fallen world, where innocence is often equated with stupidity, might regard overt sympathy with the victim as sentimental.

The narrator's disengagement also permits him, in the Belgravia interlude, to add an unusual dimension as he steps back from his story to comment interpretively on his own art, temporarily breaking the artistic illusion in a way typical of romantic irony.[2] This brief digression, strategically placed midway in the novel to show how incomplete Paul's education still is, allows the narrator to play ironically with both the central character and the reader about the nature of reality.[3] For a few hours Paul emerges from the disjointed world into which ill circumstances have thrust him to reenter a civilized milieu where he believes a gentleman can feel at home, although the betrayals he has suffered in Oxford and West End London would seem to belie his trust in such an environment. His conviction that he is once again a solid person in a solid world is also contrasted ironically with his fading memory of recent misadventures amid the "sham" of Llanabba as if they were only "nightmares." But the narrator, while confirming the dichotomy of Paul's two worlds, offers no clear resolution of which is reality and which is illusion. He merely explains that he is obliged to return Paul to the shadowy subworld, where the extraordinary adventures which are "the only interest about him" will be resumed.[4] Implying that a passive character like Paul is incapable of the heroism expected by readers of 1920s thrillers, the narrator comments that the "book is really an account of the mysterious disappearance of Paul Pennyfeather, so that readers must not complain if the shadow which took his name does not amply fill the important part of hero for which he was originally cast" (163).

In presenting the circumstances that lead eventually to Paul's "disappearance," the narrator, whose customary stance is almost complete objectivity, can indicate the confusion in Paul's life merely by detailing the physical objects in a certain environment as clues to the actions and characters associated with it. In such cases, metonymy functions ironically by indirectly conveying ideas about people and places without ever stating them. Although Waugh had toyed with this technique in *The Balance* by hinting information about Adam's friends through the contents of their rooms, he developed it fully for the first time in *Decline and Fall*. The particulars of Silenus's Bauhaus renovations at King's Thursday suggest the architect's own sterile, mechanically oriented mind. The description of Margot's "Sports Room" in her London home proclaims the kind of jobs being offered to the "young ladies" whom she interviews there: the lights are in testicular glass balls; the furniture is "ingeniously" constructed of phallic bats, polo sticks, and golf clubs; and a wall is decorated with the painting of a prize ram, presumably a symbol of male potency. The masters' common room at Llanabba, which Paul surveys apprehensively upon first encounter, provides him as well as the reader, through its material jumble, with a foretaste of the school's zany teaching staff. Scattered about in defiance of order are pipes, academic gowns, "golf clubs, a walking stick, an umbrella and two miniature rifles . . . a typewriter . . . a bicycle pump, two armchairs, a straight chair, half a bottle of invalid port, a boxing glove, a bowler hat, yesterday's *Daily News*, and a packet of pipe cleaners" (19-20).

Lack of cohesion also exists in social relations. Paul, an orphan, has no real family, and his uncaring guardian exploits him and his inheritance whenever possible. In the Fagan and Trumpington families the generations show little understanding of each other, and the elder Circumferences seem to have no genuine love for their son. Marriage becomes just another contractual business to Margot Beste-Chetwynde, Maltravers, Silenus, and Grimes, while the many instances of casual sex provide no lasting connection. The relations between instructors and students, at both Llanabba and Oxford, are a burlesque of the ideal, for each group takes advantage of the other. Paul's best friend, Potts, betrays their friendship, and Philbrick's tales suggest that there can be no trust between any men. Members of the upper class—the Circumferences, Peter Pastmaster, and the parvenu Maltravers—ignore their traditional obligations of leadership in favor of self-interest. Members of the Bollinger Club, in their destruction of items symbolizing music, art, and poetry, prove themselves not just indifferent but hostile to culture. From the perspective of the ironic narrator, all this indicates a civilization that has lost its bearing—one in which traditional bonds no longer hold it together. Hence Silenus's analogy of a turning carnival wheel is an apt symbol of frenzied circular motion with only centrifugal force and no advancement. As

Yeats put it, "Things fall apart; the center cannot hold;/ Mere anarchy is loosed upon the world."[5]

Even Scone College—that Oxonian Eden from which Paul is banished and to which he returns only in reincarnation—is itself part of the fallen world. Yet until its evil is thrust upon him, he is as oblivious as was the youthful Waugh, who reminisced in his autobiography about an Oxford that seemed "a Kingdom of Cokayne," where he "was reborn in full youth" after a cocoonlike development in a public school.[6] Blind to the perils that surround him, Paul is rudely shaken out of his chrysalis existence and then borne along on a stream of events that, at every turn, frustrate his hopes and desires. Naively assuming that external appearances are the indications of ultimate validity, he discovers to his repeated sorrow that people are not what they seem. Inexperienced and highly vulnerable, he becomes the victim of many schemes and situations in a world ruled not by justice or reason but by capricious fortune.

Paul's true education begins with the opening episode at Scone. This fast-moving sequence of events, seen from several perspectives, serves as catalyst for all subsequent action and, as a particularly successful display of ironic artistry, merits detailed analysis. Even the names of the characters seem unsuitable. "Pennyfeather" symbolizes an insignificance at odds with the main character's central position. "Sniggs" and "Postlethwaite," by their ludicrously undignified sounds, hint at the fraudulent nature of these college dons, while the uncommonly pretentious names of Bollinger members (Alastair Digby-Vaine-Trumpington and Lumsden of Strathdrummond) imply a boastfulness not in keeping with true aristocrats. Other touches of irony intrude through inappropriate words, phrases, or tones. "Lovely" is the narrator's term to describe both the depredations of the Bollinger Club and the subsequent meeting of college officials to assess punishment. The hyperbolic "What an evening that had been!" (1) characterizes destruction during the Club's previous reunion. When the drunken Lumsden encounters Paul, the laird's primitive instincts are implied in an analogy likening him to "a druidical rocking stone" (5). Another irony pivots upon the mention of *"outrage,"* which the college dons fear may occur if they interfere with the Bollinger attack on Paul, whereas an outrage of a different sort does occur because they do nothing. When Paul is described as one who "does the College no good" (7), the ostensible reference to academic reputation cloaks an actual allusion to financial gain. The chaplain's enigmatic suggestion that the "ideals" Paul has "learned at Scone" may be of use in the business world is subject to several interpretations. It may insinuate that someone like Paul, whose values seem to be less than ideal, should do well in a profession not noted for idealism. It may imply that what Paul has recently learned in college about human behavior is contrary to what a university ought to teach. Or it may indicate the naiveté of a chaplain mouthing his usual, but in this case highly inappropriate, platitudes to a departing student.

The action of the Scone episode also abounds in contradiction, some of which cuts in more than one direction. The willful and extensive damage to several college rooms during the Bollinger Club's rampage, for which its members are assessed relatively low fines, contrasts with the damage noticed in Paul's room—two slight, certainly unintentional, cigarette burns, for which the bursar assesses comparatively high charges. These minor burns, in turn, contrast with the colossal injury done to Paul himself by that same bursar, who witnessed yet did not interfere with Paul's debagging; and the moderate fining of the Bollinger members, compared with Paul's expulsion for something of which he was completely innocent, represents a further miscarriage of justice. In the realm of cause and effect, substantial losses to the unpopular students—china, a piano, a Matisse painting, and a manuscript—result in only minimal benefit to the dons of some Founder's port. Conversely, the seemingly insignificant mistaking of Paul's tie, the stripes of which differed only by a quarter of an inch in width from those of the Boller tie, sets off a chain of disastrous occurrences that result in the complete obliteration of Paul's identity.

Underlying and controlling these sharply contrasting events at Scone are broader incongruities of perspective; and the hilarity of the episode derives largely from the clash between the distinctive attitudes of Paul Pennyfeather, the college authorities, and the Bollinger members about Paul's inadvertent fall from innocence. The wielders of academic power—the bursar, the junior dean, the master, and the chaplain—think and behave, in view of their obligations, contrary to what the reader and Paul would expect. Even the porter, by assuming Paul's guilt, echoes their demoralizing point of view. The dons who gleefully watch the Bollinger mayhem from a darkened window, without any intention of halting it, dwell upon their own potential benefit from the anticipated fines—the more horrendous the destruction, the greater the gain. Hence Sniggs can utter, according to his own logic, the illogical prayer,

"Oh, please God, make them attack the Chapel" (3). A hypocritical conscience besets them momentarily when they think a titled student has run afoul of the Bollinger members but evaporates when they realize that the victim is only Pennyfeather, "some one of no importance" (6). The same double standard is exhibited by the master, who decides to expel Paul ostensibly for running through the quad *"without his trousers"* but actually because he is not wealthy enough to profit the college through substantial fines. In a burlesque of sweetness and sympathy, the chaplain bids Paul look on the bright side of his disgrace—that he has discovered so early his "unfitness for the priesthood" (8). But the porter's juxtaposed observation—that most students who are "sent down for indecent behaviour" (8) become schoolmasters—implies Paul's suitability for a profession usually thought to abide by principles as high as those of the clergy.

Members of the Bollinger Club, far from living up to their aristocratic titles, prove themselves to be barbarians. Their overweening sense of self-importance is skillfully undermined in the opening passages describing the gathering of old members for the annual "beano." Through repeated wrenching of tone involving overstatement deflated by pejorative adjectives or demeaning nouns, the narrator alerts the reader to the discrepancy between their social status and their true character: "Epileptic royalty from their villas of exile; uncouth peers from crumbling country seats; . . . illiterate lairds from wet granite hovels in the Highlands" (1-2). Their behavior at reunions suggests their belief that they are above the gentlemanly code, just as Lady Circumference's defiance of grammar implies her assumption that she is not bound by conventional rules. Liberated by alcohol, the Bollinger members give vent to their atavistic hunting instincts, perpetuated, long after being essential for survival, in the ritualistic sport of county families. Their quarry may be a caged fox, which they pelt to death with champagne bottles, or unpopular students, whose prized possessions they destroy. To indicate the bestiality of their reversion to habits of primitive ancestors, the narrator employs animal analogies— "confused roaring" (1) and "baying for broken glass" (2). The absurdity of their pretensions is further exposed when the oafish Lumsden, whose dubious distinction stems from wild chieftain forebears, becomes incensed at Paul for wearing what appears to be a Boller tie. In Lumsden's way of thinking, such presumption in a middle-class Englishman merits public disgrace.

Paul's acquaintance with Dionysian forces has been more theoretical than actual, and his confident unawareness of the evil around him has reduced his ability to cope with it. So oblivious has he been to the very existence of the Bollinger Club that he cannot conceive of having done anything to incur the wrath of its members. What transpires in his mind while he is being debagged or what his response is to the college authorities when they expel him is never recorded. The detached narrator so rarely delves into characters' innermost thoughts that the reader is often held in a state of uncertainty that heightens the irony of this crucial situation. Although it is possible to deduce from external evidence that neither the guilty Bollinger members nor the witnessing dons, who presumably offer only partial and therefore misleading evidence to the master, have the slightest interest in justice, the bitter reaction of their abused, maligned victim is revealed only when Paul utters his valedictory curse on all the malefactors.

The world into which Paul is thrust also evaluates according to outward manifestations rather than true worth. Every phase of his life as a schoolmaster is fraught with discrepancies. He is initially forced to seek employment because his guardian views expulsion from Oxford as sufficient reason to abrogate Paul's inheritance; the employment agency, though euphemistically recording "indecent behaviour" as "education discontinued for personal reasons" (12), uses Paul's disgrace to refer him to a school of the lowest category; and his employer finds it an excuse to hire him at reduced pay. Even the appearance of the Llanabba school building, misnamed a castle, accentuates the discrepancy between the genuine and the sham, for what had originally been a Georgian country home (and remains so from the back) has had a pretentious medieval fortress superimposed upon its front. Compounding the incongruity of the structure is the irony of Paul's inability to notice it because he arrives at night in a closed taxi.

The instructional system itself is a jumble of contradictions, for Llanabba is dedicated not to teaching and learning but to the semblance of education for wealthy boys who cannot gain admission to a reputable public school. The disparate assessments of young Lord Tangent, first by the unctuous headmaster, Dr. Fagan, and later by Tangent's brutally candid mother, stem from the conflict between rosy façade and harsh reality. Fagan, explaining that "many of the boys come from the very best families," characterizes "little Lord Tangent . . . , the Earl of Circumference's son," as "such a nice little chap, erratic, of course, like all his family, but he has *tone*" (16). Lady Circumference cuts through the veneer with "The boy's a dunderhead. If he wasn't he wouldn't be here" (85). Although Fagan may equivocate about the quality of his pupils, his less guarded statements and actions expose his fraudulence. While spouting the positive philosophy of educationists, paying lip service to "professional tone," "vision," and the "ideal of service and fellowship" (15-16), he encourages his masters to practice something quite different. Under his tutelage, Paul learns to "temper discretion with deceit" (24)—passing himself off as an expert in athletics or organ playing even when he has no competence whatever. On advice from another master, Paul forgets about teaching the boys anything and concentrates upon merely keeping them quiet with busywork. While he struggles with the down-to-earth problems of his situation, the high-flown educational theories offered by his pompous friend Potts further emphasize the discrepancy between educational philosophy and its misapplication at Llanabba.

That Fagan's choice of masters is dictated not by pedagogical considerations but solely by the impressions they make on his patrons is clear from his comments on unsatisfactory employees. Fagan tells of one master "who swore terribly in front of every one" (76) when bitten by a parent's dog; of another he states, "He is *not* out of the top drawer, and boys notice these things"; of a third, "He used to borrow money from the boys . . . and the parents objected" (16). Fagan's primary concern is to perpetuate the scholastic charade, which is staged to gain financial support from the school's affluent patrons. The masters, therefore, as part of "the act," must be favorably received on the superficial level; and their real characters do not matter. When Fagan declines to inquire into the details of Paul's "indecent behaviour," he lays bare his cynicism and contempt for ideals in his most self-betraying remark: "I have been in the scholastic profession long enough to know that nobody enters it unless he has some very good reason which he is anxious to conceal" (15).

Against this background, the incident of the £20 offered Paul by Alastair Trumpington to compensate for the ruination of his Oxford career is presented through a delightful series of ironies undermining the inviolable honor code of English gentlemen. Paul's moral dilemma occurs when Potts's incensed refusal of the money is countermanded by less idealistic colleagues at Llanabba. In fact, when Paul admits with double entendre that the £20 represents "a temptation," the Rev. Prendergast, following through in the religious vein with advice unexpected of a clergyman, replies that "it would be a sin to refuse" (52). Paul's subsequent struggle with his conscience, in which temptation is overcome by the need to keep his self-respect and to prove "the durability of . . . ideals" (53) bred into him as a gentleman, appears incompatible with his facile accommodation to Fagan's dishonest ways. Since Paul seems to feel no guilt for having compromised educational values, his belief that it would be dishonorable to accept compensation for personal damages becomes particularly absurd. New dimensions in the irony are introduced when the unscrupulous Grimes resolves the problem quite simply. Having forged an acceptance in Paul's name, Grimes explains: "I'm a gentleman too . . . and I was afraid you might feel like that, so I . . . saved you from yourself" (54). Paul's delighted response, "in spite of himself," with a toast "to the durability of ideals" (54) explodes the original meaning of these words. In this altered context a tribute to the undeviating code that Grimes ignores signifies (whether or not Paul realizes it) a more pragmatic orientation toward ideals. Waugh's narrator makes a final comic pass at this episode during the later sports event, when Lady Circumference tells Paul that, according to her sister's account, her nephew Trumpington has recently been fined £20. Only Paul and the reader can deduce the unstated—that Trumpington, to allay his conscience for a previous wrongdoing, has committed another by getting the money under false pretenses.

Though Waugh's account of the Llanabba sports event provides verbal pleasures and unexpected occurrences of small dimension, the main ironic thrust in this section is on a much grander scale. The conflict between assumed appearance and underlying reality is, in fact, presented on two levels—the chaotic sports themselves serving as a microcosm for the competitive tensions of society at large. While Fagan virtually ignores matters necessary for the actual sports (a defined racing course, proper equipment, and rules for judging), he lavishes attention on unessential trivia (flags, fireworks, gilded programs, and champagne cup) designed to curry favor with influential parents. But his elaborate preparations have an uncanny way of backfiring by inducing consequences opposite to what he intends. His desire to effect style by using a real pistol for starting the races brings about the accidental wounding of Lord Tangent. His hope of lending dignity with a band results in unbearably monotonous music and the bandmaster's attempts to pimp for his sister-in-law. The predetermination of athletic winners from among boys of prominent families, which obliges Grimes to declare Clutterbuck a winner despite his cheating, precipitates the embarrassing scene in which Lady Circumference refuses to award the prize. Thus Fagan's misguided hopes of gaining favor turn the gala into a fiasco, and the fraudulence with which the sports are staged totally destroys the sportsmanship supposedly generated by healthy competition.

The visiting parents also lack any sense of fair play in their social competitiveness, as the unresolved tensions among three class-conscious groups illustrate. The Clutterbucks, with a brewing fortune but as yet no seat in Parliament, are defensive about their nouveau-riche status. The obtuse Earl of Circumference and his horsey, outspoken countess exude the smug self-confidence of landed aristocrats. Margot Beste-Chetwynde, fortified by beauty, extraordinary wealth, social standing in Mayfair, and a son who is heir apparent to an earldom, feels so secure that she dares to challenge conventional standards of propriety. She defiantly flaunts her black American lover, whose unconvincing claims to culture further add to the incongruous situation in which everyone seems to be jockeying for position. Amidst expressions of racial prejudice, social antagonism, and political bias, the parental gathering is wrecked by the very people Fagan expected to beguile.

The other principal characters whom Paul meets at Llanabba are also at variance with their outward aspects. The two masters, Grimes and Prendergast, each of whom possesses a serious defect that periodically upsets his equilibrium, are to some extent ironic inversions of one another. Prendergast is well-bred and well-meaning, but his basic inclination to do good is thwarted by lack of strong belief in anything, including himself. Consequently he cannot carry through his intentions or deal with simple problems such as sharing the bath. Unable to resolve theological doubts, he has given up his vocation as parish priest. Yet he fares no better at Llanabba, where his self-pitying, defeatist attitude makes it impossible for him to keep order among the students, win their respect, or associate easily with the other masters. In contrast, Grimes, though vulgar by nature and confirmedly hedonistic, has the self-assurance to be outgoing with his colleagues and to discipline the boys, who respect him partly because his artificial leg has led them to conclude, erroneously, that he was wounded in the war. Most crucial, he has no "doubts." He is as confident of his "old boy" connections with Harrow as Browning's Pippa is of providential care and knows they will repeatedly get him out of "the soup." Hence a distinguished public school, the traditional breeding ground of English gentlemen, serves paradoxically as a perpetual safety net for one who is clearly no gentleman.

If the Rev. Prendergast is a burlesque of the questing Anglican clergyman and Capt. Grimes of the immoral schoolmaster, the butler Philbrick is a caricature of the criminal on his way to success. He seems to have no fixed identity but delights in playing different roles in a kaleidoscopic monodrama. The various autobiographical tales he offers to create a protean, polymorphous self are so imaginative as to indicate a superb con artist. All one can be sure of is that a butler with diamonds, pistol, and police on his trail is no ordinary servant. Although Prendergast's overdeveloped conscience is instrumental in his undoing, an ironic detachment from conventional morality enables Philbrick, like Grimes, to flourish, at least for the time being, in a mad world.

Grimes's eventual downfall provides an excellent example of what Muecke labels an irony of events in which the very act designed to prevent an unwanted result becomes the instrument for producing it.[7] Just as Fagan's efforts to impress his patrons at the sports event have the opposite effect, so Grimes's marriage to his employer's daughter Flossie turns into agony. Having become engaged to her as a means of protecting his job the next time his homosexual indiscretions are discovered, he weds her when in danger of being fired, not knowing that his consequent unhappiness would destroy his ability to stay in the job. He realizes with horror that, despite his lack of sexual interest in women, his primrose path of dalliance has led him directly, in another irony of events, to revolting domesticity; and his fears are reinforced by the vicar's nuptial sermon on "Home and Conjugal Love," which becomes farcical when viewed against the cynicism that brought the couple together.

Grimes's changed status generates further ironies. Especially with his father-in-law constantly belittling him, he suffers a marked alteration in personality. Just as Prendergast, under the influence of drink, had once become self-confident enough to cane twenty-three boys, so Grimes, under the impact of marriage, becomes despondent, self-pitying, and paranoid. While he at first sees a painful irony in the fact that the elder Clutterbuck's letter about an attractive job in the brewery arrives too late to prevent the marital fiasco, the reader sees an even more poignant irony in Grimes's subsequent misinterpretation of this genuine offer as only a cruel hoax perpetrated against him—one to which any response would be useless. Flossie's attitude toward the unsatisfactory relationship with Grimes is divulged ironically when she refuses to wear mourning after his ostensible suicide. Her cryptic explanation—"I don't think my husband would have expected it of me" (148)—sidesteps her real reason. A hidden irony, of which neither Flossie nor the reader could be aware at this point, arises from the fact that Grimes is still alive.

Whereas the first book begins by focusing on the fall of an innocent, the second book begins by developing King's Thursday, Margot's country home, as an ironic symbol of progress. The Bauhaus monstrosity that Paul finds at the end of an avenue of great chestnuts presents modernity at its worst. Not only is this combination of concrete, steel, and glass quite unappealing in itself, but it is further diminished by comparison with the fine example of Tudor architecture that had until recently stood on the same spot. Although Waugh implies amusing inconsistencies about the earlier mansion—that its original character had been "preserved" by the inaction of indifferent, impecunious earls, and that its crumbling beauty had been most admired by modern preservationists who did not have to cope with its discomforts—the main thrust of the irony is directed toward the new building and the bad taste of its rich new owner. Margot, contrary to the assumptions of neighbors and antiquarians that her wealth would surely restore the ancient structure, demolishes what she considers "bourgeois and awful" to replace it with "something clean and square" (155-56).

Just as illogical is her choice of an architect whose chief qualifications are a rejected factory design and the decor for a film without any human characters. Prof. Silenus's preference for the machine over man, shown in his parody of Hamlet's praise of humanity, has caused him to reduce architecture—domestic as well as industrial—to a problem of accommodating machines rather than people. Since he considers human beings to be only inferior machines, he tells Paul that in ten more years Margot "will be almost worn out" (169). Believing that the machine is the perfection to which humanity should aspire, he makes himself ridiculous by imitating its actions as he tries to eat a biscuit. His fixed expression and the regular motion of his hand and jaws illustrate the assertion of Henri Bergson, one of Waugh's favorite philosophers at the time, that "the attitudes, gestures and movements of the human body are laughable in exact proportion as that body reminds us of a mere machine."[8]

The mystery surrounding Margot's wealth is presented as an evolving irony, with both Paul and the reader initially in the dark. Gradually through a series of clues the reader is enlightened, whereas Paul, dazzled by Margot's beauty and glamorous world, remains blind to all indications that she is engaged in international prostitution. Grimes's explanation that he got a job with her syndicate because he had no problem controlling himself around women should have suggested to Paul the sexual nature of her enterprise. Her incisive manner in questioning prospective employees could have alerted him to the type of women she is dealing with, while her preference for inexperienced girls, who do not even need to know Spanish to work in Latin America, might have aroused more than mild curiosity or puzzlement. Certainly Philbrick's warning that the League of Nations Committee will soon be after Margot, to which Paul ingenuously replies, "I haven't the least idea what you mean" (196), should have raised serious suspicions. But Paul interprets everything according to his erroneous perception that Margot can do no wrong. When sent to Marseilles, where some of the girls are having emigration difficulties, he naively assumes, upon finding them in a red-light district, that Margot is showing her usual concern for the welfare of employees "unwittingly exposed to such perils" (203); and the officials' oblique allusions to the League of Nations and its efforts to stop white slave traffic are totally lost on him. Comprehending neither the girls' situation nor the winks and innuendos of the authorities, he concludes his negotiations with the perfectly innocent remark, which they take to be ironic humor, that the League of Nations seems "to make it harder to get about instead of easier" (207).

The involvement of Arthur Potts in the exposé of Margot's syndicate is another ironic thread running through this section of the novel. Having once been Paul's best friend, he becomes his nemesis. Had Paul been shrewder, he might have attached some significance to Potts's recurring appearances as a League of Nations representative just when Margot is transacting business—at King's Thursday with Grimes, in London with the interviewees, and in Marseilles through Paul's assistance. But not having learned enough about either Margot's profession or Potts's work, Paul sees no relationship and cannot fit the pieces of the puzzle into one another. Indeed it seems unlikely to him that, as Potts apparently thinks, his journey to France could interfere with his forthcoming wedding. Yet it is Potts's evidence at the trial that convicts Paul and does prevent the ceremony from taking place. Paul's expectations of a bright future, indicated by his toast to Fortune as "a much-maligned lady," are shattered by his arrest and prison sentence while the guilty Margot, whom the judge calls "a lady of . . . stainless reputation" (216), goes scot-free.

Much of the irony in Paul's prison experience is satiric, for Waugh attacks avant-garde theories of penology that seem to lack practical value. He appropriately names the first house of correction to which Paul is sent Blackstone Gaol, after one of Britain's most famous legal theoreticians, Sir William Blackstone; and for his prime target he creates the character of Sir Wilfred Lucas-Dockery, a former sociology professor turned prison governor. Sir Wilfred, who dabbles in psychoanalysis for the rehabilitation of prisoners, is one of Waugh's fatuous do-gooders whose theories crumble upon contact with reality and who therefore do more harm than good. Disapproving of Paul's request for continuation of the solitary confinement to which he had happily adjusted, the governor, believing that Paul has become misanthropic as the result of inferiority feelings, devises a complicated scheme "to break down his social inhibitions" (234). In trying to apply another of his favorite ideas—that inmates should continue the professional interests of their former life—Sir Wilfred is completely frustrated because Paul's alleged profession, white slave trafficking, cannot be carried on in prison. Even so, the self-deceived governor assumes that, in addition to bringing about a revolution in sociological statistics, he can improve Paul's self-image by removing prostitutional crime from its customary "sexual" classification and placing it in the less reprehensible "acquisitive" category (226).

One of Sir Wilfred's hypotheses—"that almost all crime is due to the repressed desire for aesthetic expression" (226)—has most unexpected results throughout the prison. There are several attempted suicides in the arts and crafts school because of easy access to sharp tools, and the men in the bookbinding shop eat the library paste because it tastes better than their porridge. Finally there is a murder—of Prendergast, now prison chaplain, who has reappeared as a "Modern Churchman" with no need to "commit himself to any religious belief" (188). That he should be done in by a bloodthirsty religious fanatic who considers him "no Christian" is certainly ironic, though possibly not inappropriate, justice. But that the saw with which the former carpenter cuts off Prendergast's head should have been supplied by prison authorities is the climactic example of Sir Wilfred's theories gone awry. Although the saw may have provided the carpenter a means of self-expression, the result is the opposite of what the governor intended.

While Paul is in prison, his comprehension of both human nature and moral complexity is enhanced to the point that he ceases to be a naïf. Since his reflections about Margot during many weeks of solitary confinement lead him to conflicting conclusions, he is forced to step back from his infatuation with her and take a more realistic view. Though sure that by shielding her from prosecution he has done what the code of an English gentleman demands, he also realizes that, despite her gifts of books, flowers, sherry, and exotic food, she has not done right by him. Moreover, he suspects that there is "something radically inapplicable" about the gentlemanly code when the woman he has protected is so obviously guilty and therefore unworthy of his sacrifice (252). But in trying to imagine Margot adapting to prison life—"dressed in prison uniform, hustled down corridors by wardresses, . . . set to work in the laundry washing the other prisoners' clothes" (253)—he is convinced that such circumstances would be inconceivable. Interpreting the troublesome contradiction in terms of "one law for her and another for himself" (253), he is able for the first time to approach a problem ironically, acknowledging that there is no absolute right or wrong in either of the radically disparate perspectives.

Even so, Paul is still not sophisticated enough to perceive the deviousness of Margot's thinking, which she never elucidates. Waugh's superb use of irony, however, makes it possible for the reader to surmise what transpires in her mind without ever requiring the narrator to explain. While one cannot be certain which choice Margot expects Paul to make—being released immediately if she marries Home Secretary Maltravers or waiting until he has served his sentence to marry her himself—Paul's decision to wait is apparently not what she wants. Although the reader is never told why she finally goes to see him in prison, one can deduce that she wishes to conclude their relationship in an amicable fashion. Yet her method is so oblique—she herself admits "how difficult it is to say anything" (263)—that Paul fails to comprehend. The clues to Margot's underlying thoughts are two seemingly unrelated, though juxtaposed, statements—that Lady Circumference has snubbed her and that "poor little Alastair" is falling in love with her (260)—first expressed in her letter to Paul and later reiterated in their prison conversation. But Paul sees no connection between these assertions or any significance beyond their literal meaning, nor can he follow her subsequent reasoning. Since his replies reveal his own very different train of thought, the conversation takes place on two planes that never intersect.

His inquiry about Alastair leads Margot to lament that she is being cut socially by people who no longer regard her as "a respectable woman" (261); but this response then prompts Paul to ask about her "business," to which he would logically attribute society's rejection. Although in answering his direct question Margot asserts that she is selling out because "a Swiss firm" has created difficulties, she insists that the ostracism must be caused by her age. When Paul again fails to grasp the connection she is trying to convey—that high society thinks her too old to be carrying on with young men such as Alastair—she abandons indirection and simply announces her decision to marry Maltravers. Since she never explains why such a marriage would be the best solution to her multifarious problems, all that Paul learns from their meeting is that, to his astonishment, he is pained not by the breaking off of their engagement but by his own failure to care. The reader, on the other hand, is able to conclude, from what is already known about Margot and Maltravers, that Margot needs married respectability and political influence to protect her prostitution syndicate from the law and that Maltravers would also be the sort of husband to ignore her nymphomania if she shared her income with him. Clearly, what is never explicitly stated in the conversation is far more important than what is said. This disparity between thought and spoken word, in combination with the characters' divergent ways of interpreting the same ideas and with the basic discrepancy between pretense and reality, creates an unusually ingenious way of presenting the episode.

But if resignation is the key to Paul's survival, such is not the case with Grimes, whose free spirit cannot bear restraint. His marriage to Flossie, which was expected to save him and his career from homosexual disgrace, has instead landed him, through conviction for bigamy, in a prison from which no inmate has successfully escaped. In a burlesque of adventure-story flights from incarceration, the narrator offers a mock-heroic account of Grimes's disappearance that is bolstered by the author's sketch of

Grimes riding a white charger into the heavens and bearing a pennant inscribed "Excelsior." Although circumstantial evidence points to the likelihood that the prisoner perished in the bog, Paul confidently believes that Grimes is immortal—an elemental life force, indeed the sex drive itself. In a parodic imitation of Pater's imaginative criticism of La Gioconda, Paul employs wildly extravagant allusions to convince himself that a man who "had followed in the Bacchic train of distant Arcady, . . . taught the childish satyrs the art of love," and withstood divine wrath "while the Citadels of the Plain fell to ruin about his ears" (269) will follow his usual pattern of turning up alive elsewhere. While Pater's ecstatic eulogy of the Mona Lisa as the embodiment of eternal life and the summation of all human experience is appropriate for da Vinci's masterpiece, Paul's hyperbolic reveries about Grimes as undying sexuality become ludicrous when placed in the same framework. Furthermore, in the light of Paul's belief in the immortality of Grimes, whose fate is never determined, the chaplain's self-reproach for not having prevented Grimes's death adds another ironic twist to the episode entitled "The Passing of a Public-School Man."

Paul's escape from prison is a carefully orchestrated charade of death, about which he knows nothing in advance. A number of inexplicable occurrences lead Paul, as well as the reader, to suspect that he may be headed for execution on the operating table. His scheduled appendectomy seems ridiculous since he no longer has an appendix; he is asked to sign a previously witnessed last will and testament leaving his worldly goods to Margot; the warder who escorts him to the nursing home makes ambiguous winks and sly innuendos about the possibility of death; and the drunken surgeon utters maudlin lamentations. Since Prendergast and Grimes have been finally disposed of in the two preceding episodes, the reader has even more reason to think that the hero will be finished off in the chapter entitled "The Passing of Paul Pennyfeather." But all aspects of the "death," arranged by Home Secretary Maltravers and Alastair Trumpington in the service of Margot, turn out to be fraudulent: the nursing home is run by Dr. Fagan (now M.D. rather than Ph.D.), no operation is performed, and the surgeon signs a fake death certificate. In this manner, some of the very people who contributed to Paul's downfall and imprisonment achieve his liberation; by staging his "death," they give him a new existence.

Imbedded in the account of Paul's demise are numerous ironic comparisons, both parallel and inverse, with his aborted wedding.

At the luncheon preceding the nuptial ceremony, he is "the centre of interest of the whole room" (209); but while Fagan, Alastair, and the surgeon deal with the legal documents, "no one [pays] much attention" to him (275). Each occasion results in a dramatic change in Paul's status, but while the first one, about which he has great expectations, plunges him from fame into disgrace, the second, about which he suffers considerable apprehension, turns his imprisonment into freedom. Fagan's toast to "Fortune, a much-maligned lady," recalls Paul's previous tribute to that fickle goddess just before his arrest. This time Margot assumes the role of Fortune and, instead of bringing bad luck, aids Paul with all her resources, while Alastair, in managing details of the "death" and in accompanying Paul to Margot's waiting yacht, plays a role analogous to his earlier function as best man. In another ironic comparison, Paul's transition into apparent death is cleverly set up as a parallel to Tennyson's account of the passing of Arthur. The farewell on the seashore, in which Sir Alastair is recast as Sir Bedivere watching the dying King Arthur embark for Avalon, places Paul's unromantic escape from imprisonment in the context of hallowed legend. Just as Arthur is spirited away to an island paradise to be healed of his wound and possibly to return, so Paul is carried off to Corfu to be resurrected with a new identity. But the mock-heroic manner of his departure and the inappropriateness of the allusions serve to emphasize the unheroic nature of the old Paul Pennyfeather.

After Paul's legal extinction, it is incongruous that one of the most profound judgments on his past life should be uttered by the pompous fool Silenus. Despite having failed in all his undertakings (including a belated decision to marry Margot), this self-deceived, self-styled "professor" pontificates with characteristic lack of humility on how Paul went wrong. According to his mechanistic theory, life is like a giant carnival wheel surrounded by a seated audience, and humanity is divided into two species—the dynamic, who scramble onto the revolving wheel, and the static, who merely watch. The majority of those on the wheel are repeatedly thrown off by centrifugal force; the successfully hedonistic, like Margot, cling tenaciously to the rapidly moving outer rim for maximum thrills, while those whom Silenus enigmatically labels "the professional men" make their way with determination toward the hub, where it is easier to stay on. In Silenus's opinion, Paul's error was to have climbed onto the wheel at all; his place should logically have been among the spectators. The most obvious error, however, is

Silenus's own assessment of himself. Unable to distinguish between the stability of the wheel's fixed center and the immobility of the stationary audience, he thinks he has arrived very near the center when he is most certainly on the sidelines.

However Paul's mistake may be interpreted, he does not repeat it. The subtle montage of the last section, whereby his altered responses are superimposed on recollections of his earlier Oxford existence, shows that Paul has profited from the intervening experiences without becoming radically different. Oxford itself is unchanged: the chaplain and Paul's scout continue to judge his "distant cousin," the "degenerate" Pennyfeather, solely on erroneous hearsay. Paul, again the ordinand but this time heavily mustachioed, gravitates toward a friend who, like Potts, is also interested in the League of Nations Union, penal alleviation, and theology. Yet Paul's attitude toward all this has matured from what it was in his previous incarnation. Though he continues to be concerned with social and religious causes, he has become more cautiously conservative toward life and religion.

That Paul deliberately severs detrimental links to his past is clear. By placing Fagan's book *Mother Wales* beside Stanley's *Eastern Church*, an account of religious schism, he tacitly implies rejection of both. By not responding to the now opulent Philbrick's invitation and by falsely identifying him as Arnold Bennett (in an ironic allusion to another con artist who had parlayed questionable talents into wealth), Paul denigrates that connection as well. In dealing with Peter Pastmaster, now the embodiment of the Bollinger, he concedes his own folly in having become involved with Margot and her "dynamic" breed; but, with the observation that Peter has already drunk too much, he brushes aside the proposal of a toast to "Fortune, a much-maligned lady." Having previously allowed himself to be buffeted by fortune, Paul is determined to wrest control of his own destiny whenever possible. Ironic detachment, even if it means withdrawal from the whirligig of life, can serve as a practical defense against the world's corruption. Experience has taught him something about where to engage and where, in the interest of survival, to disengage himself. True sophistication, he has discovered, depends on knowing which strategy to employ.

Vile Bodies

*I*n the scene in which Nina and Ginger look down upon their country from an airplane as they depart on their honeymoon, the objective narrator in *Vile Bodies* ironically juxtaposes their radically differing perceptions of England. Ginger, possibly influenced by a background of military service in Britain's imperial forces and by romantic expectations for their marriage, recalls John of Gaunt's tribute to England's heroic greatness. Nina, however, is incapable of associating that passage from *Richard II* with what she sees below—sprawling suburbs, decaying factories, and humanity reduced to meaningless existence. Far from moving her to poetical inspiration, the depressing terrestrial scene, combined with her sickening realization that she has married a man she does not love, prompts her to vomit, although the narrator's superficial reporting seems to link her temporary illness only to a rough "current of air."[1]

By placing these antithetical views side by side without editorial comment, Waugh is able to encapsulate the novel's irreconcilable conflict—basically one between reality and illusion—which affects all the characters in the sociohistorical setting of the late 1920s. Playing off idealistic notions of England's former glory against what he considers to be her present state of degradation, the author portrays an entire society oblivious to the gravity of its true situation. Not only does he poke fun at the Bright Young People for their obviously unrealistic approach to life; he also ridicules their supposedly more sensible elders—such as the wealthy and powerful traditionalists of the Anchorage House set and, with gentler irony, the anachronistic Lottie Crump—for blithely living in the illusions of the past while disaster looms in the future.

The consequences awaiting the young hedonists on whom the novel focuses seem particularly out of proportion to their original intention of merely amusing themselves. But their chase after elusive pleasure grows into a frenetic search for excitement; and their endless succession of parties, though masquerading as hilarious comedy, becomes a frenzied dance of death. As this frivolous lost generation heads for catastrophe, the mood of the novel darkens and repeated allusions to bad weather emphasize the ominous gloom.[2] Correspondingly, Waugh's irony moves from the comic to the tragic and ultimately to the nihilistic.[3] Whereas Paul Pennyfeather learns to survive in a chaotic environment, Adam Fenwick-Symes and his friends seem doomed by forces beyond their control. One by one, through some mishap, the Bright Young People disappear from the social scene. As Nina remarks to Adam, "There seems to be none of us left now except you and me . . . and Ginger" (295). Then the war disposes of Adam.

Because Waugh described the young people of that era in a sober, straightforward manner in two 1929 articles, it is possible to reconstruct his opinion of them more definitely than it is for most of the other subjects he treated only through irony. In "The War and the Younger Generation,"[4] he divided society into three age groups having only "superficial sympathy" with each other—those whose convictions had been formed well before World War I and who were too old to fight, those whose faith in the old order had been shaken by military service, and those who had grown to maturity in the 1920s. Most members of this last group he declared to be "totally lacking in any sense of qualitative value." While their "undiscriminating and ineffectual" character might partially be attributed to the wartime circumstances of their adolescence, their elders deserved some of the blame for not having rigorously disciplined them. Many returning veterans, whose ideals had been shattered by the war, became tolerant toward anything "modern" and, instead of instilling traditional values in the young, encouraged independent thinking. Some young people were allowed so much money and freedom that their natural rebelliousness had nothing further to revolt against except common decency. Consequently, their behavior often assumed the form of "perverse and aimless dissipation." Yet it was not just the young in years but also some Peter Pans of middle age who refused to grow up. In "Too Young at Forty" Waugh lamented that "in Society indefatigable maiden ladies of Chelsea and Mayfair, dyspeptic noblemen and bald old wits still caper[ed] in the public eye as 'the Bright Young People.'"[5]

In translating his views into novelistic form, Waugh was able to approach this fashionable, permissive society with an ambivalence highly conducive to irony, because from about 1924 to 1929 he had participated in its festivities. During that time and even earlier at Oxford he was not averse to a dissolute lifestyle; but eventually the shallow inanity of drunken, often mindless, revels began to pall.[6] Especially after the collapse of his first marriage in July 1929, by which time roughly half of *Vile Bodies* had been written, he withdrew in disgust.[7] Much later, in a 1956 essay honoring the urbanity of Max Beerbohm, he recalled, by way of contrast, the deliberate insolence, disdain for good manners, and social outrages perpetrated by the "rowdy little set" to which he had belonged in the late twenties.[8] In retrospect he observed that the most admired accomplishment among that group had been some successful challenge to conventional standards. At the time of composing *Vile Bodies*, however, his fascination with wily rogues and decadent pleasure-seekers had not yet been overwhelmed by growing revulsion. He was therefore superbly qualified in 1929 to depict uninhibited hedonists at play even while prophesying the likely consequences of their irresponsibility. It is this ability to identify with the irrational as well as the rational, the disorderly as well as the orderly, and to be both antagonistic and sympathetic (as a true satirist could not be) that makes his ironic presentation of the Bright Young People extraordinarily rich.

In order to carry off this dual perspective successfully and to deal with a large cast of major figures, Waugh manages his narration differently than in *Decline and Fall*. In *Vile Bodies* the narrator is more detached emotionally from the characters themselves yet more involved technically in recounting their escapades. These shifts in stance and function are partly necessitated by the dissimilar positions of Waugh's heroes in the two books. While Paul is at the center of coherent action built around him, Adam serves largely as a continuous thread holding together discrete episodes, so that in the second novel the narrator must assume a more important role in presenting the loosely strung story. It is through some of his evaluative comments that the reader may catch glimpses of the author's bitterness at the betrayals and machinations of society. In accord with Waugh's ambivalent feelings, the narrator seems generally to have withdrawn farther from Adam, who has succumbed to the values of his social set, than from Paul, an innocent with whom both author and narrator more readily empathize. Despite intermittent tinges of sympathy, especially with Agatha Runcible's demise and Adam's mistreatment by other characters, the narrator remains essentially aloof. Moreover, by portraying the Bright Young People as an entire group, the narrator is better able to maintain a disinterested attitude than he can toward an individual like Paul, on whom he must constantly focus. This greater distancing in *Vile Bodies* not only permits a balanced view of the twenties phenomenon in which the author had been participating; it also enhances the artistry of the novel by accentuating the desperate situations of Adam and other hopeless characters through an almost brutal refusal to become emotionally involved in their misfortunes.[9]

To depict the social context in which the characters move, the narrator begins with an amusing montage, or counterpoint, showing how a boatload of travelers respond to the shared experience of an unsettling Channel crossing. With a minimum of commentary and editorial glue, he shifts from one vignette to another, allowing passengers to expose more about themselves than they would willingly divulge. The drug-induced sleep into which Walter Outrage retreats as a means of coping with the choppy seas foreshadows his subsequent ineffectuality as a lover and a statesman, while his dreams of delicate oriental luxuriance seem at odds with his public "macho" image. Father Rothschild betrays himself as a master of intrigue by his diplomatic pass, his concern with international affairs, and his false beard in a borrowed suitcase.[10] The Bright Young People unknowingly disclose their party-to-party existence and its accompanying ennui through their precious vocabulary and the bibulous similes—"exactly like being inside a cocktail shaker" (9)—with which they describe the effects of the pitching ship. While the "commercial gents" try to deceive themselves about their queasy stomachs, it is apparent from the deterioration of their bridge game that mal de mer is overwhelming them; and Adam's attempt to be sociable with a garrulous journalist belies his growing seasickness. The captain and the chief officer, unaffected by rough weather, reveal their indifference to the suffering of their passengers by amusing themselves with a crossword puzzle. Mrs. Melrose Ape, the

American evangelist, even takes advantage of the desperately ill for her own financial gain: likening the stormy crossing allegorically to man's progress toward death, she organizes a hymn singing and passes the hat.

For some of the subtlest reporting in this episode, Waugh employs the conversations of gossipy twin sisters, Fanny Throbbing and Kitty Blackwater, whose naughty names jar with their social status as Edwardian grandes dames. In the manner of Ronald Firbank's conversants, they suggest by innuendo what social etiquette forbids them to utter directly. Their brief observations about former prime minister Outrage furnish an excellent example of such lightly comic irony. Through glancing references to subjects they obviously know more about—"just like poor Throbbing . . . we all used to think it was drink," "*one* person . . . at the Japanese Embassy," "but *his age*, and the bull-like type is so often disappointing" (6)—they titillate the reader's imagination. Presumably in the back of their minds they both find it difficult to reconcile the reality of Outrage as an old drug addict, seemingly devoid of mental acumen and sexual appeal, with rumors of his romantic involvement with the wife of the Japanese ambassador. But they understand each other so well that the crucial ideas underlying their disjointed banter need never be put into words. In order to comprehend the remarks of these risqué ladies, who reappear peripherally throughout the novel, the reader attuned to Waugh's ironic mode must deduce what unexpressed thoughts give coherence to their choral commentaries.

Mrs. Ape, who dominates the action on the Channel boat, becomes the object of satiric irony as the personification of debased religion. The reader is first introduced to her fraudulence through the depiction of her troupe of hymn-singing angels with detachable wings. Their stage names, such as Chastity, Prudence, and Temperance, are ill suited to their offstage conduct; and Mrs. Ape, in trying to control them, must sometimes assume the role of a madam struggling to keep her wayward "girls" in line. Her advice to them aboard ship, "If you have peace in your hearts your stomach will look after itself" (3-4), typifies her incompatible mixture of trite religious sentiment and mundanity, while her celebrated hymn, "*There ain't no flies on the Lamb of God*," which they sing in an unsuccessful attempt to avert nausea, epitomizes her vulgarity and irreverence. The collection Mrs. Ape takes up after her own charismatic performance among the seasick passengers exemplifies the perversion of her calling into profiteering, for she exploits the human desire to buy one's own deliverance. But her observation that "salvation doesn't do them the same good if they think it's free" (20) cuts ironically not only against her but against her audience as well, since both the deluder and the deluded use religion for selfish ends.

Hypocrisy of a more sophisticated nature preys ironically upon Mrs. Ape when Margot Beste-Chetwynde, now Lady Metroland, gives a London party in her honor. Although Margot's motives are never precisely divulged, they can be deduced from ensuing events. With her penchant for mischief-making, she is presumably eager to see the impact of Mrs. Ape's soul-searing antics upon her guests—an unusual and daring combination of Bright Young Things and establishment figures. That Margot also has professional designs on the angels surfaces when she underhandedly recruits Chastity for her South American enterprise. At this point, what appears on the surface to be a straightforward contrast between a beautiful, charming hostess and her coarse, mannish guest of honor can also be seen as an ironic analogy; and Lady Throbbing's realization that the term *procureuse*, which she had applied to Mrs. Ape, should not be uttered in the Metroland household obliquely confirms the underlying similarity. While the evangelist is planning to capitalize on the wealth and prominence of the elite assemblage, Margot, the shrewder and more predatory of the two, is appraising Mrs. Ape's girls for the purpose of offering them entertainment opportunities of a different sort. The final irony about the angels is that for some of them Margot's jobs would not be a radical change; Mrs. Ape herself calls them sluts when she lets her Christian benevolence slip.

The scene in which Mrs. Ape gets her revivalistic performance off to an impressive start with her celebrated injunction, "*Just you look at yourselves*" (137), is described with exaggerated emotion. Under the sway of her booming voice and searching eyes, she appears, as one angel puts it, to have "got 'em again." However, the guests' uneasy consciences do not lead to the expected result of open confessions and open purses; for Lady Circumference, whom the narrator characterizes hyperbolically as "the organ voice of England, the hunting-cry of the *ancien régime*," breaks the hypnotic spell by calling the evangelist "a damned impudent woman" (138). Again the irony cuts in two directions, demeaning both Mrs. Ape and the guests whom she almost succeeds in disgracing. But her spectacular failure spawns additional ironies through a peculiar train of events. A frustrated gossip columnist, unable to glean from Margot's party the scandals he had anticipated, invents lurid confessions for his newspaper; and Mrs. Ape, corroborating his story about the wild outpouring of guilt and jewels as testimony to her powers, snatches a fraudulent victory from defeat.

The Bright Young People are, to some extent, as phony as Mrs. Ape, but they are neither as successful nor as reprehensible, for they do not share her calculatedly hypocritical approach to the pursuit of self-interest. Though one could hardly call them innocent, they are strangely naive about their relationship to the rest of the world. Determined to be free from what they regard as the outmoded morality of their elders, they assume no obligations except to themselves and feel entitled to experiment with drink, drugs, sex, or anything else that quickens the pulse. Considering themselves a breed apart from traditional society, they communicate with a special coterie vocabulary ("shame-making," "too divine"), unaware that their favorite pejorative adjective, "bogus," is particularly applicable to themselves. Indeed their tenuous existence is predicated upon a number of inconsistencies. Since most of the Bright Young People, including the two titled gossip columnists, have only proletarian incomes, their delusions of living as cavalierly as French nobles before the Deluge must be sustained through the manipulation of someone else's money. By borrowing houses, servants, and cars from family members, they belie their avowed independence; and by courting wealthy déclassé outsiders, who can afford to give lavish parties and provide transportation, they discredit their own pretensions of social superiority. Consequently, the struggle to lead an insouciant lifestyle brings them not the pleasure they expect but constant anxiety. In every respect they seem to be both the perpetrators and the victims of self-contradiction.

Their claim of being liberated from duty is invalidated by the negative consequences their actions sometimes inflict upon others. A marvelously funny example is the incident at 10 Downing Street. In a case of high contrast between cause and effect, what begins as an impromptu early morning breakfast after a costume party elsewhere is so embellished by the gossip columnist in the group that the prime minister, Sir James Brown, is forced out of office amid rumors of scandal. It never occurs to his thoughtless daughter Jane that bringing this smart set into her home could have political

repercussions; and her self-absorbed guests are totally unconcerned that reports of "Midnight Orgies" at the official residence
might topple her father's government. Climaxing this explosive situation is the dramatic moment of revelation when Agatha
Runcible, having spent the night at the Browns' and still in Hawai-
ian dress, reads in the morning paper about the supposedly wild
party there and realizes for the first time (as does the reader) exactly where she is. Her spontaneous reactions thereafter are instrumental in further ironies. Her suggestion that a complaint from Sir
James might result in the gossip columnist's dismissal actually foreshadows the prime minister's own downfall because of the unfa-
vorable publicity; and her flight into the street while clad only in
her scanty costume provides the waiting reporters with evidence
for their wildest assumptions.

From her first wriggles of delight before the Channel crossing to
her final hysteria in the nursing home, the Hon. Agatha Runcible is
often at the center of the novel's most amusing or bizarre occurrences; and the narrator, by presenting her madcap progress in a
detached, nonjudgmental manner, permits the reader to share
Waugh's mixed feelings toward the wacky set she symbolizes. One
might, for example, scoff at the stupidity of her assumption that
the Independent Labour Party is a social event to which she has not
been invited but nevertheless find the candor of her reaction to be
refreshing. While her unreflective actions at the auto race—such as
smoking amid open fuel containers—might be deplored as evidence of mindless immaturity, her defiance of restraints—whether
by violating safety rules or wearing trousers in disregard of twenties' propriety—appeals to the latent anarchy in all of us. And her
recklessness in taking the wheel of a race car because her arm band
(intended only as a ruse to get her into the pits) reads "Spare
Driver" must be weighed against her kindhearted intentions of saving a disabled driver from being eliminated. Nevertheless, her fool-
hardy entrance into the race, with its perils and repetitive
circularity, has to be seen as a parallel to her social set's plunge into
aimless amusement. Her hallucinations after the crash—of driving
faster and faster without being able to stop—represent the group's
headlong rush toward destruction, which in Agatha's own case is
brought about quite inadvertently by her friends' riotous party at
her bedside.

Some of the blame for the Bright Young People's shocking behavior rests on the unhealthy symbiosis between them and the

press. Inherent in this strange alliance is an absurd disparity between pretense and actuality, since habitués of the smart set profess to dislike publicity and complain about reporters at their
parties yet eagerly seek out newspaper accounts and photographs
of themselves. This inconsistency is particularly exemplified in the
escapades of Agatha Runcible. Despite saying to Adam that she
"can't *tell*" him how she has been strip-searched by customs officials, who mistake her for a gem smuggler, she can hardly wait to
reveal *all* the "too shaming" and "shy-making details" to the press,
who immediately put her story in headlines. Although feigning
embarrassment while wandering half-naked around the prime
minister's residence, she clearly delights in performing before
stunned audiences—for the Browns inside and the newspeople
outside 10 Downing Street. And in the aftermath of Mrs. Ape's fiasco, Agatha's numerous court appearances—first as plaintiff,
then as witness, spectator, intruder in the press gallery, and finally
as prisoner being sentenced for contempt of court—engender
enough press clippings to fill two albums.

Since many antics of the Bright Young People are motivated by a
desire for notoriety, journalists, whom the narrator subjects to
acerbic irony, abet the folly of these partygoers by writing glamorized accounts of their frolics. The gossip columnists themselves
are impelled to transform what they privately regard as colossally
boring occasions into fascinating copy in order to sell their newspapers and keep their jobs. In this pernicious web of falsehood and
self-interest, readers who feed on sensational journalism are also
shown to be culpable; and the narrator indicts them not only for
encouraging irresponsible conduct among the young but for causing the press, in a highly ironic turn of events, to become the victim
of its own money-making strategies. Publishers, steering between
their own fears of libel and subscribers' voracious appetites for excitement, make such conflicting demands upon their employees
that the result is often disaster. In a grim twist of fate, Lord
Balcairn, as the columnist Chatterbox, confronts his impossible dilemma by concocting outrageous slander about real people in the
fashionable world and then committing suicide. Adam, upon becoming Chatterbox, resolves the problem more genially by inventing socialites and fads that do not exist; and his method is for a time
so successful that real socialites pretend to know his creations and
rival gossip columnists embroider additional fabrications about
them.

The inversion of human values reflective of an ironic universe creates insurmountable difficulties for Adam in his star-crossed love affair with Nina. Although society pays lip service to traditional virtues, it does not reward them. Adam's purposeful ambition to become a creative writer is thwarted by the customs official's unreasonable confiscation of his first manuscript and by his publisher's exploitive contract. His honesty and trust are repeatedly betrayed—most egregiously by Col. Blount and the Major to whom he entrusts his £1,000. But while Adam's integrity yields no tangible benefits, his journalistic deceit wins him approval. In such an atmosphere of perversity, injustice, indifference, and uncertainty, Adam and his fiancée can find no secure or productive place. Nor can their love flourish in a superficial environment that regards the acquisition of wealth as paramount—that prevents an impecunious marriage even while permitting extramarital sex and the begetting of a child. Adam's seemingly caddish act of selling his share in Nina, in order to pay his hotel bill, and her acceptance of a loveless marriage to a man with inherited means represent the lovers' final surrender to a money-centered world.

Against the background of Adam and Nina's unsatisfactory relationship, the narrator offers ironic perspectives on romantic liaisons outside the circle of the Bright Young People. The rendezvous of Outrage and Baroness Yoshiwara at Lottie Crump's hotel is an amusing exercise in frustration, since neither participant understands the subtleties and signals of a different culture well enough to interpret the other's desires. A more sophisticated example is the passionless engagement of Edward, Lord Throbbing and Lady Ursula, daughter of the Duke and Duchess of Stayle. In this instance it is Ursula's domineering mother who provides the discrepancies through her expert dissembling. Claiming, with some truth, that Edward would not have been her choice because of his family's tarnished reputation and lack of substantial wealth, the Duchess hints covertly at Ursula's inability to attract suitors by asserting that "there seem so few young men about" (180); but her feigned reason for not interfering with the undesirable union—that the "headstrong children . . . seem so fond of each other" (179)—is revealed as a lie when Ursula at first refuses Edward's dilatory proposal. Nevertheless, the Duchess persists, using a subtle back-door method that incongruously transforms her assurances of support for her daughter's wishes into inferences encouraging the marriage: "It's a matter that only you can decide. . . . No one is going to make my darling girl do anything she doesn't want to. . . . Papa shall see Edward in the morning and make everything all right . . . dear Lady Anchorage was only saying tonight what a lovely bride you will make" (189).

Anchorage House, as a symbol of the ruling classes, provides the narrator with an extremely different perspective for his objective reportage on the Bright Young People. Having examined the rebellious set at close range, he also surveys them from the more distant vantage point of their elders. Lady Anchorage's soiree— juxtaposed for maximum effect to the simultaneous but very dissimilar party in the captive dirigible—evokes a wide spectrum of opinion about the younger generation. Not surprisingly, Margot Metroland, without making any overt comment, unmistakably shows her identification with unconventional youth by deserting the formal reception for the orgies in the dirigible. From what the Edwardian twin sisters obliquely imply, it is obvious that, despite the disparity of age, they too are kindred spirits with the young people of the twenties. Wistfully longing to participate in the wild entertainments, Fanny and Kitty console themselves with the rationalization that being naughty now could not be as much fun as in the days when they had to work very hard "to be even moderately bad" (181).

Father Rothschild's defense of modern youth, while thoughtful and well-meaning, appears to involve some flawed reasoning; and its absurdities may possibly be an ironic commentary on his supposed wisdom.[11] Seeing the predicament of the younger generation in historical terms—because they are caught between the disruptions of a past war and an imminent one—he concludes quite plausibly that they long for something enduring in which to believe. But that their desire for permanence should be evidenced, as he infers, by an increase in divorce seems an internal contradiction that would deconstruct the very assertion of it. Moreover, this extraordinary deduction is based on the inversion of a familiar precept; according to the Jesuit, the young maintain that "if a thing's not worth doing well, it's not worth doing at all" (184).

In contrast, most of the Anchorage House guests—representing the old aristocracy, Parliament, the commercial plutocracy, and the Church of England—are so bogged down in tradition as to be completely out of touch with the young rebels; and it is evident from the narrator's tone that he is not offering the stodgy ways of the old order as a solution to contemporary ills. Mr. Outrage, presently the prime minister, and Lord Metroland can only deplore that the young seem to be in open conflict with the establishment and are not preparing themselves for future leadership. But Outrage's angry refusal to understand them and Metroland's inability to deal directly with them (by deliberately avoiding his wife's lover and attempting to pamper his drunken stepson) imply that the elders, through either excessive intolerance or permissiveness, are largely responsible for the collapse of normal relations between age groups.

The failure of the generations to solve their mutual problems on the world stage is contrasted ironically with the skill displayed by Lottie Crump in conducting the business of Shepheard's Hotel. Her unique institution, where, as the narrator observes, one can still draw "healing draughts from the well of Edwardian certainty" (41), is a relic of the era when aristocrats knew how to enjoy their pleasures without flaunting them in public view as do the Bright Young People. In appearance the hotel jars with the contemporary scene. Its parlor, for example, is full of autographed pictures showing the illustrious patrons of bygone days. But if Shepheard's clings in some respects to a time made obsolete by the social and economic changes after the First World War, Lottie manages her affairs with a timeless practicality. Through shrewdness and cockney bravado, she turns human strengths and weaknesses to the advantage of her enterprise, providing whatever her guests require; and her services may include not only lodging, food, and an abundance of champagne but at times sympathy, privacy, and even anonymity.[12]

The psychological acumen with which Lottie effects these accomplishments lies beneath an unlikely facade of forgetful eccentricity, but the narrator's objective stance precludes the possibility of fathoming her inner consciousness. Her seemingly poor memory—which now and then can flash with uncommon clarity—may be her way of tuning out the inconsequential; or it may represent a habitual, possibly subconscious, self-defense in a business where it is wise not to show how much she actually knows. That the obtuse chatter with which she sidesteps inconvenient confrontations may be another means of self-protection is illustrated by her conversations with Adam concerning the Major to whom he has entrusted his £1,000:

> "What major?" said Lottie. . . . "I never saw a major."
> "The one you introduced me to in the corner."

"How d'you know he's a major?"

"You said he was."

"My dear boy, I've never seen him before. Now I come to think of it, he did look like a major, didn't he?" (55-56)

Many pages later, when Lottie reminds Adam about the Major, her memory is surprisingly intact: "He's a chap who used to come here quite a lot. . . . He was here the night that . . . You ought to remember him, dear. He was the one made that bet for you on the November Handicap" (281-82).

Lottie's cunning succeeds most superbly when she plies the police with cheap champagne in order to avoid scandal involving the death of a drunken prostitute who had been swinging on a lighting fixture at Shepheard's. The obituary euphemistically describes the deceased as a woman of *"independent means"* who fell while trying to mend a chandelier in an unnamed West End hotel; and its finest touch of irony—because it implies much more to the initiated than the words alone convey—characterizes her as *"well known in business circles"* (100-101). Lottie, as Adam realizes, is far more adept at preventing adverse publicity than Prime Minister Brown. In this and other delightful instances her pragmatic sophistication triumphs where the naiveté of the young and the stupidity of the old fail.

However unpredictable Lottie may be, her motives are more readily fathomable than those of Father Rothschild, the elusive Major, and Col. Blount, Nina's father. The narrator's ambivalence toward these characters suggests not only that he is playing with them but that Waugh, as ironist, is playing with his readers by withholding information. Our fascination with Rothschild, a caricature of the politically involved Jesuit, is partly due to the persistent aura of secrecy surrounding him. Though his benevolence is apparent, his worldly interests and behind-the-scenes plotting jar with his priestly vocation, and his objectives are never revealed. He surfaces periodically throughout the novel (aboard ship, over the telephone, and at the Metroland and Anchorage parties) only to retreat into obscurity as dark as the night into which he finally disappears on his motorcycle. In contrast, the drunken Major, who promises to bet Adam's £1,000 on a horse and return the winnings, tantalizes the reader by appearing and disappearing numerous times as the discrepancy between his pretenses and his true character gradually unfolds. Without repaying the money, he keeps up enough genial palaver to make his professed honesty at first seem plausible; but after he cons Adam out of a "loan" and then gloats about his victim's gullibility, the reader concludes that he must be something of a scoundrel. The Major's final actions on the battlefield, offering Adam a worthless check and copulating with Chastity, show him to be utterly unconscionable about taking advantage wherever he can.

More enigmatic and humorous than either the Major or Father Rothschild is Col. Blount. Not only are the workings of his mind impenetrable; his behavior lacks any consistency from which the reader may draw irrefutable deductions. The fantasy world in which the Colonel lives is as odd as the film venture in which he performs and even invests, and one can never be sure whether he is playacting. Such an ambiguous presentation gives him a complexity and an individuality that he would not otherwise possess. At times he is a caricature of the stereotypical eccentric—a bumbling, blustering old fool whose absentmindedness is so chronic that acquaintances comment on it. At other times he is extraordinarily sharp-witted. These fluctuations in his personality are best portrayed in his three encounters with Adam, whom he seems to regard as three distinct individuals. During their first meeting, the Colonel, even while persisting in the notion that Adam is a vacuum-cleaner salesman, asks astute questions about his prospective son-in-law's financial situation. There is little incoherence in the conversation; the Colonel's queries are right on target and progress logically toward culmination in his gift of a £1,000 check. The dislocation arises from his bogus signature—"Charlie Chaplin"—which invalidates the check and shows him to be capable of an ironic jest that neither Adam nor the reader fully comprehends until later.

A particularly good example of Col. Blount's mental aberrations occurs when Adam, during his second trip to Doubting Hall, tries to explain that he has a job with a newspaper. Whatever Adam says is misinterpreted. Blount's replies slide past Adam's thoughts without contact; the only link is a word or idea disconnected from the original context and reconnected in an unrelated context. In the following contracted exchange one false assumption is built upon another:

> "I'm afraid you've forgotten me, sir. . . . [Nina] wanted me to tell you that I'm Mr. Chatterbox now."

"... I'm afraid I don't remember you. ... There's a Canon Chatterbox at Worcester I used to know. ...."
"Mr. Chatterbox on the *Daily Excess.*"
"No, no, my dear boy, I assure you not. ... He was never on the *Daily Excess* in his life."
"No, no, sir, I'm on the *Daily Excess.*"
"Well, you ought to know your own staff, certainly. He *may* have left Worcester and taken to journalism. ...."
"... You don't understand—I want to marry Nina."
"... I happen to know she's engaged already. There was a young ass of a chap down here about it the other day. ... So I'm afraid you're too late. ... Well, good-bye. ... Remember me to Canon Chatterbox. ... Writing for the papers, indeed, at his age." (210-12)

Thus Col. Blount thwarts Adam a second time and, according to the narrator, retires "victorious"; but it is still unclear whether his disjointed responses are deliberate.

During the Christmas visit the Colonel's enthusiastic acceptance of Adam in the role of Nina's wealthy husband Ginger is also suspect, though without concrete evidence one can only speculate on the workings of his mind. When he refers to the salesman and the journalist as Nina's previous suitors, neither the characters nor the reader can determine for certain what he really believes; and whomever he takes this supposed son-in-law to be, the reader must question his motives for trying to sell the young man one-half interest in an unsuccessful film enterprise. Whatever the Colonel may think, he plays the ironist in all his encounters with Adam, whether his strategies are premeditated or impromptu; and he can get away with teasing and tricking his helpless victim because Adam, in the vulnerable position of either a prospective son-in-law or an impostor, cannot afford to confront him.

Adam and Nina's happy but illicit honeymoon at Doubting Hall, which is uncomfortably juxtaposed to her miserable wedding trip with Ginger, climaxes the on-again, off-again love affair that holds the novel together. While the episode is couched in the framework of a traditional Christmas in the country, it becomes an elaborate charade fraught with multiple ironies stemming from Adam's impersonation. All the characters participate in the hoax, though for different reasons. Col. Blount, showing no signs of recognizing Adam, receives him as Ginger, congratulates his daughter on her choice, and inappropriately predicts a good life for the couple. The servants unquestionably detect the imposture but, not daring in their position to expose Adam as a fraud, are obliged to wish him and Nina a happy marriage. The rector plays along with the pretense because he draws several false conclusions from inadequate evidence. Recognizing Adam from his first visit to Doubting Hall, he naturally accepts the young man as Nina's husband; but also remembering Adam's uncontrollable laughter on that occasion and puzzled by his complete denial of the visit, the rector thinks him so unhinged as to require humoring. If Adam and Nina achieve peace and marital happiness under the playacting conditions of this "ideal" Christmas, they do so against the background of impending war and the reader's knowledge that this fraudulent marriage is the only one they are destined to have.

The last chapter of *Vile Bodies*, ironically entitled "Happy Ending," represents the nadir of Waugh's disillusionment with the society of his day. Moving from positions in which positive stances can be deduced even from negative depictions, the conclusion finally passes into the realm of what Booth has called unstable irony.[13] As Adam, lost and forlorn, surveys the ruins of a gigantic battlefield, the values of Western civilization have suffered total collapse, and nothing in this modern wasteland has any significance or coherence. All norms seem to have been dissolved; and there are no longer contradictions to reconcile, judgments to suspend, or stands to take on any issues. Since the author offers no remedy, even by implication, to rectify the tragic absurdity of the situation, the scene moves toward complete nihilism. The drunken Major, now elevated to the rank of general, continues his exploitation of others for his own diversion. Chastity, having sunk from her angelic status to camp follower, takes whatever pleasure she can as the fighting draws nearer. With nothing to live for, Adam grows oblivious to all that is going on around him and merely falls asleep, becoming one more sacrificial victim in a world gone mad.

Black Mischief

*P*robably because of his penchant for incongruities, Waugh seems to have been especially fascinated with those areas of the world where
widely divergent cultures overlap—"where ideas, uprooted from
their traditions, become oddly changed in transplantation."[1] In
Black Mischief he not only represents the contradictions inherent
within particular societies but emphasizes those arising from encounters between disparate ways of life. By showing primitive African culture and European civilization existing side by side, he
brings into bold relief all the bizarre consequences of their interaction, thereby producing some of his sharpest and most intricate ironies. In shaping the novel, Waugh profited tremendously from
having previously written about the African scene as a journalist—
reporting to three London journals on the coronation of the Ethio-
pian emperor in 1930 and recording subsequent travels in *Remote
People* (1931). Hence he already possessed the raw material that
needed only imaginative exaggeration to be heightened into uproarious fiction, and his professional distancing from the subjects
in the factual accounts translated well into the extremely disengaged narration of *Black Mischief*.

Although the nonjudgmental approach of his narrator increases
enjoyment for the sophisticated reader, it tends to invite gross misinterpretation by the literal-minded. Waugh particularly suffered
from the refusal of Ernest Oldmeadow, editor of the *Tablet*, to review the novel even on its artistic merits while editorializing that its

author could not be a man of Catholic principles.[2] Such a charge cannot be substantiated, however, by thoughtful analysis, for if one reads the irony of *Black Mischief* properly—questioning the literal meaning and searching for a more plausible intent, as Booth recommends—the author's norms become clear on every topic from progressivism to casual sex.

Indeed Waugh's architectonic abilities are so adroitly used to counterpoint incompatible elements that the need for editorial comment is virtually eliminated. In *Black Mischief*, more than in any other Waugh novel, irony functions heuristically by inviting the reader to discover what the narrator implies but does not express. Primarily through uncomfortable juxtapositions, language inappropriate to its context, unacceptable points of view, and incongruities between appearance and reality, Waugh not only discloses his own thoughts but strives to elicit similar reactions from a morally responsible audience. The reference to the gallows used for "trivial, domestic executions"[3] necessary in the palace reveals, chiefly through the wrenching of tone by the word "trivial," exactly what the author's attitude is toward palace justice. Basil's request for more whiskey, after subjecting the frightened British colony to stories of Sakuyu savagery intensified by alcohol, forces the intended conclusion about his own barbarism. The dispassionate image of Prudence's body "stewed to pulp among peppers and aromatic roots" (300), to which Oldmeadow took particular offense, emphasizes the irreconcilable discrepancy between a cannibal gourmet's delectation and a civilized observer's revulsion. In each instance, nonchalant reporting is more shocking, and therefore more effective rhetorically, than any subjective condemnation could be.

As Waugh explained in self-defense against strictures in the *Tablet*, the theme of *Black Mischief* is "the conflict of civilisation, with all its attendant and deplorable ills, and barbarism."[4] This clash, presented in the novel through antithetical forces in unresolved opposition, exposes as fantasy the colonialist belief that civilization as conceived in Europe must prevail over African barbarism by virtue of being more enlightened or ethically superior. In many instances the technology and theories offered by the developed countries are so alien to primitive modes of life that Azanian efforts to adapt them to their own situations become not only ludicrous but highly disruptive. When the disparity is so great that neither culture can comprehend the other, the customs remain intransigently distinct. For example, the insular British Courteneys and the feudal chieftain Ngumo tolerate almost no change in their accustomed ways of life. The most disconcerting situation, though the most fruitful for the ironist, arises when each culture, in trying to bridge the differences between them, assumes as correct a viewpoint that the other regards as fallacious. Consequently, in the matter of cruelty to animals both Dame Mildred and the Azanians turn each other's ideas upside down.

But Waugh's narrator does not preach about the mutual failure; with noncommittal amusement he portrays the naiveté and bafflement of Africans encountering unfamiliar concepts and the folly of Western idealists ignorant of the practical realities in non-Western societies. Though his acerbic irony is merciless toward blatant opportunists, he is generally tolerant of the well-intentioned, if misguided, members of both races. He is possibly even gentler toward the misunderstandings of the native populace, whose fantastic adaptations of foreign culture marvelously deflate European fads and pretensions. Such incompatibilities, Waugh realized, could not easily be eliminated. Given the fallen nature of man and the chaos of his environment, as exemplified in Azania, genuine civilization could be attained only through gradual transformation; and barbarism, ever present in the human heart, would lurk as a constant threat from within as well as without. As Waugh later asserted: "Barbarism is never finally defeated. . . . we are all potential recruits for anarchy."[5]

As exemplars of the contrasting worlds in *Black Mischief*, two central characters whose individual personalities embrace conflicting elements are played off against one another. The emperor Seth upon returning to Azania to assume the throne is, even more than Waugh's earlier heroes, a misfit in his own land. His rejection of African culture combined with an imperfect assimilation of European ideas and practices has so suspended him between the two societies that he cannot function effectively in either. Having lost contact with his natural heritage and having become too advanced for the needs of his people, Seth is torn between despising the native Azanians for their savagery and trying to enlighten them. Upon learning that Wanda tribesmen have eaten his father, he declares them to be "totally out of touch with modern thought" and, to rectify their lack of education, proposes to "start them on Montessori methods" (57-58).

What Seth gains from his own education at Oxford proves inadequate in another sense: he so focuses on the surface manifestations of Western culture that he becomes overcivilized to the point of decadence. Captivated with European society, he adopts its externals—elegant dress, refined manners, titles of nobility, ceremony, literature, social change, machinery—in the mistaken belief that these outward signs of advancement will instantaneously transform his backward nation into a twentieth-century marvel. But without sufficient awareness of the concepts upon which civilized institutions are built, he interprets his newly acquired knowledge according to primitive instincts, illogically creating a fetish out of modern progress. Deceiving himself that his alignment with civilization makes him invincible, Seth proclaims hyperbolically:

> "Defeat is impossible. . . . I have seen the great tattoo of Aldershot, the Paris Exhibition, the Oxford Union. . . . at my stirrups run woman's suffrage, vaccination, and vivisection. I am the New Age. I am the Future" (22); "The world is already ours. . . . We are Light and Speed and Strength, Steel and Steam." (54)

Contrary to his faith that "Progress" and an armored tank will win the civil war, his forces emerge victorious through the most unprogressive of weapons—spears and lies. The tank, unsuitable for battle in equatorial heat, proves useful only as a punishment cell for his own unruly soldiers. In an even more striking contrast, Seth's intense belief in superior knowledge is juxtaposed to his nocturnal terrors, which reveal how close he actually is to atavistic fears of the jungle. Inside this ironic comparison is another— between Seth's naked ancestors, huddling together for strength against enemies outside their mud huts, and the royal Seth, clad in silk pajamas, desolately alone among spies and traitors within his own fortress. Even as emperor, he is weaker than his ancestors: he possesses neither the full power of barbarism nor the wisdom of civilization. Trapped in events he cannot control, he becomes a tragic figure whose idealistic attempts to impose a pseudocivilization bring about his ultimate destruction.

The other protagonist of the novel, Basil Seal, though the scion of a proper upper-class family, is less than civilized and often semibarbaric in his ruthlessness. Whether he cashes a bad check, scrounges money from his mistress, steals his mother's jeweled bracelet, goes on drunken binges, or behaves insolently to distinguished people, he permits few scruples to restrain him. From his mother's point of view, he is an immature, ungrateful spendthrift, unmindful of obligations toward his parliamentary constituency. Yet his virile qualities fascinate women, and his defiance of convention appeals to men who subconsciously long to kick over the traces. The contemptible and the estimable are so mixed in Basil's personality that one might condemn his rebellion against duty as the contrariness of a spoiled child while commending it as the determination not to be stifled by a straitlaced environment. Although his attraction to the effete wastrels of the Trumpington set indicates self-indulgent tendencies, his revulsion at their parasitic lifestyle denotes some strength of character. When he decisively rejects the whole London milieu to pursue adventure in Azania—"Every year or so," he claims, "there's *one* place on the globe worth going to where things are happening" (112)—he becomes positively admirable, if a shade opportunistic.

The strong bond of friendship that develops between Seth and Basil results to a great extent from the peculiar attraction of opposite personalities—the aesthete and the rogue,[6] the overcivilized and the undercivilized, the idealistic theoretician and the cynical utilitarian. Whereas Seth is virtually obsessed with attiring himself in striking clothes and shows no interest in Youkoumian's offers to "fix" him with a woman, Basil cultivates a slovenly, unkempt appearance and gratifies his own variety of narcissism through sexual conquests. The description of their initial acquaintance at Oxford also points up the contrast, for Seth had been classed among the foreign nonentities, whereas Basil had been famed for his brilliance, sophistication, and political acumen. Even though their relative positions are reversed, the emperor still looks upon his Oxonian contemporary with awe, as "the personification of all that glittering, intangible Western culture to which he [aspires]" (147). In addition, similarities of circumstance and purpose contribute a degree of kinship. Each protagonist is in revolt against the values of his fathers, and each considers himself to be "liberated"—Seth, from the savagery of his ancestors, and Basil, from the demands of an overrefined society. Although neither suspects that he could become embroiled in the environment that the other has spurned, such an ironic reversal does occur when Seth is hopelessly entangled in the trappings of "Progress" and Basil is caught up in the practices of a jungle culture. Mutual need draws the two men even closer together, for each sees in the other the way to his own fulfillment. Basil is the *"one* man" who can implement the emperor's plans for Azania, and Seth is the means by which Basil gains virtual control over the island nation. Although their characters may be paradoxical and their relationship unusual, their combined efforts to achieve certain aspirations become almost heroic, and their defeat against overwhelming odds makes them tragic victims with whom the reader can sympathize.

Partly responsible for the downfall of both protagonists is the nature of Azania itself—a mélange of ethnic, religious, economic, and architectural components, typical in its incohesive disorder of Waugh's ironic environments. Among its inhabitants are cannibalistic aborigines, Western speculators and diplomats, Arab traders, Indians, Armenians, and Greeks. Their religious faiths include native African beliefs, Islam, Judaism, Hinduism, and Christianity. The currency of other nations serves as legal tender in the commercial areas, while barter and primitive media of exchange persist in the hinterlands. Even the assorted styles of buildings in the capital—"a haphazard jumble of shops, missions, barracks, legations, bungalows and native huts" (19)—testify to the cultural forces at war.

The collision of such irreconcilable elements is dramatically epitomized at Seth's victory ball, attended by the elite from all segments of Azanian society. In a superficial atmosphere of party hats and false noses that mocks the intended imitation of a European court, various groups and individuals follow their own inclinations, which jar with the earnestness and dignity of the emperor. The English diplomatic corps play childish games while their French counterparts indulge in self-deceptive espionage. A high government minister escorts a notorious courtesan and becomes obnoxiously drunk. Climaxing the occasion, the fierce Earl of Ngumo, clad in gaudy jungle regalia, arrives late and, finding no table vacant, threatens to clear a place by force. His confrontation with Seth, impeccably dressed in evening clothes, affords a moment of high ironic contrast, both visually and symbolically. The abyss separating them is later acknowledged in Seth's own mind when he thinks of his subjects as "insupportable barbarians" (150). With no unifying tradition and only a thin overlay of civilization, the Azanian heterogeneity will not congeal.

The novel's opening episode, detailing Seth's precarious situation and subsequent triumph in the civil war, is saturated with a complex interweaving of ironies that provide, in addition to amusement and intellectual exercise, the semblance of high adventure. Such techniques as double entendre, indeterminacy, and unexpected events are used to create surprises, suspense, and mystery. As the emperor's regime appears to crumble, the narrator focuses on three unscrupulous opportunists—his Indian secretary Ali, the Armenian entrepreneur Youkoumian, and Major Joab—who betray not only their sovereign but each other as well. Crucial information about their plans is carefully manipulated so that it is withheld sometimes from certain characters and sometimes from the reader, each of whom must fit the pieces together in order to deduce the unstated. Even when essential facts become clear, intentions that are never acted upon remain indeterminable. The first hint of Ali's disloyalty, and Seth's mistrust of him, is the emperor's surprise that his secretary has not already left the island kingdom with other fleeing officials. Ali's uncharacteristically ingenuous admission that there was no room in the boat and his wry observation that the weight of so many important people might have caused it to sink seem designed to be facetiously disarming. Seth's response that Ali's loyalty will be rewarded is correspondingly equivocal and proves to be more prophetic than either the characters or the reader could yet know.

The ironic clues to the reciprocal treachery between Ali and Youkoumian are their extravagant protestations of friendship, through which they unintentionally betray themselves. Youkoumian's assurance to Ali—"I trust you as I'd trust my own father" (26)—turns ambiguously on whether or not the Armenian does indeed have faith in his father. Although Youkoumian's assertion is presumably designed to win the secretary's confidence, Ali, equally experienced at lying and aware that Youkoumian is too crafty ever to trust anyone, perceives a very different truth than he was expected to believe. Such statements, which can be interpreted two ways, alert the reader to the insincerity of the characters' promises—Youkoumian's, to transport Ali to the mainland in his hidden launch; Ali's, to pay for petrol and tell no one about the boat. Youkoumian's plans for his wife are also uncertain. Whether (as she suspects) he would abandon her to make room for the extra passenger or whether (as he assures her) Ali would not really be taken aboard, that choice never has to be made. But later, while bargaining for his life with Major Joab, Youkoumian does make a similar decision without hesitation only to discover that he himself is the one left behind. Ali reveals the magnitude of his own perfidy by ordering Joab in the emperor's name, though without Seth's knowledge, to execute Youkoumian. It is less clear what the treacherous secretary intends by his unsuccessful attempt to extort money from Seth on the pretext of buying a boat for the emperor's escape. Although Ali apparently means to pocket the money and then steal Youkoumian's launch, his promise to aid Seth remains problematic since his own death precludes any possible course of action.

Major Joab's initial designs are even more obscure; one never discovers the thoughts behind his enigmatic comment that the victorious army encamped in the hills "is what we have waited to see" (28). He may believe it is Seth's forces, or he may plan to sell Seth to the conquering enemy, as Ali later suspects when Joab refuses to buy a chance of escape after everyone assumes Seth's defeat. But Ali is self-deceived; neither he nor the reader realizes that the announcement of Youkoumian's death is a trick and that at this point Joab has the option of departing with the Armenian. Indeed Joab's conniving skills are underestimated by everyone. While accepting Ali's bribe for safe passage out of the fort, he arrests him for stealing the imperial regalia. Even after Seth releases the double-crossing secretary, Joab secretly strangles him and absconds with both crown and launch. But Youkoumian, though left unconscious on the seashore, emerges as the most fortunate of the three conspirators through the unexpected triumph of Seth's army. Youkoumian's inability to flee, despite attempts to do so, makes him ideally situated to ally himself with the victorious regime.

Painfully obvious is the discrepancy between what one might expect of those hailed as "soldiers of Progress and the New Age" (46) and the rabble of tribesmen who exultantly pour into the coastal city of Matodi. In an excellent example of chaos reflective of the ironic world, the narrator describes the motley collection of warriors, marching in disarray to brass band and jungle drums, carrying every sort of weaponry, dressed in tattered uniforms and native garb, with booty in their pockets, spoils of live animals driven before them, and members of slain enemies dangling from their necks. The incongruous nature of this military rout is intensified when General Connolly, privately referring to the troops as his "menagerie," publicly extols their prowess in behalf of emperor and empire as though he were a Roman commander praising his legions. A similar disparity can be seen between his orders that the men refrain from looting, raping, murdering, or burning and his correct prediction that these "lucky bastards" will unrestrainedly "make whoopee" (50).

A more civilized kind of disorder, though more absurd, prevails among the foreign diplomatic corps in the capital at Debra-Dowa. The British legation, "a stockaded compound" (65) in the mountains far from the town, represents by its insularity and inaccessibility the staff's detachment from their essential obligations. Most of the aides prefer playing games to deciphering coded messages from London or learning native languages, thereby severely limiting communication in either direction. The minister, Sir Samson Courteney, is completely out of touch with the political upheavals in Azania; and Lady Courteney's chief interest in this false paradise is the maintenance of an English garden that not only removes her from the realities of African life but is symbolic, with its "immature maze" (67), of the community's introversion. At the time of the coup d'etat, Sir Samson banishes all responsibility toward the British refugees, while his wife carries on as though she were the hostess at a country house party. During the civil war official indifference even foils the Anglican bishop's attempt to gain information about a possible massacre of civilians, for his pointed requests are met with domestic news. In this instance the juxtaposition of superficial tea-time chatter to the narrator's account of bloody atrocities not far away illustrates more dramatically than could editorial comment the legation's incredible nonchalance toward the threatening danger.

In contrast, the French make themselves ridiculous by over-zealous involvement. M. Ballon, having himself learned Sakuyu, operates an elaborate spy network to uncover all that transpires in Azania, as well as in the British legation, with which he feels in desperate competition. Deluding himself that everyone must be as conspiratorial as he, Ballon assumes that Sir Samson and his compatriots are all secret agents; and from this misapprehension arises one of Waugh's most amusing ironies, in which a false premise logically leads to an erroneous deduction. Two French secretaries, instructed to watch every move of the British at Seth's ball, conclude that writing on a menu card—actually a preposterous fantasy concocted during a party game—is evidence of an affair between Gen. Connolly and Mme. Ballon; and further references to the matter, which surfaces in various contexts almost to the last page, increase the pleasure of this joke on French espionage. Ultimately, through a train of political events, Ballon's meddling backfires to the detriment of French power, while the British, totally unconcerned with Azanian affairs, achieve the dominant role in the protectorate set up after Seth's fall.

Unfortunately the Courteneys' daughter, inappropriately named Prudence, does not muddle through the Azanian chaos successfully; a malevolent fate, treated ironically, seems to hang over her and her affair with Basil. The narrator's cynical attitude toward the couple's first assignation, as well as the unromantic nature of their lovemaking, is obliquely conveyed through the description of Basil's disgusting cigar: "He threw the butt of his Burma cheroot into the tin hip bath," where it "floated throughout the afternoon"—a "soggy stub of tobacco [emanating] a brown blot of juice" (185-86). The horrifying end of Prudence's life is handled impressively through interrelated ironies. It is foreshadowed in a playful conversation between the lovers—when he remarks, "I'd like to eat you" and she replies, "So you shall, my sweet" (237)—though the reader is initially unaware that the metaphorical cliché will be translated into literal reality. It is accomplished through unforeseen occurrences when the plane intended to take her to civilization delivers her into the hands of cannibals, who serve her as stew to the unsuspecting Basil—fulfilling in a contorted manner his farewell promise, "We'll meet again somewhere" (282). The tragic irony in Basil's case is sharpened by the fact that Prudence's death is brought about, inadvertently, by his own act, of which he too becomes an innocent victim. Not knowing that she is held captive by the natives making ready for Seth's funeral, he orders them to "kill [their] best meat and prepare a feast" (296-97). The episode also involves an element of dramatic irony: while the cannibals know all along what they are eating, Basil and the reader make the sickening discovery only after the meal.

A different series of ironic events brings about the collapse of Seth's reign, an outcome which can be seen from the beginning as inevitable. Caught between cultures but oblivious to his predicament, the emperor is in an impossible situation such as Muecke calls an irony of dilemma.[7] Most of his intentions go awry in some unanticipated fashion. Even his well-planned triumphal departure from Matodi is thwarted by indignities that deflate his imperial style: a wrecked vehicle blocking his car forces him to proceed to the train station by mule, and a runaway engine temporarily strands the passengers. The futility of Seth's attempt to turn native Africans into cultivated Europeans by mere change of title is illustrated in the renaming of Black Bitch as the Duchess of Ukaka. While Seth reasons that the racist-sexist connotations of her nickname might be publicly embarrassing, no one else takes her transformation very seriously. Connolly, indicating that he will always think lovingly of his wife as Black Bitch, continues to introduce her as such. The French ladies, who court her in order to win the general to their side, become so friendly that they too drop the "Duchess" and use her sobriquet. Black Bitch, while pleased with the nominal elevation, refuses to be anything but herself; and her genuineness both endears her to the reader and creates riotous incongruity, especially when a magnificently uniformed messenger from the French legation delivers a formal invitation to Her Grace as she is washing her husband's socks, spitting into the soap suds, and drying her hands on her knickers.

While Seth pursues his fascinated, and sometimes frantic, study of European catalogs, books, and newspapers to learn of other "improvements" he should impose upon his people, Basil, as minister of modernization, virtually manages the country, assisted by Youkoumian as financial secretary. But instead of reshaping Azania into the constitutional monarchy Seth had envisioned, Basil creates a socialist dictatorship, which he justifies as more "modern." His ministry's original function—"*to promote the adoption of modern organisation and habits*"—becomes "the right of interference in . . . public and private affairs" (157). However, in his interference with the military, Basil allows childish egotism to override common sense and thereby adds his own miscalculations to those of Seth. The irony in this clash of authority is one of Waugh's choicest. The thousand pairs of boots, which Youkoumian sells at a profit and Basil forces upon Connolly's barefoot troops in order to provoke a showdown, are mistaken for extra rations by the soldiers, who boil and eat them to Connolly's delight and Basil's chagrin. The conflict is brought to a head in a play on words when Basil, as yet unaware that his plan has miscarried, taunts the general about how well the boots "went down" with the men; for Connolly's repetition of the metaphor gives it a literal rendering, confirmed by his additional remarks about "no cases of lameness" but "one or two of belly ache" (181). Subsequently, the seemingly minor affair of the boots, which alienates Connolly, has monumental repercussions as a principal catalyst for the ensuing coup d'etat.

That Seth, as a naïf, comprehends only superficially the grandiose projects by which he expects to civilize Azania is presented almost exclusively through ironic means. His hope of eradicating all disease through decreed physical exercises and "community singing" is exposed as an idle dream by its juxtaposition, without authorial comment, to Prudence's soap-opera reveries about "*a woman in love*" (187). His interest in German *Nacktkultur* (nudism) after an edict mandating trousers demonstrates that imitation of European fads can deconstruct his aspirations. His desire to give his people an instantaneous museum leads to an incredibly unwise act—the appropriation of Ngumo's town mansion—that contributes directly to his downfall. The discrepancy between the theoretical and the possible becomes pronounced in his determination to rebuild Debra-Dowa according to a design that necessitates razing the almost indestructible Anglican cathedral. Indeed, when the reader last sees him alive, Seth is totally engrossed in the valiant though irrational effort to demolish with his own hands the granite structure that blocks his vision of progress. The rift between his imagination and reality seems complete when, without the knowledge of his ministers, he prints money that has no fiscal backing and creates an Imperial Bank of Azania out of a cupboard stacked with fiat currency, the circulation of which helps to fuel the uprising against him.

In none of his innovations is Seth so politically inept as in the campaign for birth control, which ultimately unites the opposition against him. Not surprisingly, cosmopolitan blacks, Europeans, and Arab intellectuals display indifference, while strong disapproval comes from the conservative landed gentry led by Ngumo and religious groups headed by the Nestorian patriarch. Overwhelming support comes, unexpectedly, from ordinary tribesmen, though only because of their colossal misinterpretation of a colorful and widely displayed poster. Designed to enlighten even the illiterate about the benefits of limiting population, it depicts the squalor and illness of a family with eleven children as opposed to the prosperity and health of a couple with only one child. Yet the cultural tradition equating success and happiness with fertility causes the Azanian populace to misread Seth's meaning so that they believe the contraceptive device, affectionately termed "the emperor's juju," to be a new means of achieving fecundity. Seth's good intentions are further mocked at the gala birth control pageant, when the courtesan Mme. "Fifi" is enthroned on a float representing the place of women in the modern world and advertising culture through sterility.

The introduction of Dame Mildred Porch's perspective on events in Azania permits delightful ironic comedy since even the most logical deductions of an outsider tend to distort the truth for which the narrator has already prepared us. Dame Mildred considers Youkoumian "very obliging" to change her British money into the Azanian paper notes that both he and the reader know to be worthless. Unaware that the pageant celebrates birth control, she is perplexed by the seeming inability—actually the modest reluctance—of the Anglican bishop and Youkoumian to explain its purpose. Unprepared for the unexpected, she peremptorily brands as "absurd" her traveling companion's inference that the well-dressed young man chipping away at a cathedral archway might be the emperor, although that identification is confirmed for the reader by the description of his clothing and by Seth's earlier remark that the cathedral would be removed even if he had to do it himself.

Her references in conversation with Seth to Achon's existence in a monastery and Ngumo's mission to free him not only produce ironies at her expense but set the stage for a more striking, and very poignant, irony about the state of Seth's mind. Her obtuseness in assuming the emperor knows his uncle is alive and her naiveté in mentioning a rival claimant to the throne are compounded by misjudgments about Achon himself. Ignorant of information the reader will soon discover—that the man whom everyone thought dead has been chained for years in a dark cave and that the monastery in charge of him has allowed pagan superstitions to make a mockery of Christianity—Dame Mildred believes Achon has been a monk and endorses his liberation from the contemplative life, which in her biased view is useless and selfish. But Seth is oblivious to what should be a startling revelation: he is too abstracted from reality to grasp the inadvertent warning that might have saved him from his enemies.

Waugh's ridicule of the two Englishwomen who champion the rights of dumb animals involves not only their fanatical devotion to a cause but also the misunderstanding of their crusade by the Azanians. Although Dame Mildred is correct in assessing the barbarism of some hunters, her extreme solicitude for jungle beasts shows her to be more naive than the people she hopes to enlighten. So obsessed does she become with the welfare of domestic animals that she condemns as *"greedy little wretches"* (207) the hungry children who try to take the food she gives to stray dogs. When the parade is attacked, she fears for the safety of oxen pulling the floats rather than for the human beings involved. But Dame Mildred is so blinded by the rectitude of her cause that she does not realize the need to explain it unambiguously. Hence semantic confusion among the natives, combined with their environmental conditioning, creates the outrageous misconceptions revealed at the banquet given to welcome her and her companion, Miss Tin. On the gilded menu cards designed by Seth, the title of the women's organization, "Society for the Prevention of Cruelty to Animals," is drastically altered in meaning by being abbreviated as "Cruelty to Animals," while the list of foods consisting primarily of meats also seems to contradict their mission. In his toast to the honored guests, Viscount Boaz not only reverses the purpose of their work by introducing them as "renowned throughout . . . Europe for their great cruelty to animals" (225); he incongruously fuses his own junglewise logic with Seth's progressivist catchwords by asserting what amounts to an internal contradiction—that the women have come to teach Azanians how to be more "modern" and "refined" in their cruelty.

As all hope of Seth's New Age evaporates with his abdication and prospects for another Azanian regime dim with the death of Achon, the country disintegrates into the shambles of "murder, loot and fire" (261), from which it is only superficially rescued by the imposition of European power. During the interim, one of the novel's major ironies becomes clear as the contrast between Seth and Basil grows more pronounced. Without conscious intention or even self-awareness, each character reverses, through his own actions, his original expectations of himself. Seth's confident anticipation of guiding his people to enlightenment comes to naught, since his ability for effective leadership has ceased long before his assassination. Although no details are given about Seth's flight from the capital or about his mental state during his wait for Basil in a jungle village, the reader can easily imagine that the emperor's mind is still a ferment of untenable ideas. On the contrary, Basil, whose ambitions for a bit of adventure in Azania are by comparison modest and casual, becomes what he has not envisioned—an efficient, masterful leader. To cope with the crisis, he rallies his practical instincts, and his capabilities seem to flourish in adversity as never before. His single-minded approach to problems focuses on immediate solutions, and he allows neither idealism nor apprehension to throw him off course. Worrying, as he tells Prudence, is "one of the things there's no sense in at all. . . . it doesn't get [people] any-where" (276).

While Seth's heroism lies in his unwavering, if misdirected, de-votion to an ideal, Basil's heroism lies in solid accomplishment and in his loyalty to Seth. Whereas in England Basil had shirked re-sponsibilities to family and country, in Azania he assumes and exe-cutes many duties—civilized as well as primitive. He takes charge of preparations for defense at the disorganized British legation, braves a horrendous journey by camel into the interior to meet Seth, persists in discovering the cause of the emperor's death, engi-neers retribution for his murder, and escorts his body to the Wanda city of Moshu for a royal funeral, at which he delivers the oration. That Basil does all this clothed in the robes of a native merchant symbolizes his descent into barbarism, to which his ascent to lead-ership is an inverse parallel. In fact, it is the barbaric tendency in his own nature that enables him to adapt easily to the customs of a savage environment until, when he reaches its nadir, the cannibal feast proves to be more than he can stomach.

Lesser, sometimes lighter, ironies punctuate the gravity of Basil's last adventure in Azania. His graphic descriptions of atrocities have unplanned consequences at the British legation: though intended primarily (and rather wickedly) "to scare the old women" (276), they are reenacted as a game by the children and rouse the adults to the need for self-defense. Prudence's logical concern for Basil's welfare as she is about to be airlifted from the compound to sup-posed safety becomes ironic when she perishes and he survives a circuitous overland journey. Boaz's purpose for killing Seth—to win favor with Achon's supporters—backfires when the pretender dies; and Boaz's frightened, drunken attempts to concoct plausible scenarios for the emperor's death are punctured by Basil's perspi-cacity. The irony concerning Joab lies not so much in his surprising reappearance among the imperial guard as in the discrepancy be-tween the real and pretended motives for his actions. Essentially an opportunist serving his own interests, he professes soldierly avoid-ance of politics as the reason for not interfering with Boaz's murder of Seth, yet implies duty to a dead master as the incentive for exe-cuting Boaz. High ironic comedy characterizes Basil's memorial tribute to Seth, who has accomplished none of the superlatives at-tributed to him. Though grounded in a genuine appreciation for his noble qualities, the eulogy becomes a mock-heroic fabrication, through hyperbole and poetic license, designed to meet the expectations of the Wanda tribesmen:

"Thousands fell by his right hand. The words of his mouth were like thunder in the hills. Weep, women of Azania, for your royal lover is torn from your arms. His virility was inexhaustible, his progeny numerous beyond human computation.... When he led you to battle there was no retreating. In council the most guileful, in justice the most terrible, Seth the magnificent is dead." (299)

Thus Seth, who had renounced the barbarism of his country, is buried as a savage by a civilized man presiding over the barbaric rituals.

An unusual and subtle infusion of irony into these final Azanian episodes is achieved through the recurrent monsoon rain that modifies the expected by its literally dampening effect. It extinguishes the fires in Debra-Dowa and discourages the rioters; it so delays Basil's arrival at the rendezvous that, as the reader infers from Boaz's oblique but repeated reference to lateness, it may have determined events there; it muffles the death cry of Boaz; and it puts an end to the cannibal revelry.

The denouement of *Black Mischief*, which restores Azania to a semblance of order, returns Basil to an England substantially changed by the economic slump of the early 1930s. Diminished finances have reduced his former chums the Trumpingtons to a tiny servantless flat and ended the social whirl around which their hollow lives revolved. Impoverished circumstances have also shrunk their personalities into a state of childish self-absorption, which contrasts with the expanded, more mature outlook forced upon Basil by responsibility and tragedy. Consequently, when the friends meet again, they perceive each other's reality as illusion. The Trumpingtons, rejecting as unreal anything outside themselves, refuse to hear of Basil's "far-flung stuff" (305). Sonia, believing that he is about to spin tall tales, even forestalls him with teasing about the proverbial adventures of travelers in uncivilized lands—running "the whole country," falling "madly in love," having "a court official's throat cut," and attending "a cannibal banquet" (304)—little realizing that these are the actualities of his Azanian experience. Basil, in turn, rejects the realities of the Trumpingtons' vapid existence as illusory. To Sonia's suggestion of "some parties like the old ones," he replies, "I'm not sure I shouldn't find them a bit flat after the real thing. I went to a party at a place called Moshu . . ." (305). But the Moshu "party" to which Basil refers has implications for the reader beyond the Trumpingtons' comprehension.

Narrowness of vision and preoccupation with trivialities also infect the predominantly British administration of Azania under a League of Nations mandate, and British influence is as insubstantial as the Gilbert and Sullivan songs carried through the night air of Matodi. Though certain advances have been made in the cities—children vaccinated, stray dogs eliminated—beneath the veneer the same fractured society continues virtually unchanged. Arab gentlemen still stroll the waterfront, tribal natives still dominate the interior, and that perennial survivor Youkoumian still sells boots to the army. Although the new, more conventional civil servants are unlike the eccentric Courteney set by actually being involved in the political affairs of the island, they are just as socially isolated and even more race-and-rank conscious. In their indifferent, uncomprehending observations on the deportation of Connolly and the unacceptability of his black wife, Waugh offers a final oblique commentary on the "civilized" values these Europeans represent.[8] While we may laugh at the clash of two cultures and their continuing failure to tolerate one another's assumptions, the ironic presentation compels the reader to perceive that some solution is needed beyond this endless round of confrontations.

A Handful of Dust

*F*rom the conflict in *Black Mischief* between pseudocivilization and barbarism, it may seem only a short step to the opposition in *A Handful of Dust* between moribund aristocratic traditions and rapacious materialism. Yet that move helped effect a sophistication in Waugh's fiction that had not existed previously, for it necessitated realistic depictions of conflicting realms that Waugh knew more intimately than Africa—country-estate life, with its anachronistic ideals, versus fashionable London society, with its zeal for self-gratification. To examine these warring incompatibilities, irony was the ideal mode. Fortunately, too, the novel was written at the point in Waugh's career when his philosophical view of the universe as unpredictable, devoid of moral order, and largely beyond human control (much like Mrs. Rattery's card game) was not only at its most profound but coincided with the zenith of his rhetorical expertise.

If the shift in subject matter created advantageous opportunities, it also set up new obstacles to be overcome. Waugh was required to present far more complex characters, coping with the intricacies of personal and social dilemmas, than those he had depicted earlier. As he admitted, the novel was "very difficult to write because for the first time" he was dealing "with normal people instead of eccentrics."[1] Whereas contradictions between appearance and underlying reality might be wildly exaggerated for comic, fantastic, or anarchic characters, discrepancies in the personalities of "people [such as] one has met and may at any moment meet again" had to be subtle enough to portray real life.[2] Possibly the most challenging problem involved objective distancing from deep emotional wounds and anxieties—not only the bitter recollection of Evelyn Gardner's infidelity and desertion but also of Teresa Jungman's more recent refusal to marry him.[3] These painful experiences, mirrored in Tony Last's rejection by Brenda and then Thérèse de Vitré, were traumatic not just because they undermined his self-esteem but because they boded ill for any future hopes of Catholic marriage, family, or settled home. The transmutation of such feelings into fictional art from the perspective of a detached, often bemused, narrator required a more determinedly ironic stance than had any of Waugh's earlier autobiographical material. Tony could not be overwhelmed by the author's self-pity or reproach but had to be depicted with a modicum of both—as an essentially admirable person unable to liberate himself from the circumstances in which he is trapped. Waugh describes him as "a Gothic man in the hands of savages."[4]

Waugh's dual perspective on both Tony and the urban society against which Tony is pitted so increases the complexity of the irony that the reader cannot react in a completely unambivalent way. Although Brenda Last's London friends constitute the basic ingredients of a sparkling comedy of manners, Waugh, in addition to having fun with their follies, turns them into villains who triumph over the rather unheroic hero. While Tony is inherently decent, his weaknesses, especially blind faith in his wife and cultural heritage, dampen the generally favorable response from the reader, who concludes that Tony is well rid of Brenda and other destabilizing forces. Indeed Waugh shows himself very adept in *A Handful of Dust* at eliciting the reader's reactions through manipulation of authorial attitude, and critics have generally agreed on the superb control of tone in this novel. Robert Murray Davis in particular has shown how Waugh improved the manuscript and serial versions to achieve the right balance between sympathetic involvement and impersonal detachment.[5] This careful distancing—which permits the ironic blending of comedy and tragedy, empathy and rejection, good and evil—is largely responsible for making the work a masterpiece of realistic fiction.

Waugh had already concocted the embryo of *A Handful of Dust* for his short story "The Man Who Liked Dickens" (1933). But herein Dickens has no specific relevance to the bland, dilettantish explorer Paul Henty; and Waugh may have just been taking a fling at a then unfashionable writer, toward whom he seems to have had curiously mixed feelings. He had read Dickens's works avidly in youth and heard his father read them aloud at home; later he reread some of those novels he chanced upon in the South American jungles, Abyssinia, and Yugoslavia.[6] Yet, despite a certain fascination, Waugh harbored serious misgivings about Dickens, whose exaggerated emotions and characters palled on him as early as 1920. After seeing a film of *Little Dorrit*, he recorded in his diary: "Dickens always seems so fantastic and grotesque on the cinema with all his doddering old men and semi-imbeciles. The plot too seemed peculiarly inconsequent and insipid."[7] By 1934 Waugh evidently considered the Dickensian philosophy of benevolence a hopelessly inadequate bulwark against savagery and possibly even a wallowing in sentiment that led nowhere beyond enjoyment of itself.[8] Significantly, the last word on Dickens in *A Handful of Dust* is uttered by the mad Mr. Todd, who returns to *Little Dorrit* for the best of cries.

Waugh's original version of the novel, published in book form after a serialized adaptation, incorporates as its penultimate chapter the situation from his short story and represents a kind of mental backtracking from it. Reflecting on how Henty came to be "trapped in the jungle, ending his days reading Dickens aloud," Waugh began studying "other sorts of savage at home and the civilized man's helpless plight among them."[9] In creating Tony's background, experiences, and mindset, he turned the enforced reading of Dickens into a remarkably apt and disturbing irony. While Todd revels in the imaginary realm of Dickens but does not allow it to have any influence on the realities of his life, Tony, who has lived by a secularized religion of benevolence, suffers the ultimate psychological torture of having to revive the Dickensian ethos in an environment especially inimical to it. To be reminded again and again of a just world, in which virtue ultimately triumphs and villainy is defeated, while he languishes in undeserved imprisonment, transforms his idealistic dream into a nightmare. Tragic irony, therefore, predominates in this version, since Tony, as the sympathetic victim, is not only overwhelmed by barbarism but is subjected to a punishment far in excess of any transgressions against society. Other critics have measured Tony's disproportionate suffering by the standards of classical tragedy. Northrop Frye, for example, asserts that the novel is "close to a parody of tragic irony, as we can see in the appalling fate of the relatively harmless hero."[10] James Carens, conceding that the novel is actually ironic rather than satiric, claims that its irony is closer to that of tragedy than that of satire, even though the characters themselves are not of tragic stature.[11]

Waugh was obliged, however, to compose an alternative ending for the novel's serialization in *Harper's Bazaar* (1934) because the serial copyright to "The Man Who Liked Dickens" had been sold to enable the short story to be published in British and American magazines the previous year.[12] Even if, as Christopher Sykes maintains, "the American magazine which published a serialization [did ask] for a happy ending,"[13] serial copyright would in any case have required a new conclusion. Although this so-called "happy ending" of the serialized version, entitled "A London Flat," provides more twists and turns of a comic nature, the general tone of the irony becomes more nihilistic, since Tony finally succumbs to the corruption of a society to which he was once morally superior.

Whereas Brenda moves back to Hetton and becomes the model wife, Tony, contrary to all expectations, is on the verge of becoming the philandering husband. The narrator, in truly objective fashion, does not allow us insight into how they feel about their reconciliation but permits their actions to betray them. Despite Brenda's claim to have given up the flat because its smell was unbearable, one senses that she had no choice except to return home. The reader can also deduce that by the time Tony comes back from a pleasure cruise his love for his wife has cooled. Displaying neither happiness at being met by her nor continued anger about what she casually terms "that nonsense with Mr Beaver,"[14] Tony simply falls asleep in the car and dozes off again after dinner without asking Brenda the crucial question about their future. His later decision to keep the London flat for his own private use shows that he has indeed turned the tables on Brenda. Whether Waugh thought that such an ending would please the largely feminine readership of *Harper's Bazaar* in America or whether it reflected his own sexual promiscuity after the breakup of his first marriage may be debatable, but, unlike the book version, it makes light of Brenda's adultery and certainly undermines Tony's integrity.

The brilliant ironic coup of this alternative ending pivots on the conversation between Tony and Mrs. Beaver concerning disposition of the flat. Although the speakers never express the crucial ideas motivating their discourse, the reader can tell from their replies that the thoughts have been unequivocally communicated.

Tony's stated reasons for keeping the flat—because it is cheaper and more convenient than his club—at first seem perfectly plausible and straightforward. But Mrs. Beaver's assertion that having such a place "is *necessary*" (264) implies what they both realize about its advantages beyond mere usefulness. Her knowing response, "I *quite* understand" (264), to Tony's concern about Brenda's probable reaction, as well as her readiness to keep his name off the tenants' listing as a "precaution," throws additional light on the secret plans which Tony seems to have and to which the shrewd Mrs. Beaver only alludes in innocently ambiguous terms. In the same way, her obliging offer to sell him "some little piece of extra furniture" (265) conceals her underhanded way of extracting money for unspecified services. Tony, thoroughly conversant with her tactics, understands this subtle blackmail as her price for "absolute discretion"; and his reply—"Yes, I suppose I had better" (265)—hints at his awareness of possible consequences should he not buy the expensive, unnecessary writing table. An unsuspecting Brenda, believing Tony's lie that Mrs. Beaver has disposed of the flat "*very* decent[ly]," utters the final word on the subject: "So that's the end of that" (265). But the reader can surmise from the foregoing conversation what Brenda does not comprehend—that use of the flat, far from being ended, is about to provide a new beginning in Tony's life. Such predominantly flip comedy in the alternative ending shows Waugh to be in prime form as an ironist, but it does weaken the serious import of the novel.[15]

In its darker aspects, *A Handful of Dust*, more than any other work by Waugh, reflects acquaintance with Oswald Spengler's *Decline of the West* (1918-22) and actually illustrates some of Spengler's theories in an English setting.[16] According to Spengler, it was during the nineteenth century that the West passed from a vital, creative period of development into a decadence that signaled the end of its organic life cycle. Whereas in the earlier stage society was guided by the "soul" of the countryside, in the ultimate phase, which he terms "civilization," it is dominated by the "intellect" of a few world cities. Inevitably the mass of nomadic, parasitical urbanites, oriented primarily toward commerce, are antagonistic toward the landed gentry, inheritors of aristocratic traditions and good taste. "Civilized" humanity has become obsessed with technology, material comfort, and money as the prime means to power. Even what appears to be a renewed interest in religion emphasizes the symbols of an earlier epoch rather than the true faith that they represent. As the vital structures that once provided stability have deteriorated, a new fascination with the occult has arisen, and with it, a new savagery. Since man by nature is neither rational nor idealistic, he has reverted under these conditions to being a beast of prey governed by animal instincts. In this final stage of intellectualized barbarism, Spengler postulates, traditional Judaic-Christian morality is ineffectual and in fact weakens humanity, hastening the inevitable downfall.

Many of Spengler's ideas assume concrete form in the characters and episodes of the novel, and Tony Last particularly bears out Spengler's dire predictions. Although from one perspective Tony appears to be a kindly, sensitive country gentleman unfairly treated by his wife, her urban friends, and fate, he can also be seen by the reader who grasps the most sophisticated irony as a spineless, if well-meaning, idealist. In a different time or location his honorable principles might have won him unquestioned esteem in society, but in a Spenglerian frame of reference the vulnerability of his guileless virtue contributes to his defeat in the last barbaric stage of civilization. He becomes a victim of irony insofar as he does not even begin to perceive until too late the situations in which he is captive—metaphorically in England, literally in the Brazilian jungle. So sure is he of the rectitude of his own beliefs and behavior that, as a typical *alazon*, he remains confidently unaware of their shortcomings. Whereas in conventional tragedy the hero experiences "discovery and recognition" of what went wrong, Tony may never fully realize the causes of his fall. But the reader's awareness of them adds another facet to the irony. By passing a kind of moral judgment on Tony's imperceptiveness, the reader finds himself unexpectedly in the company of Tony's detractors, though for different reasons. This quandary of indecision between sympathy and disapproval reflects Waugh's own difficulties in dealing with autobiographical material in *A Handful of Dust*. Although he projects his suffering onto Tony, Waugh does not offer a solution to the character's predicament, as he would be able to do later for Charles Ryder in *Brideshead Revisited*.

To understand Waugh's ambivalence, the reader must comprehend how Waugh felt about Tony's self-defeating chivalry and grasp what he meant by calling his character "the betrayed romantic."[17] Romanticism, as Waugh denigrated it in his critical biography of D. G. Rossetti, was a trusting, self-deluding perspective that by its very nature invited betrayal. In contradistinction to the

more commonsensical Victorian views—one view fatalistically re-
signing itself to uncertainty, the other seeing life as part of an integrated whole—Waugh described the "romantic outlook" as one
that perceived "life as a series of glowing and unrelated systems"
and valorized *the picturesque* as the only true authenticity.[18] Accordingly, during the Gothic Revival, stimulated in architecture by
Pugin and Ruskin, "Romance threw up her frail machicolations
against the inexorable advance of the industrial system"[19] and enabled the Victorians to invest a crumbling religion, threatened by
scientific skepticism, with visual charm designed to conjure up an
age of genuine belief. In their attempts to revive the earlier Gothic,
however, the Victorians concentrated on outward manifestations,
especially the picturesque features, and slighted the spiritual essence, thereby emphasizing symbol at the expense of substance.
Such pseudomedievalism, or Victorian Gothic, Waugh considered
not a positive affirmation but a romanticist's retreat into illusion—a determination to see the world as it had never been rather
than face up to present reality.

That Waugh continued to be scornful of Victorian Gothic architecture is evident from his note to Tom Driberg with a presentation
copy of *A Handful of Dust* in September 1934: "At any rate the fron-
tispiece [of Hetton Abbey] might amuse you. I instructed the architect to design the worst possible 1860 and I think he has done
well."[20] "English Gothic," which Waugh uses to designate three of
the seven chapters of the novel, refers not to the vital form that existed in an earlier stage of our culture but to the spurious imitation
that arose in what he considered to be its winter—typifying a fragmented, insubstantial, and ultimately deceptive outlook on life.
When Tony's illusions about Brenda and his own chivalry are shattered by her demands for an unreasonable divorce settlement, the
narrator observes: "A whole Gothic world had come to grief . . .
there was now no armour, glittering in the forest glades, no em-
broidered feet on the greensward; the cream and dappled unicorns
had fled."[21]

Tony's ancestral home, Hetton Abbey, serves as tangible symbol
of that bogus neo-Gothic ethos. Rebuilt in 1864 from the destruction of an authentic abbey, it is presented from conflicting perspectives that cannot be reconciled. Assorted friends and relatives
characterize it negatively as "pretty ghastly" (133), "huge and quite
hideous" (7), or "authentic Pecksniff" (43) in allusion to Dickens's
fraudulent architect. Brenda's intense dislike of the house, which

she calls "appallingly ugly" (45), contributes to the formation of several ironies. Her disastrous attempt to modernize the morning room with white chromium walls and natural sheepskin carpet, according to Mrs. Beaver's execrable taste, points up the absurdity of superimposing modish renovations on it. Brenda's feeling of being held captive there is even more significant, for it ironically foreshadows her husband's eventual imprisonment in Todd's jungle habitat.

Tony's fascination with Hetton, which he is determined to preserve at all cost for his descendants, transcends any rational analysis, since his love of every "glazed brick" and "encaustic tile" (13) is inconsistent with his knowledge that the place is also run-down, uncomfortable, and financially ruinous. One aspect of the house that virtually drips with ironic possibilities is the naming of the bedrooms for Malory's Arthurian characters, though with Tennyson's spelling to imply Victorian corruption. Ostensibly a contribution to the mansion's romantic atmosphere, the names become portents of Tony's future. His bedroom, "Morgan le Fay," a repository of early memorabilia, suggests not only the enchantment of his own childhood but that of the young Arthur under the spell of an evil sorceress, while Brenda's occupancy of "Guinevere" hints at her infidelity. Tony's emotional attachment to Hetton, which may seem commendable in theory, must be deplored in view of the havoc it wreaks on his marriage and himself. Indeed it is another example of enthrallment to concepts that in the modern world are equated with fantasy.

Much of Waugh's depiction of Tony is achieved through the contradictory opinions of other characters, who perceive his personality traits as either admirable or deplorable according to their individual biases. Mrs. Beaver refers to him as "a stick" (6) and "a prig" (7), while Brenda's fashionable London acquaintances regard him as a pompous bore; but he is admired by his best friend, Jock, who at the beginning of the novel declares him to be "one of the happiest [of] men" (11). Such differing views tend to heighten and ironize one another, especially when they emanate from characters who are themselves subject to conflicting evaluations. Hence the reader's response can never be a simple resolution of incongruities but one that holds various possibilities in suspension.

Tony's own actions may be interpreted variously. When he accedes to his wife's desires about accepting an invitation, putting pleasure before business, or renting a London flat, he can be seen either as considerate and tolerant or as weak and vacillating, though as events transpire such uxorious indulgence proves detrimental to both of them. When against his better judgment Tony also allows himself to be overruled by his son, his wife's brother-in-law, and his stable groom, his compliance ceases to be virtuous and becomes ill-advised. While the rightness of his intentions is beyond question, Tony's failure to translate them into positive effects sometimes makes him appear foolish. For example, his lecture to his son, John Andrew, on language appropriate to gentlemen has no impact on the boy's vulgar speech and actually confirms Brenda's view of Tony as "madly feudal" (49). He is truly unselfish at the time of John Andrew's death, while suffering intensely himself, to be concerned about other people involved in the accident; but his anxiety about Brenda's distress is clearly misplaced. His belief that losing their son will "be so much worse" (148) for her than for him underscores his blindness to their temperamental differences; and his overconfident assertion to Mrs. Rattery, "You see, I know Brenda so well" (149), is a rapier stroke of self-deceptive irony. Even his refusal to sell Hetton in order to pay Brenda's alimony—although a decisive action applauded enthusiastically by the reader—can also be viewed as an expression of loyalty to a false ideal.

Underlying Tony's failures, Waugh implies, is the character's sole reliance on rational self-sufficiency, which ultimately proves inadequate to sustain him against the onslaught of the barbarians. Presented as a humanist, Tony is shown to have little contact with the kind of spirituality that might have strengthened him. His regular Sunday morning church attendance is merely part of an inherited obligation, and during services his mind dwells on mundane matters. He regards the Church of England simply as an organization for the improvement of social and ethical behavior; hence he considers the vicar's attempt at consolation after John Andrew's death to be painfully inappropriate. As he tells Mrs. Rattery, "the last thing one wants to talk about at a time like this is religion" (158). Much later, in response to Todd's question of whether he believes in God, Tony ingenuously admits, "I suppose so. I've never really thought about it much" (291). In accord with Waugh's statement in "Fan-Fare" that A Handful of Dust contains all its author "had to say about humanism,"[22] the novel therefore is presumably intended to illustrate, as does St. Augustine's Confessions, the folly of placing humanity, rather than God, at the center of one's uni-

verse.[23] The idolizing of human reason, to the neglect of the supernatural, can be seen as reducing characters to a merely human level
or, in the case of those less principled than Tony, even to bestiality.
That Waugh believed this humanist rejection of divine guidance to
be a prelude to religious liberalism is also substantiated in a comment to his brother Alec; upon reporting the dissolution of his own
marriage, Evelyn added: "The trouble about the world today is that
there's not enough religion in it. There's nothing to stop young
people doing whatever they feel like doing at the moment."[24]

What Waugh regarded as secularized and atrophied religion is
portrayed in the character of Tony's parish priest, Mr. Tendril,
whose leadership consists largely of maintaining formalities that
lack spiritual substance. Through a series of discrepancies built into
this inherently ironic situation, Waugh is able to depict both the
good intentions and the ineffectuality of the Anglican clergyman.
As a preacher Tendril is admired for the wrong reasons: a "noble
and sonorous voice" (38-39) and the habit of excluding from his
sermons any comments that might disturb the consciences of his
flock. In fact, his oft-repeated homilies, once suitable for British
garrisons in India decades earlier, have little relevance to the England of the 1930s. At Christmas, for example, Tendril laments the
lack of cold weather under an "alien sun," the absence of loved
ones in a heathen land, and the presence of "the ravening tiger and
the exotic camel" in place of the traditional "ox and ass of
Bethlehem" (79). Some of his references—to parishioners' "distant
homes" and to "our Gracious Queen Empress" (39)—even take on
totally different meanings from what they were designed to convey
years ago. Thus Tendril's credibility is completely demolished
without direct attack; he is revealed as not only incompetent but
blissfully unaware of his incompetence.

Brenda Last's personality is presented with even greater ironic
detachment than that of her husband. Initially the reader, like
Tony, sees her as a lovely, gracious aristocrat who for seven years of
marriage has done all that her husband and society expect. Yet this
superficial, deceptive view has been deliberately foisted upon the
reader, who gradually comes to see, through Brenda's own words
and deeds, that his early evaluation was erroneous. Her clichéd
thoughts, vapid conversation, immature diversions, and refusal to
confront serious issues give hints of a deeper irresponsibility as yet
undemonstrated. Although she has occasional twinges of conscience about relatively unimportant matters, she has no qualms

about deceiving Tony concerning her London activities or directing outrageous lies against him in the divorce suit. Abandoning her marriage vows as nonchalantly as her maternal obligations, Brenda demonstrates that her only strong commitment is to herself. By means of this evolving irony, the narrator, without offering any editorial condemnation, shows her character to be radically different from what he at first led the reader to believe.

Brenda's response to her child's death, which dispels any illusions the reader might have had about her, is handled through the obliquity of several ironic techniques that, converging in the act of her self-betrayal, disclose her real attitudes without any verbalization. The frivolous setting in which she receives the news—Polly Cockpurse's home, where gossipy friends amuse themselves with the latest fad, a fortune-teller who reads the soles of their feet—is deliberately contrasted with the gravity of the situation; and the fact that Jock is prevented from interrupting Brenda's reading even to inform her of the tragedy illustrates the transposition of values in an environment which elevates the trivial and downgrades the significant. Serving as a prelude to Brenda's shocking reaction and heightening the drama of this critical scene is her anxiety that John Beaver might have an accident on his flight to Paris. Her worrying over his safety has so obliterated all thought of her son, about whose participation in the hunt she had earlier been concerned, that when Jock tells her of the "very serious accident" that has befallen "John," even the reader cannot at first be sure who Brenda thinks has been killed. Only after Jock explains that he himself has been hunting at Hetton does she gradually awaken to the knowledge that her son is dead. Caught off guard, she utters the few words that betray her: "John . . . John Andrew . . . I . . . Oh thank God . . ." (162). Despite her subsequent attempt to palliate that subconscious revelation, both Jock and the reader understand her underlying, unexpressed thoughts. Brenda's departure from Hetton soon after the funeral in order to attend a house party provides an anticlimactic twist typical of Waugh. While Tony, as the betrayed and self-deceived husband, naively postulates that his wife needs to be among people who do not remind her of her lost child, Jock's failure to respond reveals to the reader the unspoken truth that she has gone to be with her lover.

The fashionable urban society in which Brenda chooses to live is depicted primarily through ironies that depend upon some kind of deception. In many instances the effect is double-edged, as members of this group, in their efforts to deceive others, unknowingly delude themselves or inadvertently betray their nefarious designs. Brenda's talent for misrepresenting the truth seems to make her well suited for such company. In addition to her calculated duplicity toward Tony, she shows an amazing ability to reshape her own perceptions of reality. Her assertion to Jock after the divorce falls through—"I'm very fond of Tony . . . in spite of the monstrous way he behaved" (239)—indicates that she has actually come to believe her distortion of the facts. But if she has succeeded in disregarding her own culpability, she is also blind to the fact that her new London acquaintances are using her more successfully than she is using them. The irony of their "friendship" becomes sharply apparent when in her subsequent poverty they all abandon her. Mrs. Beaver refuses to give her a job. Jenny, who had earlier declared, "I shall stick by you whatever happens" (173), dispenses only hollow commiseration; instead of offering to buy Brenda a meal, she comments, "I hear they are putting in bathrooms at Hetton—while you are practically starving" (249).

The way these urban barbarians prey upon one another is first illustrated in the account of Mrs. Beaver's luncheon party, which Brenda and her sister Marjorie happen to encounter. A microcosm of the social scene Brenda is about to enter, it represents, like other examples of Waugh's ironic world, an incohesive society devoid of tradition and ethical standards. Its members are petty opportunists whose pursuit of self-interest creates transient alliances with those who can be useful and ruthlessly rejects those who cannot. Among the guests invited because they are "in" with this society is Polly, Lady Cockpurse, about whom the narrator contributes his own ironic observation that a woman with such a questionable past should have climbed the social ladder to become the doyenne of London society. However, her elevation to countess does not expunge her natural vulgarity, as with brassy hypocrisy she shouts across the room to invite Brenda and Marjorie to a "very small, secret party" for "just old friends" (51). Like others in her set, who regard themselves as being quite different from what the reader sees, Polly does not comprehend her self-betrayals. An even more crucial invitation comes to Brenda from Mrs. Beaver to discuss a possible flat; but Marjorie's assessment of this chance meeting as "luck" must, in the light of subsequent events, be radically reinterpreted.

Although Mrs. Beaver tries to cloak her real motives with social amiability and the appearance of doing favors for her clients, the discrepancy between pretense and actuality is obvious in the opening scene of the novel. Eager to turn into financial gain a house fire in which two servants perished, she exposes her callousness by regretting that the damage was not more extensive so that her redecorating might be more lucrative. For a price she provides customers with whatever they desire, whether by remodeling a residence, leasing a flat, or launching a new fortune-teller; and while they perceive her dissembling and avarice, she succeeds because she caters to the weaknesses of human nature. Ironically, only Tony's heir, Richard Last, who knows nothing of Mrs. Beaver's character, profits from her supposed "helpfulness" without paying for it. Unable to see through her claim to having been "one of Tony's closest friends" (307), he considers her suggestion of a memorial "most considerate." Yet to the delight of the reader, who by then understands the strategies of this aggressive entrepreneur, Richard declines her offer to arrange for the redecoration of the Hetton chapel as a chantry—an idea as inappropriate for Tony as the chromium and sheepskin decor was for the morning room. Instead, the new owner of Hetton selects a simple stone monument, fashioned on the estate, from which Mrs. Beaver gains nothing. The observation by Lady St. Cloud that Tony "would have preferred" the stone extends the irony even further, since neither she nor Richard could have known how pleased Tony would have been that someone had managed to thwart Mrs. Beaver.

The ironies surrounding John Beaver can be seen principally as reversals of the expected. At the beginning of the novel the reader, agreeing with Brenda's first impression that he is "rather pathetic" (33, 49), feels sorry for him because of his penury, his dependence on a domineering mother, his tenuous connection with the social set, and even Jock's apparent callousness in forcing him to buy drinks. But the narrator obliquely undermines that initial sympathy through a variety of ironic techniques. Under the impertinent questioning of little John Andrew, Beaver unguardedly divulges more of himself than he normally would; and the boy, sensing Beaver's fraudulence, pronounces him "a very silly man" (33). In this instance, an unsophisticated child functions as *ingénu*, expressing without adult understanding what the more worldly-wise characters have yet to discover. Another view of Beaver is provided by London society, which radically alters its opinion after his involvement with Brenda. Having formerly considered him rather ridiculous, this fashionable set promptly elevates him to fantasy status and finds in him admirable qualities hitherto undetected. Although such capricious assessments are hardly reliable, they nevertheless cast suspicion on his character.

That Brenda should choose someone of Beaver's caliber for a lover seems most unlikely, and her rationalizations for doing so appear equally perverse. While conceding that he is socially inept, snobbish, and probably "cold as a fish" (66), she imagines she can improve him. As she confides to Marjorie (who thinks him *"dreary"*): ". . . he's got to be taught a whole lot of things. That's part of his attraction" (66). But Brenda has only a superficial perception of Beaver. Blind to his opportunism, she worries that he will be bored with her aristocratic friends from debutante days and cannot see how pleased he is to be in their company. She is also unable to deduce from his Christmas thank-you note, written in "a large, schoolgirlish hand" (81), what its infantile style and content indicate about his shallow feelings. Nor does she discern the self-seeking stratagem behind his pretext that their intended marriage would be unfair to *her* unless she were "properly provided for" in the divorce settlement (207). Through an irony of unanticipated events comprising the Brighton fiasco and Tony's subsequent refusal to pay anything, Beaver's greed in demanding four times the alimony Tony had promised precipitates the collapse of the entire scheme. Brenda's realization that her lover, guided by "mumsey," has no time to waste on an impoverished divorcée finally brings her to the awareness of his true character that the reader has long comprehended.

Compounding the pathetic with the ridiculous is Brenda's London acquaintance Jenny Abdul Akbar, who presents herself as an abused and exiled Moroccan princess. Some indication of her bizarre personality can be inferred from the description of her "promiscuously" furnished flat with its conglomeration of incompatible objects, including a phallic fetish and several items used in ways contrary to the purposes for which they were created (prayer rugs on the divan, a wall covering on the floor, ivory elephants on the radiator). Thus the detached narrator, by means of what Peter Green has called the "social objective correlative,"[25] is able to debase her indirectly through ostensibly realistic reporting. Jenny herself is so fantastic—with her overdone appearance, overwrought emotions, and stories of great suffering in a mysterious past—that she seems the personification of *Arabian Nights* hyperbole. Especially melodramatic is her claim of being responsible for little John

Andrew's death because of some "terrible curse" (157) that follows her everywhere. At Hetton her proclivity toward exaggeration actually produces unintended results. Instead of seducing Tony, as she had expected, Jenny so repels him with lavishly sentimental praise that he regards her as a "joke-woman" (120); but she inadvertently captivates John Andrew by her beauty, perfume, and tales of Moorish horsemen. The reader's attitude, however, must remain in a state of ironic ambivalence, since the truth about Jenny's identity and experiences can never be precisely determined.

In presenting Brenda's brother, Reggie St. Cloud, the narrator sets him up for a monumental fall through verbal irony and graphic descriptions that hint at his inadequacies. Exaggerated language—his widowed mother's "atavistic faith in the authority and preternatural good judgment of the Head of the Family" (200) —and an account of his gross obesity undermine the reader's confidence in him. Slighting diction belittles his archeological expeditions as merely "desecrating some tombs" (200) and his trophies as nothing more than "fragmentary amphoras, corroded bronze axeheads, little splinters of bone and charred stick" (202). Although Reggie is only a peripheral figure, his sole entry upon the scene to discuss the divorce settlement with Tony becomes a pivotal point in the action that dramatically alters the future for the major characters and effects the most crucial reversal of expectations in the novel. Reggie's efforts in his sister's behalf prove disastrous. Unable to prevent the divorce by the illogical tactic of calling Tony "vindictive" for allowing Brenda to marry an undesirable lover, he bluntly demands so great a financial settlement that Hetton would have to be sold. When Tony does not capitulate, Reggie obtusely concludes that his approaches have been too tactful: "I must have put things rather badly. It comes from trying to respect people's feelings too much" (207-8). Without ever suspecting that his next strategy could boomerang, he proceeds to threaten Tony with an alimony suit based on the "infidelity" evidence concocted in Brighton. Although Brenda's friends and sister believe, quite mistakenly, that her case was lost because she trustingly allowed it to be presented to Tony beforehand, Brenda's brother-in-law, Allan, suspects the truth, which the reader already knows, and echoes Reggie's phraseology with reversed meaning by telling Marjorie: "I expect your ass of a brother put the thing wrong" (210).

Of the two men most responsible for Tony's captivity in the jungle, Dr. Messinger, who organizes the search for a fabled Amazonian city, becomes an ironic victim himself, largely through self-deception. What destroys the expedition and leads to his drowning is overconfidence in his ability to understand the natives. His assertion, "I *know* the Indian mind" (262), when he attempts to bribe them with green mechanical toy mice, proves to be as false as Tony's earlier conviction, "I know Brenda so well" (149); for the Indians, instead of being delighted, are terrified by the noisy, moving creatures and run away. Messinger's prediction that they will return is indeed fulfilled, though in a way he does not anticipate: they do creep back to the camp but only to retrieve their belongings and disappear again, leaving the Englishmen helplessly alone in uncharted territory.

While Messinger's failure results from blindly deceiving himself, Mr. Todd's success stems from his shrewdness in deceiving others; and of all the barbarians in *A Handful of Dust*, none is more sinister or more complicated than he. His mixed parentage, gold-seeking English father and Indian mother, represents the joining of civilized and primitive savagery, merged so incongruously in his personality that cruelty is dressed in urbanity and guile is masked in the appearance of artlessness. Waugh's method of presenting Todd is also ironical in that the evil in the character's nature unfolds little by little out of a semblance of goodness. Initially he seems to be a man of compassion, whose spiritual home is the world of Dickensian fiction. His motives for saving Tony from death in the jungle are ostensibly humanitarian; and the cross he erects—to mark the grave of a black man who used to read to him and also to celebrate Tony's arrival—can easily be interpreted as a sincere Christian tribute. But neither Tony nor the reader comprehends the significance of the illiterate Todd's comments on the black man or connects them with Todd's repeated injunction to Tony: "You shall read to me" (290). Tony's observation that reading through the entire Dickens library will take longer than his stay shows him to be completely unaware of his host's intentions. Nor does Todd's retort—"Oh, I hope not" (292)—seem ominous. Yet the narrator has implanted subtle hints of a darker aspect to Todd's personality—his promiscuous siring of Indians, his use of a shotgun to control them, his knowledge of harmful as well as beneficial herbs, and his obsession with Dickens. It is from his childlike desire to have Dickens read over and over again—so that he may weep at the sentimentality, laugh at the humor, and delight in virtue rewarded and vice overcome—that Todd's psychological peculiarities unmistakably emerge.

At first Tony, as the ironic victim, is oblivious to his true situation and even later does not understand the full implication of Todd's evasive or ambiguous replies to his inquiries about leaving. But his "foreboding of permanent exile" is confirmed by the discovery of a note written by the black man, stating Todd's promise to "*let him go*" (296-97); for Tony realizes that his predecessor was liberated only by death. Thereafter Tony recognizes Todd's seemingly gracious acquiescence to his demand for freedom—" . . . my friend . . . You are under no restraint. Go when you like" (297)—as a sadistic jest, for both men know that he cannot survive unaided in the jungle. Todd's most chilling behavior, while Tony is drugged and hidden elsewhere, is the way he thwarts the rescue attempt with equivocal evidence—simply by giving the English search party Tony's wristwatch and showing them the cross erected in his honor. Without lying, Todd leads the rescuers to the logical but false assumption that Tony is dead and thereby assures himself of no further interference from the outside world. Although his account of this event to Tony after the Englishmen have left contains nothing untruthful and is spoken with an air of complete innocence, Tony presumably understands the diabolical cunning that will condemn him to a living death as prisoner of a madman.

Throughout the progress of the novel, as Tony's and Brenda's lives are changed by contact with the barbarians, Waugh uses ironic foreshadowing to portend future events. This technique, well suited to the work's foreboding quality, abounds in *A Handful of Dust* more than in any other of the novels. Characters unwittingly become prophets as their casual commentary takes on, in the light of later developments, meanings that their words could not have had at the time of utterance. What is expressed in one situation may suggest, often quite indirectly, what will happen in a different context. Although Beaver, in amusing Brenda with fortune-telling, unknowingly hits upon the truth that "there is going to be a sudden death" in her life, his prediction of "a long journey across the sea," after which she will "grow a beard and die" (42), is realized in Tony's fate. The irony in Brenda's remark to Tony concerning his reaction to Beaver—"When someone's awful you just run away and hide" (43)—is that Tony, by going to Brazil, does literally what she meant only metaphorically. Tony's joking assertion to Brenda, after Beaver's departure for London, that their guest has "gone back thinking [she is] mad about him" (46) is turned into reality by events that neither husband nor wife can foresee. The deeper implications of Mrs. Beaver's observation that the London flat will "fill a long felt need" (53) do not become clear until Brenda uses her pied-à-terre for a liaison. Nor does the stationmaster's tale about a local man whose wife would not willingly return from London appear to Tony as relevant to his personal life. The belief of the poor Last cousins visiting Hetton at Christmas that (presumably because of blood kinship) "they had far more right" to be there than Brenda (80) takes on unexpected significance when they inherit the estate. Highly ironic is Messinger's warning to Tony, with respect to Thérèse, about the dangers of getting mixed up with women, for both men are later betrayed by the Indian woman Rosa. Tony's enjoyment in reading to Brenda until she confessed "it was torture" to listen (292) is a foreshadowing in reverse parallel of his own torment in having to read to a delighted captor.

Irony typical of Greek tragedy, including numerous forewarnings that assume the proportion of oracular prophecy, is prominent in the handling of events surrounding John Andrew's death during the hunt. The boy's tumble from his horse on a previous day presages a more serious fall, as does Tony's casual remark in a letter to Brenda, *"I hope he doesn't break his neck"* (135). Indicative of the future in a way that the speakers could not anticipate is John Andrew's conversation with his nanny about the hoped-for killing of the fox. To his remark, "If I'm in at the death I expect Colonel Inch will blood me," she categorically answers, "You won't see any death" (136). His response to the insistence of the groom Ben that they return early from the hunt is also in the vein of unwitting prophecy. Countering the argument that his father will then be more likely to let him ride some other day, John Andrew replies: "But there mayn't *be* another day. The world may come to an end" (140). What does end his world is an irony of events somewhat analogous to the situation of Oedipus, whose efforts to avoid his prophesied fate actually bring it about, for the back lane selected by Jock and Ben as the safest homeward route turns out to be the most dangerous. In retrospect, therefore, the narrator's initially ambiguous comment on this choice—"So John's fate was decided" (141)—takes on an ominous meaning. So do the oblique hints from both the narrator (in the role of a Greek chorus) and Jock of some catastrophe in store for Miss Ripon because of her unmanageable horse. But that she, traveling the same back road as John Andrew, should cause his accident is contrary to all the characters' expectations. The rankest irony in the episode is expressed in the narrator's final choric comment—"Everyone agreed that it was nobody's fault" (143)—because everyone involved in trying to protect the boy contributed to an outcome beyond anyone's power to avert.

Less somber instances of innocent unawareness occur in conversations. One or more characters may be in the dark about the real meaning of what is said, though the reader will understand if he discerns the unexpressed thoughts that prompt the spoken words. In an exchange with Jenny, John Andrew, not knowing her habit of mistaking people's names, wonders why she calls his father "Teddy"; but her reply, "Because I hope we are going to be great friends," is evidently based on the assumption that the child questions her first-name familiarity. Unable to interpret her statement of intent, and therefore her logic, John Andrew concludes that she gives "a funny reason" (116) for using the wrong name. The reader is also obliged to follow childlike reasoning in order to comprehend why, after Beaver admits to being "very poor," John Andrew should ask him whether he is "poor enough to call people tarts" (32). The boy's association of poverty with the vulgar language used by the stable groom is based on his father's reprimand for calling nanny a "tart." When John Andrew argues that Ben often applies the word to "people," Tony explains proper speech as a function of class: the "less fortunate" are permitted "certain expressions" that gentlemen do not use (25). Hence John Andrew apparently wants to find out whether Beaver is allowed the colorful language he himself is forbidden.

Implications hidden from one conversant can be clear to another who possesses more information about a subject. Since Jock knows about Brenda's affair with Beaver and the use to which she puts the London flat, Tony's unsuspecting comments have significance in his friend's mind that they could not have in his own. When Tony asserts that Brenda's flat is too small for the two of them to spend the night, Jock knows that to Brenda it is too small only if the second person is Tony, not if it is Beaver. References to Brenda's supposed studies figure in other ironies that arise from this discrepancy in knowledge. Jock, going along with Tony's concept of his wife's London endeavors, asks whether the new acquaintances she invites to Hetton are from the economics school. Tony, explaining that he has postponed renovations at Hetton in order to lease the flat, remarks in an amusing wordplay that he must "econ-omize because of Brenda's economics" (87). In both instances the term "economics," shifted into the context of Brenda's actual life in London, takes on unorthodox meanings for both Jock and the reader. A more unusual form of irony occurs when a character, in order to deceive, speaks the truth as if in jest. Brenda's jocular response to Tony's question of what she found to do in London—"I've been behaving rather badly" and "carrying on madly with young men" (70, 71)—presumably relies on two assumptions: that anyone guilty of such indiscretions would conceal rather than reveal them, and that anything couched in a humorous context is unlikely to be taken seriously. She expects, therefore, that her "confession" will be interpreted as a declaration of innocence, as indeed it is by Tony, though not by the reader. With Beaver she indulges in a similar tac-tic; certain that he is too self-satisfied to see the truth about him-self, she puts him down in a bantering fashion:

Beaver: "I'm awfully fond of Tony."
Brenda: "Don't let that worry you, my beauty, he doesn't like you *at all.*"
Beaver: "*Doesn't* he? Why not?"
Brenda: "No one does except me. You must get that clear . . . it's very odd that *I* should." (77-78)

By means of such devices, the narrator demonstrates Brenda's ma-nipulation of both men without openly accusing her of being devious.

At times the narrator operates as a calculating ironist himself, deliberately misleading the reader to false assumptions. After Brenda says it is pointless to have a large house if one does not en-tertain and Tony delivers a lecture on the primacy of his inherited obligations, the narrator provides no dependable clues to the cou-ple's relationship. Instead, by referring to their conversations as "scenes of domestic playfulness" (19), he grossly misconstrues both Brenda's denial that Tony would even "know how" to be pompous and her avowal that she too is glad no guest is coming. Still main-taining his seeming obliviousness to the tension building up be-tween an increasingly resentful wife and her contentedly unaware husband, he condones the immaturity of their eating games and praises Tony's willingness to put Brenda's amusements before estate business by declaring: "What with Brenda's pretty ways and Tony's good sense, it was not surprising that their friends pointed to them as a pair who were pre-eminently successful in solving the problem of getting along well together" (28). Since the narrator's unreliability is not easily detectable except in retrospect, it is understandable that Cyril Connolly, after reading only the first serial installment of the novel, should have believed it to be "all about a happy county family."[26]

Later in the novel the narrator drops his pose of naiveté and in the very process of expressing a certain point of view shows, through verbal irony, that it is untenable. In representing the attitude of Brenda's London set toward her liaison with Beaver, he first employs overblown diction to transform the sordidly drab affair into fairytale glamor: ". . . for five years she had been a legendary, almost ghostly name, the imprisoned princess of fairy story, and now that she had emerged there was . . . enchantment in the occurrence" (75). But the narrator then interweaves such highly derogatory terms among the exaggerated metaphors that the inflated illusion collapses. The description of Brenda's "choice of partner" as a "touch of fantasy" and Beaver himself as "[catching] up to her among the luminous clouds of deity" is shot down by the reference to him as "the joke figure they had all . . . despised." The "realm of poetry" to which the affair has been elevated is debased by the word "escapade," and Brenda's new friends are denigrated as a "gang of gossips" (75). Thus, while seeming to praise the romanticism of "Polly and Daisy and Angela," the narrator reduces it to absurdity.

Some of the most memorable irony in *A Handful of Dust* is contained in the plot structure, accompanied by occasional verbal wrenchings. Disparities between reality and either appearance or illusion dominate the scenes depicting the divorce procedure, in which Brenda assumes the role of plaintiff—"the innocent and injured party" (176)—while Tony gallantly takes the part of defendant and provides evidence of infidelity against himself. Imbedded in these public deceptions is Tony's continuing self-deception about Brenda, whom he still trusts, despite her previous betrayal, to keep their unwritten agreement about the alimony. When Tony must choose someone to serve as his partner in the trumped-up adultery, appearance is again emphasized, especially in the solicitor's tale of another client who was so rigidly moral that his own wife, disguised in a wig, finally had to act as the corespondent. Tony selects the prostitute Milly because she *appears* to be a lady; as another prostitute puts it, "You have to have a *lady* for a divorce" (180). But although Milly plays her part in the charade superbly—dressing elegantly for dinner in the hotel dining room and for breakfast posing in bed with Tony to validate their "intimacy" before the hotel servants—one mishap after another occurs, making the Brighton episode the high point of comedy in this rather uncomical novel.

Winnie, Milly's eight-year-old daughter, whom Tony is trapped into taking along despite his repeated objections, is at the center of much that goes wrong. Her behavior as an obnoxious brat is played off against Tony's attempts to placate her—almost always to his disadvantage. Her very presence is highly inappropriate in a situation of supposed adultery; and one of the private detectives hired to corroborate the evidence declares it to be "most irregular," adding with a touch of verbal irony that it "sets a nasty, respectable note bringing a kid into it" (185). From his standpoint, any appearance of respectability could jeopardize a case that "depend[s] very much on making the right impression" (187). Tony's open socializing with the detectives also disturbs their professional sensibilities, and the senior detective remarks admonishingly, "Mr. Last, sir, this is all *wrong*. . . . You haven't no business to recognize us at all" (186). His lament to his colleague that too often clients do not "realize that divorce is a serious matter" (188) suggests that the seriousness of divorce may have very different meanings. To the detective it represents adherence to the outward formalities of the law, but to clients like Tony it represents an internal emotional rupture of which the detective seems unaware.

That Tony's mind is not even on the most crucial issue to be established in a British divorce at that time is shown by the incident of the two breakfasts; for, having eaten with Winnie in the dining room, he must be reminded by the detective to do so again while in bed with Milly. Winnie's repeated taunts thereafter about his "eating two breakfasts" (198) call attention to the ironic discrepancy in their points of view. While Tony tries, rather ambiguously, to explain his real reason for the second meal by telling Winnie, "It's the Law," her juvenile logic misinterprets his motive as greediness. His intentions are also grossly misconstrued by the other people on the beach where Winnie demands to swim despite the unsafe condition of the sea. The spectators, unaware of the true situation, believe that he is a monster who wants to drown his child. But not even as a subconscious desire could this imputation be applicable to Tony, although the reader, knowing Winnie's mistreatment of him, might think it her just desert. At this point neither the reader nor any character suspects what will later be revealed as the culminating irony of the Brighton episode—that such an enfant terrible, who would share her mother's bed while Tony sleeps in an adjoining room, would unintentionally become his salvation by invalidating the evidence.

Tony's romantic friendship with Thérèse de Vitré on the ship bound for South America is treated with ironic obliquity insofar as the most important thoughts of the would-be lovers are never expressed. Although they obviously enjoy talking, swimming, sightseeing, and dancing together, the extent of their personal feelings for one another is not apparent to the reader until the relationship reaches its turning point. Except for giving Thérèse a kiss, Tony shows no indication that he might be falling in love; and the signals Thérèse gives him seem to be mixed. She speaks ingenuously about her probable marriage of convenience to someone from another rich creole family, yet several times she suggests that Tony visit her in Trinidad—to see her father's fine house, to eat creole cooking, and to meet her parents. One might suspect that this talk of her future marriage, to which both she and Tony keep returning—although she is not as yet engaged to anyone in particular—may be an indirect way of addressing their own growing attraction to each other.

When the climactic moment occurs on their visit to the island of Barbados, it too is underplayed as if nothing consequential is happening. To Tony's admission that he has an estranged wife in England, Thérèse only replies, "Somehow I didn't think you were [married]" (231). But the surprising news apparently brings a halt to the devoutly Catholic girl's interest in Tony, for she immediately desires to return to the ship and comments about their idyllic day on shore as if in farewell. Her superbly disciplined emotions are further revealed when, realizing that she has lost the stuffed fish they had bought earlier in the day, she laconically states, "It doesn't matter" (231). Christian marriage with Tony, of which she had evidently entertained hopes and which the fish symbolized, has thus been tacitly consigned to the impossible. Tony's unspoken sadness may be seen symbolically in the narrator's observation that blue water ended after Barbados and muddy seas surrounded Trinidad. But the final comment on Tony's thwarted romance has a sharply ironic twist: a fellow passenger remarks that, according to his own experience, those poor but proud creoles may be friendly on board ship but never invite one to their homes. In Thérèse's case such a plausible interpretation is totally wrong.

Tony's quest for a fabled Inca city in Amazonia provides some of Waugh's most imaginative and sophisticated displays of irony.[27] Numerous juxtapositions and collages, implying connections amid disparities, create a literary fabric rich in humor, pathos, and psychological insights. Tony's suffering from jungle discomforts is accentuated by his own recollection of pleasant London dinner parties, which the narrator then counterpoints with a description of Jock and Brenda presently dancing at Anchorage House. While Messinger is trying unsuccessfully to negotiate with Indian women whose men have gone off hunting wild pigs, Jock in Parliament has an analogous communication problem in presenting a question about pig breeding. Such a linkage suggests that life in London has more similarities to life in the bush than Londoners would like to admit and forces the reader to reconsider Jock's complacent assertion that "the whole world is civilized now" (238), for jungle tactics seem to prevail even in the highest levels of English government. The insecurities of Brenda and Beaver in London are counterpointed with the increasingly precarious situation of Tony and Messinger in the Amazonian jungle, so that each circumstance serves to emphasize the seriousness of the other. Similarly, the paralleling of Brenda's desertion by Beaver, lawyer, and friends with Tony's isolation after Messinger drowns heightens the poignancy of each character's desperation.

The conflation of some of Tony's thoughts also permits greater understanding of his subconscious mental processes. His prefiguration of the lost Inca city as thoroughly Gothic—indeed "a transfigured Hetton" (222) with all the panoply of medieval romance—obliquely suggests that he has transferred his loyalty from one ideal, now fallen, to another equally insubstantial. His consciousness of being in a different time zone in Brazil evokes the fanciful notion that the sun reaches him "second hand and slightly soiled after Polly" and her friends have "finished with it," rather "like Polly's dresses which Brenda used to buy" (237). Through this unusual analogy the narrator shows, without ever expressing the thought directly, that in Tony's mind Brenda's London acquaintances sully everything they touch.

Tony's delirious perceptions, whereby disordered recollections of past experiences in England are interwoven with more recent ones in Brazil, resemble dreams in that the elements constantly shift, blend, disintegrate, or become transformed, often with a logic neither realistic nor rational but implicitly true. His first hallucinatory sighting of Brenda occurs in the canoe; and when she accompanies him to shore, Tony, recalling her usual train from London, tells Messinger: "I am so glad she could come. She must have caught the three-eighteen" (270). Brenda reappears thereafter in various guises. When wearing a tattered, dirty cotton dress or slipping away in the night with her hammock and food ration, she is fused with Rosa, appropriately since both are women who have betrayed him. When she takes the canoe and does not return as promised, she is associated with Messinger. Tony's assumption that she is "staying with one of her new friends in Brazil" (285) reveals his unstated belief that she prefers to live among savages.

At the height of Tony's malarial fever, phantasmagoric mélanges of previous experiences and conversations, transformed and wrenched out of context, pass through his mind. A condensed illustration involves the unlikely assemblage of Reggie, Polly, Milly, Winnie, and Brenda at a County Council meeting, deciding to widen a road for Green Line buses that turn into mechanical green rats, while Mrs. Beaver is awarded the construction contract and her workmen get two breakfasts. Yet if Tony's delirium liberates the anxieties ordinarily suppressed by his rational censor, it also makes possible the only fulfillment his quest is destined to have. Still superimposing his Gothic dream on the lost Amazonian City and imagining that his butler Ambrose offers to "serve it directly . . . in the library," Tony sees it, as from the windows at Hetton, and struggles from his hammock toward its ramparts, turrets, and spires as the "gates . . . open before him and trumpets . . . [salute] his arrival" (282-83).

But at the nadir of despair, when ragged, scratched, and very ill as he reaches Todd's squalid village—actually a burlesque of the City he has sought—Tony speaks bitterly of what he has "learned in the forest" (288). Of Brenda he concludes: "She will say nothing cruel. . . . But she will leave you. . . . Let us kill in the gentlest manner." Of the City he concedes: "There is no City. Mrs. Beaver has covered it with chromium plating and converted it into flats. . . . Very suitable for base love. And Polly will be there. She and Mrs. Beaver under the fallen battlements . . ." (288). By means of these jumbled distortions Tony conveys his fear that Mrs. Beaver and her kind have beat him to the City, wrecked it, and remade it in their own image. Civilization, he seems to imply, has been destroyed by the barbarians.

In the final chapter, "English Gothic—III," Waugh draws together the various strands of his subject. These few pages of narration about Hetton's new owners, interspersed with their ordinary conversation, may seem dramatically flat after Tony's horrifying experiences in the jungle, but they are packed with ironies that offer oblique commentary on characters, actions, and thematic developments in the novel. Although the juxtapositions and parallels are so subtly contrived that their components drop casually from the remarks of narrator and characters without apparent design, they stand out sharply against the low-key matrix once the reader has made the necessary connections.

The silver foxes being raised as a business by the inheritors of Tony's estate form the basis of several derisive comparisons— ironic because the implied analogies seem bizarre and the author's judgments are conveyed without direct expression. The foxes, as representatives of humanity's animalistic nature, reintroduce the theme of savagery, as well as the folly of confronting it with a civilized response. Although they live in pairs and sometimes appear tame, their rapacity is satisfied only by devouring gentler animals and their treachery is manifest in attacks on each other and unwary caretakers. Reference to the vixen that had her tail bitten off when she stuck it into the adjacent cage not only underscores the viciousness of the species but suggests Brenda's behavior. The fact that the vixen has suffered only minimally provides a sly, underhanded dig at the amorality of a society in which Brenda is scarcely worse for her indiscretion because she has married Jock, long considered by her friends to be a suitable mate.

The silver foxes also undermine the aspiration of returning Hetton to Gothic splendor, for it is through raising and selling them that the Richard Lasts intend to acquire the necessary funds. The narrator's closing remark—that by means of these stinking creatures Cousin Teddy expects "to restore Hetton to the glory that it had enjoyed in the days of his Cousin Tony" (308)—reveals not only that Teddy knows little of Hetton's decline during Tony's ownership but also that he must resort to commercialism to achieve his goal. This third section centering on the values of "English Gothic" shows them reduced to a state of even greater degradation than they suffered in two previous sections of the novel, since the aristocratic way of life, if it is to survive at all in modern society, must resort to money-grubbing tactics that Tony had considered inimical to his beliefs. Quite obviously, Hetton, as the tangible symbol of his high-minded principles, will fall to ruin unless it is sustained by wealth.

In a world governed by mammon, Gothic idealism, whether represented phenomenally by Hetton or noumenally by Tony's vision of the lost City, would seem to be a bankrupt illusion that cannot stand up to barbarism. Yet Tony's romanticism is not necessarily absurd for contributing to his defeat any more than society's predatory materialism is commendable merely for proving successful. Herein lie the paradoxes that are brilliantly exploited in the novel through dramatization of ironic conflicts. What permits society to carry off reprehensible behavior with impunity is a dubious value system, in which the externals are all that matter. So long as the desire for self-gratification is camouflaged by social respectability, the armor of hypocrisy is virtually invulnerable to direct criticism. But society's self-contradictory nature is an ideal target for irony. Hence, in portraying the human dilemmas that result from this skewed environment—and for which there are no facile solutions—the most satisfactory aesthetic approach is neither satiric reduction nor sentimental exhortation but an appropriately distanced ironic perspective. Indeed Waugh's outstanding success as an ironist in *A Handful of Dust* owes much to his ability to challenge the assumptions of both commercial and chivalric codes. By showing the disorder wrought through living according to either instinct or hollow tradition, the novel demonstrates, by negative implication, the need for something higher than man-made ideals.

CHAPTER SIX

Scoop

Waugh's ironic vision of the world in *Scoop* is not so menacing as in previous novels; and the narrator approaches its abundant anarchy, not with horror or fascination, but with playful, even jovial, amusement. Although William Boot, like Paul Pennyfeather, undergoes a rude awakening and a circular progress that ends where it began, the evils encountered are much less malignant, the fates of the characters are less horrendous, and the overall tone is considerably more cheerful than in *Decline and Fall*. Despite William's failure in love and his awareness of having been taken advantage of, he does not allow disappointments or predators to overwhelm him, as do Waugh's earlier tragic victims. Instead, he returns home with greater consciousness and stronger convictions about what is really significant to him. By coming to terms with contingencies over which he has no control and by taking charge of his own destiny insofar as possible, William is able to make a rational decision about where and how he will live. This more hopeful mood of *Scoop* may well be attributed to Waugh's happiness, during the time of its composition, with Laura Herbert, to whom it is dedicated. Begun a few months after their engagement and completed within the first year of their marriage, the work reflects a measure of the contentment and well-ordered stability that she brought to his life.

Besides offering more optimistic views on some of the recurrent dilemmas in Waugh's fiction, this novel also recasts in a new vein some of the author's own experiences. Whereas for *Black Mischief* Waugh had turned his recollections of Ethiopia into serious and often tragic irony, his reuse of the same material in *Scoop* is light to the point of farcicality, revealing his ability to see the comical aspects of that African country. During his first visit there in 1930, he observed a "peculiar flavour of galvanised and translated reality" that he associated with the fantasy world of Lewis Carroll.[1] Indeed he described his first sojourn in Addis Ababa as a "preposterous *Alice in Wonderland* fortnight." Since for *Scoop* he compounded these impressions with remembrances of his bizarre experiences as a war correspondent there in 1935, it is not surprising that an atmosphere of make-believe should pervade the novel. By liberating time, place, and action from the ordinary expectations of reality, Waugh created a fanciful realm that was highly conducive to the workings of irony. Accordingly, he drew on many of the devices that Lewis Carroll had derived from fairy tales—wish fulfillment, dream logic, nonsensical sequence of events, the mixture of sense and nonsense, and mistaken identities.[2] The debt to Carroll is especially evident in the irrational logic and semantic confusions throughout the novel and specifically in the character of Salter, who burlesques the White Rabbit with repetitions of "Oh dear" and persistent worries about being late.

The novel also owes much to the inventions of another favorite Waugh author, P. G. Wodehouse, whose fictional world is as imaginary, though not as improbable, as that of Carroll's work, and whose characters Waugh praised for having no "identity with the real life of any period."[3] In *Scoop* the Boot family and others of their acquaintance are treated in such hilariously whimsical fashion as to invite comparison with Wodehouse characters.[4] This similarity is particularly obvious in the caricature of the amiable eccentrics at Boot Magna, who in their refusal to grow up retreat from the harsh realities of modernity into a never-never land of rural isolation. In fact, Boot Magna itself, surrounded by enchanted nature, may well have been inspired by Blandings Castle, with its Edenic gardens; certainly Waugh identified the milieu of Wodehouse novels with the fairy-tale atmosphere of *A Midsummer Night's Dream* and *Alice in Wonderland*—"a world," as he described it, "inhabited by strange transmogrifications."[5]

In the wonderland of *Scoop*, implausible twists in the plot and preposterous linkages between cause and effect propel the action from beginning to end, defeating expectations and bringing about miraculous solutions. John Courteney Boot's wish to become a spy in order to escape London is redirected by Julia Stitch, who promises to find him a position as a foreign correspondent. Lord Copper's decision to hire him as a war reporter in Ishmaelia is thwarted by the *Daily Beast*'s foreign editor, Salter, who drafts William Boot for the job. William complies with Copper's summons in the belief that it concerns an error mischievously inserted by his sister Priscilla into the nature column he writes for the *Beast*. In effect, Priscilla's little joke lands her brother in Africa just as, much later, Kätchen's gleanings from Ishmaelian gossip thrust him toward his journalistic coup. The ironic disproportion becomes even more pronounced in the realization that a peccadillo in an obscure article leads directly to front-page renown. In Ishmaelia William's happiness in love is destroyed by the sudden return of Kätchen's so-called husband, and William's ebbing fortunes on the day of the Communist takeover are reversed when Mr. Baldwin drops out of the sky in response to his cries for help. Baldwin himself is blessed with an equally improbable deus ex machina: the instant he voices the need for some means of effecting immediate political change, the drunken Swede, Olafsen, bursts upon the scene on a revved-up motorcycle. In London the prime minister's reliance on irresponsible underlings to bestow a knighthood on William results in the knighting of John Boot[6]; and Salter's substitution of Uncle Theodore at the banquet to honor William brings about the foreign editor's calamitous demotion. In a world governed by mischance, Murphy's Law is the only certainty.

Many of the comic blunders in *Scoop* derive from misapprehension—as characters infer from credible premises conclusions that seem perfectly sound but turn out to be incorrect because the premises are either misleading or misunderstood. The irony lies in the fact that, as Eleanor Hutchens states, "reason itself has led to an unreasonable conclusion" or that a character has followed "a chain of logic which he believes to be based on true causality."[7] The plot first jumps the rails because Salter's plausible deductions lead him to select the wrong person for the African assignment. Ordered to find a Boot known for his "high-class style" of writing and favored by the prime minister, who is said to be "nuts on rural England,"[8] Salter logically concludes that the author of the florid, stilted prose in the nature column is his man. But during their initial acquaintance Salter and William completely fail to communicate; neither is aware of the other's intentions or clarifies his own. As William's agonies over the mistake in his column run parallel to Salter's attempts to interest him in Ishmaelia, misinterpretations bounce back and forth.

In other instances as well, the narrator sets up the irony by imparting the truth to the reader beforehand and then allowing characters with insufficient knowledge to make incorrect judgments. When Salter visits Boot Magna, his hosts, not knowing his distaste for the country or his dread of riding atop the lorry sent to meet him, believe he has walked from the train station for pleasure. Salter's collapse from exhaustion they misconstrue as drunkenness and at dinner offer him only water to drink. When he returns to London looking haggard, the managing editor thinks he has been intemperate among "heavy drinking country squires" (308). Even richer in irony is Algernon Stitch's conjecture that if John Boot is being awarded a knighthood the prime minister must be cracking up, for it not only betrays Stitch's low opinion of both men but reveals his thought processes. His reasoning that the superficiality of one man could be rewarded only through the derangement of the other appears to have surface credibility but is flawed because of Stitch's unawareness that incompetent secretaries have erred. An inductive leap over missing information leads him to an unwarranted conclusion.

Mistaken or uncertain identities contribute to the ironic comedy of *Scoop,* and indeed few characters are actually what they seem or what they conceive themselves to be. John Boot, the novelist fashionable among London's smart set, is confused with a distant Boot cousin who writes articles about country life. William, while waiting in the Megalopolitan headquarters to see Lord Copper, is mistaken for a novice reporter and sent on a trivial assignment. Uncle Theodore becomes the famed "Boot of the *Beast*" when neither William nor John can be obtained for Lord Copper's triumphal dinner. The real identity of the international financier known as Mr. Baldwin is never ascertained: while claiming to be English, he uses a Costa Rican passport, speaks many languages, and owns property in Bordeaux, Antibes, and Ishmaelia. Kätchen's nationality is equally ambiguous. Born in Budapest of Polish and Russian parents, she has lived in England and passes herself off as German. In a spoof of popular spy novels, bearded M. Giraud, the Swiss ticket collector on the Ishmaelian train, is alleged to be a Russian spy though he is actually Baldwin's agent, and the train's engineer is Baldwin's valet in disguise. These incongruities give rise to amusing situations that blur the usual distinction between seeming and being.

The mistaken identity of Uncle Theodore at Lord Copper's banquet serves as the basis for one of Waugh's most notable achievements in an evolving comic irony. Copper's gradual awakening to the awful truth that his guest of honor is not the right Boot leaves him no choice but to conceal the error. Since the discrepancy between reality and the pretense that Copper is determined to maintain is most obvious in his prepared address on the "opportunities and achievements of youth" (318), he quickly tailors it to fit the elderly Boot. The result is ingenious verbal irony. "Young in years," composed with William in mind, becomes "young in . . . service to Megalopolitan Newspapers" (317). But Copper does not realize that his rephrasing is doubly appropriate to William's replacement, who had indeed been hired by Salter a few hours earlier. As the banquet proceeds, Uncle Theodore, genuinely believing that the complimentary words apply to him, warms to an employer he had previously considered "dull," while Lord Copper, though increasingly repelled by his guest's offensive conversation, is obliged to continue his glowing eulogy despite knowing that the praise is totally inapplicable.

The central confusion of the three Boots has significance beyond its structural bearing on the plot, for each character can be seen as a distortion of a particular aspect of the author's personality.[9] Although in *The Ordeal of Gilbert Pinfold* Waugh would later project, in a somber and more complex manner, many of his vulnerable idiosyncrasies onto a single scapegoat in an effort to purge them or at least come to terms with them, in *Scoop* he playfully ironizes himself through gentle, if more or less depreciatory, caricatures that mix truth with fancy.[10] John Boot represents Waugh's ambivalent relationship to the Mayfair set and its connections with Parliament, press, and predatory women. Like the author, John writes fiction, biography, and travel accounts. His life of Rimbaud parallels Waugh's biography of Rossetti; and *Waste of Time*, a "description of some harrowing months among the Patagonian Indians" (3), suggests Waugh's reporting on life in exotic lands. William Boot represents the shy, reclusive side of Waugh, who relished the quiet, untrammeled life of the country and the peace of family life. But William's reluctance to acknowledge evil, though initially shielding him from worldly corruption, proves inadequate after he has lived in the realm of experience. Uncle Theodore exemplifies the

Dionysiac side—the raconteur, the bon vivant, the bluff country squire, and the repressed roué longing for occasional flings in the city. His continual harping on "change and decay," to the exclusion of transcendental permanence, shows a preoccupation with worldly concerns. Although William is the Boot with whom the narrator clearly empathizes, each character shows what the author saw himself capable of becoming should certain propensities be allowed free rein. By exaggerating and personifying these tendencies, Waugh has created a fantasy world from his own reality. The sliding identities and the mistakes that result from taking one Boot for another are not wholly imaginary.

In addition to members of the Boot family, a number of major characters represent something beyond their surface identities. Outstanding among those whose actions affect the destinies of others are several who, because of social or economic power and managerial inclinations, qualify as embodiments of fortune. Whereas some of Waugh's earlier novels contain a single fortune figure, *Scoop* offers three, who divide and dilute the role to the extent of burlesquing it.[11] They are particularly well suited for ironic treatment by being unaware of how much their pretensions exceed their accomplishments. Deceiving themselves that they operate in the world at large, they actually function in limited spheres of influence and therefore can have only partial success.[12]

The irrespressible Julia Stitch rules imperiously over other people with her charm, wit, and remarkable verve. Subconsciously at least, she seems to consider herself superior to ordinary mortals. That she feels entitled to freedom from sublunary constraints is indicated by her eccentric habits, which sometimes defy law as well as convention. Delighted that in her absurd "baby car" she can do things she "couldn't do in a real one" (9, 10), she propels the tiny vehicle over curbs and sidewalks and even down the steps of a men's public convenience. Unfortunately for John Boot, her endeavors in his behalf—mesmerizing Lord Copper and creating such an impressive Boot myth that Copper resolves to employ the novelist—go awry because of her own smugness. Her total absorption in the Mayfair environment blocks any awareness that people outside her social set might never have heard of her friend Boot or his writings; hence she is mystified that her carefully wrought scheme could have failed. She is equally in the dark about how John achieves his knighthood, though she accepts his misplaced gratitude with the ambiguous acknowledgment that perhaps she "did have something to do with it" since he "had been disappointed about that job on the newspaper" (265). But her original effort to make him a foreign correspondent is not so unfruitful as she may assume; it ultimately backfires when Sir John is sent by the *Beast* to track a female expedition to the South Pole—an assignment in sharp contrast to his expected covering of a war in equatorial Africa.

Lord Copper is also the burlesque of a tutelary deity; and his inflated self-image serves, by contrast, to accentuate his ineffectuality. Dominating the vestibule of his opulent Fleet Street offices, from which he presumes to dispense wisdom to the multitudes who read his newspapers, is "a chryselephantine effigy of [himself] in coronation robes" (31). Equally pompous is his oratory. Expounding on his duty to enlighten the public, he boasts with overblown rhetoric that "the vast machinery" of his "great newspaper" will give "fullest publicity" to the Ishmaelian conflict, that "microcosm . . . of world drama" (14). "We shall," he continues, "have our naval, military and air experts, our squad of photographers, our colour reporters, covering the war from every angle and on every front." But despite his extraordinary wealth and undisputed influence over a publishing empire, Copper is far less Olympian than he assumes. Not only does he fail in his grandiose ambition to give providential guidance to the world; he allows himself to be manipulated by Julia Stitch, and his control over the three Boots is subject to greater mischance than direction since in each case a subordinate's ludicrous error thwarts his intentions. The power Copper exults in does not exist; his news media and his banquets, like his statue, are simply monuments to his megalomania.

The enigmatic Mr. Baldwin, a strange mixture of sybarite, polyglot, aesthete, sportsman, and adventurer, mimics the avenging deity who sets things right. Descending to earth via parachute, he is the "god from the machine" for whom William prays and for whom even Frau Dressler's pugnacious "milch-goat reverently [makes] way" (237-38). As the most successful wielder of power, Baldwin acquires the mineral rights in Ishmaelia and, by maneuvering the drunken Swede into fomenting counterrevolution, wreaks slapstick mayhem on Dr. Benito and the Communists in the style of "an early comedy film" (252). In attaining his objectives he not only outwits the foreign agents but also beats the journalists at their own game of playing with words and distorting reality. By recasting William's homely phraseology—"Baldwin has bought country" (254)—into journalese more acceptable at Copper House, he mocks the goals and parodies the style of the professionals. But inadvertently Baldwin undermines himself as well in the long communiqué assuring the *Beast* that British financial interests have triumphed. Since, as he admits to William, he represents only his own interests, the benefits of capitalistic imperialism must be seen as extremely limited.

The uncertainties of power manipulation are not confined to Mayfair, Fleet Street, or the world of commerce. Unpredictability flourishes in Ishmaelia, where a conflict of cultures, such as Waugh had detailed in *Black Mischief*, provides fertile ground for political chicanery. According to the narrator's ironic definition, the country is "called a Republic," since there is "no form of government common to the peoples . . . nor tie of language, history, habit or belief" (106). Its administration is a travesty of democratic process: members of the ruling Jackson family, treating the country as their private fiefdom, ignore or bend its constitution, rig elections, use a rapacious army to collect taxes, and appropriate much of its wealth to themselves. What brings out the worst in these Ishmaelian politicians is the profit motive, encouraged by European commercialism; for the Jacksons, usually to their own advantage, play off economic imperialists against each other. Yet it is the Jacksons' flirtation with both the Fascist Germans and the Communist Russians over gold rights that brings about the civil war and causes the temporary overthrow of this oligarchic family.

The most ludicrous aspect of the war is the ill-suited political rhetoric adopted by opposing factions. Smiles Soum, who organizes a Fascist group with German assistance, embraces the white-superiority line of Nazi propaganda and applies it to Ishmaelia with self-contradictory logic:

> . . . the Jacksons were effete, tyrannical and alien; the Ishmaelites were a white race who . . . must purge themselves of the Negro taint . . . the Jacksons had committed Ishmaelia to the control of international Negro finance and secret subversive Negro Bolshevism, by joining the League of Nations. (110)

Reversal of these sociopolitical theories by the socialists is equally fallacious. According to their oversimplification,

> Smiles represented international finance, the subjugation of the worker, sacerdotalism; Ishmaelia was black, the Jacksons were black,

collective security and democracy and the dictatorship of the proletariat were black. (111)

Although the self-serving, exploitive first family of Ishmaelia have
never bothered much about ideology, the Marxist line provides
them with instant friends throughout the world, as leftist intellectuals in Moscow, Harlem, Liberia, and Britain identify with what
masquerades as Jacksonian liberalism.

Indeed political theorists on both sides have blown up the local
hostility, like the Spanish Civil War, as a trial match between two
ideologies struggling for global dominion; and William is afforded
a preview of this broadened conflict even in London at two
Ishmaelian legations, where the fact that neither consul is an
Ishmaelite national betrays the extent of foreign meddling. The
first consul, identifying "the patriotic cause in Ishmaelia" with the
nonwhite races and the proletariat everywhere, attributes all progress and ultimate triumph to the philosophy of "that great Negro
Karl Marx" (68). At the other legation, which boldly displays a
swastika, the black consul blames the world's ills on Genevan Jews
subsidized by Russian gold and asserts that his race is pure Aryan.
By making the rival consuls ridiculous and their propaganda absurd, the narrator successfully undermines both communism and
fascism.

The lack of any satisfactory solutions to the political strife in
Scoop suggests that Waugh was skeptical about the ability of any
political system to improve either man or society, and his disparag-
ing portrayals of government officials and ideologists evince his
distrust. Algernon Stitch, the bumbling Tory minister whose
ineffectuality endears him to Labour, is mildly ludicrous: he speaks
in fragments and cannot get his own overcoat on. The Communist
reporter Pappenhacker is even more subversive of the cause he es-
pouses; believing that kindness to proletarians only strengthens
capitalist oppression, he behaves rudely toward waiters in order to
hasten the revolution. The sharpest satire is aimed at the
Ishmaelian Minister of Foreign Affairs and Propaganda, Dr. Benito,
who persuades the falangist Young Ishmaelites to collaborate with
the Russians. Like the Italian dictator Benito Mussolini, from
whom his name is derived, he advocates nationalism not primarily
to bring about promised reforms but to solidify his personal power.
Politics, as seen by Waugh, is the opportunist's art of duping others

to achieve one's own advancement, political theory being only a lure for the gullible.

Equally reprehensible in Waugh's estimation are the vagaries of professional journalism, which he subjects to the funniest satiric irony in *Scoop*. In a memorandum to Endfield and Fisz, who in 1957 considered making a film of the novel, Waugh describes his work as "a light satire on modern journalism, not a schoolboy's adventure story of plot, counterplot, capture and escape."[13] The purpose he enunciates is "to expose the pretensions of foreign correspondents . . . to be heroes, statesmen and diplomats." Although the novel is more complex than Waugh implies, his statement points to what he considers the egregiously fraudulent aspects of journalism. As a practitioner of this often romanticized vocation, he had found it neither exciting nor intellectually stimulating; and whereas he saw its only justifiable function to be the gathering and disseminating of factually reliable information, he discovered that news was often misused to enhance reputations or promote biased opinions. Although imaginative novelists might with impunity transform fact into fiction, as *Scoop* itself bears testimony, journalists, Waugh believed, had no business taking such liberties; and those characters who pervert their calling in his novel are sharply condemned.

Lord Copper is portrayed as a self-contradictory martinet, for, even while asserting that he never interferes with his correspondents, he explicitly decrees what war news William must supply. Having decided that readers want their anxieties aroused but quickly allayed, Copper prescribes "a few sharp victories, some conspicuous acts of personal bravery on the Patriot side, and a colourful entry into the capital" (56). Most preposterous is his demand for a "first victory about the middle of July" (57). So blinded is he by his own egomania that he cannot comprehend the absurdity of his policy. Nor does he understand its subsequent failure: at his banquet honoring the wrong Boot, Copper glorifies himself as "the deserted leader" whose underlings have not shouldered "the great burden of Duty" (316). By discrediting the newspaper magnate in this fashion, Waugh shows that he had little faith in the press's assumption that it could effect social reforms, eliminate corruption, or sway the course of history.

The activities of the foreign correspondents in *Scoop* often burlesque adventure novels and films of the 1930s, which throve on the fabulous intrigues of spies and journalists; and Waugh undergirds his tale with a skewed analogy between the two professions. The fact that John Boot's request for a job in the secret service results in one with the foreign press corps indicates that qualifications for the news business and the spy trade are perceived to be much the same. That operations in the field of journalism strongly resemble those of espionage is clear from Corker's account of "the heroic legends of Fleet Street," which might have come from any spy thriller—"of the confessions wrung from hysterical suspects; of the innuendo and intricate misrepresentations, the luscious, detailed inventions that composed contemporary history; of the positive, daring lies" (91-92). The covert nature of news gathering is exposed when the reporters covering the Ishmaelian conflict resort to the fictional techniques of undercover agents. William, for example, buys cleft sticks for sending messages, hires a native boy to help obtain information, and ultimately succeeds because Kätchen is an expert Mata Hari.

Among William's colleagues in Africa are certain journalistic superstars famed for extraordinary feats of reporting. Waugh, by setting their past exploits in impossible time and space relationships or illogical cause and effect sequences, ingeniously demolishes the credibility of their profession. The renowned Sir Jocelyn Hitchcock, while on assignment in Abyssinia, is said to have dispatched "some of the most colourful eye-witness stuff" without ever having been near the fighting (41). Wenlock Jakes is reputed to have "scooped the world with an eye-witness story of the sinking of the *Lusitania* four hours before she was hit" (92). He is also credited with actually bringing about a Balkan revolution by inventing such vivid accounts of it that other reporters were afraid to refute them; and for his grisly depictions of the slaughter, he was awarded a Nobel Peace Prize.

Although Hitchcock's purported interview with the Fascist leader at Laku is a complete fabrication, it is (at least in the eyes of those who assume the city's existence) woven on the loom of possibility; and his apparent absence from Jacksonburg, designed to throw rival journalists off his track while he is holed up in his room concocting the story, is certainly within the scope of plausibility. Hence indeterminacy flourishes in the complex of ironies associated with these deceptions. Even the reader, while aware that the interview, the city, and Hitchcock's "disappearance" are hoaxes to fool the gullible, can never be certain whether Hitchcock realizes that Laku is itself a fiction. Hitchcock's failure to go there gives no

definite indication of his knowledge about it since his modus ope-
randi often includes reporting on real places from afar. His graphic
account to Olafsen and William about the supposed journey, on
which he claims to have seen gorillas where none exist, reveals
only his imaginative powers. All the reader can be sure of is that Sir
Jocelyn rarely resists the inventive urge.

The commotion surrounding Shumble's scoop—about the arrival of a Russian agent in the guise of a railway official—is intriguing because of the concatenated ironies that disparage both
reporters and editors. Through the progress of ironic developments, truth is completely vanquished. Whereas William, having
discovered that the supposed agent really is a ticket collector,
would take the logical course of simply "explain[ing] the mistake"
(138), the journalistic solution is quite the contrary. Corker, realizing that the story is a deliberate fabrication such as he himself
might have concocted, denounces William's straightforward approach as "unprofessional"; and he and the other journalists, urged
on by demands from their London offices, feel compelled to find
and report on the Russian, whether or not he exists. But the falsehood that William would have confronted with the plain truth is
actually killed by a sophistical denial from the Ishmaelian Press
Bureau. Dr. Benito's statement that there is no Russian diplomat
and that no Russian national arrived on the Saturday train is absolutely correct, though highly misleading, since a Russian agent is
already in Ishmaelia under his protection. By the time William
learns of the real Soviet spy, all the foreign correspondents, backed
by Benito's official support, have wired denials to their papers; and
William is told that making another reversal would be bad business. Corker's conviction that no one would publish the spy story
"after the way it's been denied" (144) implies obliquely that the
press's credibility could be damaged by an honest resolution of the
mystery. Moreover, in Corker's aesthetic judgment, William's ex-
clusive information, supplied by the British legation itself, does not
make as good copy as Shumble's. The irony with regard to
Shumble is threefold: he never learns that his fictitious Russian really exists; he never knows that the railway employee, M. Giraud, is
a secret agent working for Baldwin against Russian interests; and
he never suspects how close he has come to a true story.

Among the many instances of make-believe news that permeate
Scoop, one of the most flagrant involves William himself. Without
his prior knowledge and to his intense embarrassment, his own

editors, in the aftermath of his dramatic scoop, publish a supposedly autobiographical account "of his meteoric leap to fame" (267). The disillusionment William feels as a result of his journalistic experience is encapsulated in his incisively ironic remark to an aspiring student reporter whom he meets upon returning to London. Asked by the young man whether "inventing imaginary news" is good training for the profession, William truthfully responds: "None better" (272); but the cynical as well as humorous implications of this succinct reply are obvious only to the reader.

Through characters who view the antics of newsmen from outside the profession, Waugh further denigrates the journalistic mindset. Baldwin candidly points out the reporters' failure to identify Giraud correctly as typical of their oversimplification: by conflating one rumor about a Russian plotting to overthrow the government with another rumor about the arrival of a foreign agent, they have produced one falsehood out of two truths. Benito, on the contrary, cloaks his contempt with diplomatic equivocation. To William's statement that the other journalists "wouldn't listen" to his information about Laku's nonexistence, the Ishmaelite enigmatically replies: "Perhaps they have more experience in their business" (176). His use of the word "experience," in regard to the veteran correspondents that he has succeeded in duping, is an excellent illustration of what Eleanor Hutchens labels connotative irony.[14] The word's usually favorable overtones have been reversed to imply that the journalists' experience has produced not wisdom but folly. Corker's earlier reaction to being told that there is "no such place" as Laku exemplifies his colleagues' irrationality: "Well there is now," he retorts. "At this very moment it's bang across the front page of the *Daily Brute*" (164-65).

The journalists' distortion of facts is often reinforced by twisted phraseology; and in a novel that focuses on those whose professional tool is language, the manner in which they speak and write assumes considerable importance. Waugh himself emphasizes the function of style by describing his own "writing not as investigation of character, but as an exercise in the use of language."[15] Although that assertion points up one aspect of his creative work while downplaying another, it implies an interaction of the two whereby style, in its comprehensive sense of being a distinctive method for representing experience, serves as an index to the minds of Waugh's fictional men and women. Hence in *Scoop* the journalists' disregard for correct English, which is associated with a cavalier attitude toward factual accuracy, betrays their questionable character. Their most conspicuous barbarism is telegraphese, which reduces idiomatic expression to pidgin by the omission of expendable words and the creation of unnatural compounds. In this jargon, "We have received no news from you" becomes "News exyou unreceived," while information about Aden's unpreparedness for war is compressed into the ambiguous "Aden unwarwise." Such scorn for linguistic art further symbolizes their vulgar disrespect for the order and standards of civilized life, for in Waugh's view corruption of language indicates debasement of thought.

Other characters in the novel also expose their true natures or motives unknowingly through the idiosyncrasies of their discourse. John Boot's written work, variously described as "divine," "high-class," and "smutty," presumably reflects the modes of thought and expression popular among the Mayfair socialites who admire his books. Wenlock Jakes's vignettes about prominent Britishers— marked by pretentiousness, name-dropping, exaggerations, clichés, and mixed metaphors—betray his own superficiality as well as that of his intended American readers, among whom such personalized gossip is bound to sell. The style of William's ordinary speech and telegraph messages—chatty, forthright, and unpretentious—mirrors his natural personality. But the labored artificiality of his "Lush Places"—*"Feather-footed through the plashy fen passes the questing vole"* (19)—reveals, in its reflection of the poetically ornate manner of the previous columnist, William's inclination to be imitative rather than original. Salter, like a character out of Lewis Carroll, sometimes plays with language that, by not meaning exactly what it says, suggests lack of complete honesty. Through fear of offending Lord Copper, he answers his employer's questions with formulaic euphemisms—"Up to a point" rather than a definite "no" or "Definitely, Lord Copper" instead of a simple "yes."

Semantic distortions are especially prevalent in language calculated to sway opinions. Baldwin's choice of the noun "might" instead of "force" to portray British influence shows how he takes advantage of connotative differences to further his economic enterprises. In political contexts truth is warped to a much greater degree. The labels of Traitor and Patriot, in regard to the Ishmaelian factions, reveal nothing about the political affiliations of the groups themselves but only the bias of the person applying the terms. Even more obscurantist is the subjective, misleading terminology with which the warring parties distinguish their ideological beliefs; and Salter's attempt to render it intelligible results in hope-lessly delightful Alice-in-Wonderland reasoning:

"You see they are all Negroes. And the Fascists won't be called Black because of their racial pride, so they are called White after the White Russians. And the Bolshevists *want* to be called Black because of *their* racial pride. So when you *say* Black you mean Red, and when you *mean* Red you say White, and when the party who call themselves Blacks say Traitors they mean what *we* call Blacks, but what *we* mean when *we* say Traitors I really couldn't tell you." (57-58)

As in all successful nonsense, however, what appears to be absurd in Salter's analysis actually contains a logic of its own, but one that does not contribute much illumination because the propagandistic meanings are intended to conceal rather than to clarify. In all these instances, such linguistic obfuscation reflects an ironic universe since it prevents one from getting at the truth.

Although the narrator in *Scoop* occasionally indulges in language that indicates something other than what it states, his purpose is to reveal rather than to obscure. By using a word or phrase at odds with its context, he is able to effect an instantaneous reversal of meaning. When he asserts that "various courageous Europeans" in the 1870s went to Ishmaelia "furnished with suitable equipment" (105), he seems at first to be praising their practical acumen; yet his listing of that equipment ("cuckoo clocks, phonographs, opera hats") causes the word "suitable" to convey the opposite of its normal sense so that his condemnation of their folly is unmistakable. His censure of Ishmaelian Christianity is also accomplished indirectly. Through seemingly casual references to it in his account of cannibalistic practices, he emphasizes the barbarism that flourishes amid nominal adherence to ecclesiastical rules: "The better sort of Ishmaelites . . . will not publicly eat human flesh, uncooked, in Lent, without special and costly dispensation from their bishop" (105-6). To underscore the irrelevance of the civil war to most natives, the narrator resorts to a syntactical inversion by expressing his crucial idea as an anticlimax, so that its abnormal position calls attention to significance beyond its literal meaning. Countering his own ironic exaggeration about "the deep currents that were flowing in Ishmaelite politics," and about which until recently "no one in Europe knew," he adds, as if in afterthought, "nor did many people know of them in Ishmaelia" (109). Thus studded with verbal irony, his introduction to the African nation undermines the pious shams of politics and religion.

In a society and a profession so debased it seems improbable that gentlemanly William should rise to heroic stature and worldwide renown. But in defiance of all the conventions of a reporter's trade, he succeeds where the other foreign correspondents have failed. What impels his uncharacteristic fever of action, in which he overcomes the impediments of typewriter and recalcitrant wireless operator to warn the world of a communist takeover, is the coalescing of his most intense feelings—patriotic pride, the thrill of a journalistic coup, loathing for Benito, and yearning for Kätchen's lasting affection. In a vision of triumph that parodies the clichés of early cinematic melodrama, William sees Bengal Lancers and kilted Highlanders liberating Jacksonburg while he himself destroys the villainous demagogue, rescues his bride-to-be, and carries her home to Boot Magna. But his imaginings, like Tony Last's hallucinations of the City, are not fulfilled quite as he envisions them. In the actual world they are realized with exquisite irony when the hopes that inspired his 2,000-word telegram are overturned by quirks of fate. Benito is defeated not by British valor but through Baldwin's strategy, William's scoop brings him much unwanted fame for the wrong reasons, and he saves Kätchen only by helping her to escape in the company of her former lover.

In the portrayal of William's love affair with Kätchen, ironic techniques are ingeniously used to manage the disclosure of information. When the experience of first love so overwhelms William's usually open and forthright manner that he cannot verbalize his deepest thoughts, the narrator speaks for him through metaphor and analogy that communicate the state of his mind without literal reference to it. The underwater forest that symbolizes William's subconscious stirrings of passion is described in the style of his nature column; but its exotic plants with "spongy flowers" and creatures "without fur or feather, wing or foot, [passing] silently, in submarine twilight" (181) create a "lush place" totally foreign to English landscape. Through this eerie distortion of the familiar— twisting similarity into contrariety—the narrator effectively conveys an almost frightening sense of William's strange new emotions. To represent William's joy after the consummation of his love, the narrator graphically depicts a magnificent terrestrial scene full of warmth, brightness, color, and expansiveness: "The transformation . . . had taken place overnight. . . . weeds . . . had suddenly burst into crimson flower; a tropic sun blazed in the sky . . . with promise of a fiery noon, while beyond . . . the city . . . mile upon mile of sunlit highland . . . green pastures . . . rosy terraces . . . [receded] to the blue peaks of the remote horizon" (205).

In contrast, Kätchen's personality reflects an ironic world—elusive, unpredictable, changeable, illogical, and fraudulent. To achieve such a delineation, the narrator appropriately refrains from disclosing all that transpires in her mind; and by leaving much to the imagination, he enhances the enigmatic charm with which Kätchen fascinates both William and the reader. The narrator's objective reporting of her appearance and actions provides little beyond an external view; and his representation of her thoughts is accomplished mainly through innuendos in her seemingly artless conversation. At the most crucial moments he sometimes withdraws altogether, teasing the reader with insufficient clues to the truth. Although Kätchen's general purpose is obviously to ensure her own survival, her motives for specific maneuvers are often unclear. Among the unsolved mysteries is her ambivalence toward both William and her German soldier of fortune, as well as her reluctance to marry William on a permanent basis. Nor can one be certain how devoted she really is to the German or what choices she might have made had she not been imprisoned or had he not returned. Especially difficult to fathom are the reasons behind her shift in strategy occasioned by William's declaration of love, which appears to have wrecked some hidden plan and prevented her from voicing some unspecified request. While it is tempting to conjecture that Kätchen, having perhaps cast William in the role of Platonic benefactor, is genuinely upset by this romantic complication, one may conclude with equal justification that her anger and self-pity represent merely another tactic to enlist his sympathy.

The ways in which Kätchen takes advantage of William are almost invariably ironic and usually involve some kind of discrepancy between appearance and reality. Intending to conceal even more of herself than does the narrator, she presents to her new friend only what may appeal to his sensibilities; and he is so blinded by infatuation that he perceives her simply as a helpless innocent in need of assistance. The reader, on the other hand, realizes that beneath her ingenue exterior and affectionate, playful simplicity is a shrewd coquette manipulating an inexperienced, unsuspecting victim. Kätchen's devious intent is first apparent in the sale of the geological specimens, which she persuades William to purchase by playing on his conscience for having indirectly caused her to lose her room at the pension. But she perverts her implied intention of paying a delinquent lodging bill by spending the money for clothes and cosmetics to further impress William. In suggesting that he provide her with funds from his expense account, ostensibly in compensation for ferreting out political information, Kätchen rationalizes with Alice-in-Wonderland logic that, while she could not honorably accept money from a *man*, she could do so from a *newspaper*. Again, William's expectations are not fulfilled as he anticipates, for spying is incidental to Kätchen's primary aim of buying things from her knowledgeable contacts. Only by chance— and without knowing its value—does she furnish the scrap of news that leads to William's monumental scoop.

Her illogicality becomes delightfully complex after her German lover reappears. Having called herself German while claiming to be his wife, she now proposes to marry William in order to become British and then to marry her former lover so that he too will have the benefit of British nationality. Her final exploitation of William in Ishmaelia—appropriating his canoe and his aid in launching it so that she and the German can escape—is incredibly brash; but in truly ironic fashion she carries it off with a disarming reversal of blame by scolding William for being jealous instead of happy about her "husband's" return. The narrator never enlightens us about William's reaction to her further attempt to extract money from him in a letter addressed "Darling William" and signed "Ever your loving, Kätchen" (320). In the manuscript version William receives the letter at Boot Magna but, as the novel ends, postpones reading it until the next day.[16] The printed redaction, however, offers the letter at the time Kätchen is writing it. Waugh evidently realized that he could heighten the indeterminacy by concluding his story before the letter arrives.

Despite the inequities of *Scoop*'s unpredictable world, a modicum of justice does prevail, for many characters get exactly what should be coming to them. As in traditional fairy tales, the villains are vanquished and other characters have their wishes fulfilled. But Waugh, by giving an ironic twist to each well-deserved fate, turns the typical fairy-tale ending on its head. Benito and his henchman are felled in ridiculously comic circumstances by the most unlikely adversaries. The strong-arm dictator is forced to tumble from the presidential balcony, as well as from political power, by the usually mild-mannered and slow-witted Olafsen. And the swaggering welterweight is tossed ignominiously into the garbage by the milch goat, whose actions are described through inappropriately grandiloquent language: "All day she had dreamed gloriously; now in the limpid evening she . . . charged, splendidly, irresistibly, triumphantly" (218-19). Although most characters are awarded futures that they *seem* to want, the narrator simultaneously hints at the folly of their desires. Lord Copper receives an excess of what he already has—banquets, speeches, deferential underlings—as does Mrs. Stitch, with her innumerable acquaintances and possessions. Kätchen, having chosen to stay with her German lover, continues her precarious existence. Even the changed circumstances of Salter's well-regulated domesticity and Uncle Theodore's self-indulgent life in London have the ring of empty gratification. With the implication that human desires, even if attained, will not produce the anticipated happiness, the narrator subverts the fairy-tale formula to reveal a darker irony beneath the novel's farcical surface.

For William, return to Boot Magna is a destiny appropriate to his innate disposition. Sensitive, honorable, and conscientious, he holds tenaciously to his own values amid familial security and continues to write idealistically about rural life. But in opposition to his gentle view of *"maternal rodents [piloting] their furry brood through the stubble"* (320), the narrator juxtaposes an awareness that predatory "owls [hunt] maternal rodents and their furry broods" (321). Nature is not wholly benevolent, and William's Wordsworthian concept of it cannot entirely protect him from harm. That he has not been left unscarred by encounters with the outside world is shown indirectly when a moonlit night hauntingly evokes recollections of gratified love in Ishmaelia. After his disenchantment with both Kätchen and the *Beast*, however, William's choice to live in one of society's more remote places becomes a relatively happy ending. Such a resolution to his problems is also in accord with Norman Knox's defintion of comic irony, wherein the sympathetic victim triumphs.[17] Insofar as William, through his own determination, has rid himself of an environment to which he was ill-attuned, he has won a personal victory, one which, to note a further irony, unquestionably brings him greater satisfaction than the public acclaim over his scoop. The fact that he respects his old nurse's opinion more than the wishes of Lord Copper clinches this inversion of popular values.

For such a conclusion the reader should already be prepared, since William's experiences aboard the train during his first journey to London provide clues to his paradigmatic attitudes and behavior. His mistaken offering of a sovereign instead of a shilling to the steward suggests William's unworldliness; his loss of the gold coin to a con artist reveals the vulnerability of his trusting nature; and his overwhelming desire to withdraw to the safety of Boot Magna indicates his way of dealing with humiliations inflicted by "a foreign and hostile world" (29). Of particular significance to Waugh's ironic presentation is William's refusal to be fleeced a second time by the con man, for it predicts not only his response to Kätchen's letter but also the likelihood that he will never again allow either Kätchen or the *Beast* to take advantage of him. Hence the early episode on the train functions as an oblique foreshadowing of things to come.

Work Suspended

*B*y the time Waugh began *Work Suspended* in the summer of 1939, he evidently realized not only the limitations of his usual detached stance and of his spare, crisp style but also the need for a more positive orientation. To advance his fiction beyond the confines of its previous form, he apparently decided to become more profoundly involved, even at the risk of exposing aspects of his own life; and for the first time he created, in the character of John Plant, a central figure who is also the first-person narrator of the story. Plant, prior to his own account of experiences that were to alter his perspective on life and literary technique, had devoted himself to writing successful mystery novels that contained "absolutely nothing of [himself]"[1] and to maintaining superficial relations with the world. But in narrating subsequent events, he endeavors to portray deep, complex emotions that defy objectification. In the first chapter of the fragmentary novel, Plant depicts his bereavement at the loss of his father; in the second, the emotional complications resulting from his platonic love for a friend's pregnant wife. The problem Waugh had to resolve was whether, as the author, he could express these highly sentimental feelings through the narrator-character without abandoning the ironic technique he had perfected.[2] To do so he had to delve into the minds of the characters, largely from the narrator's internal perspective, yet present other aspects of the novel from an external point of view—all the while maintaining artistic unity.

Waugh's awareness that he had exploited most of the possibilities of his old style is echoed in John Plant's realization that he has reached a "climacteric" or "turning point in [his] career" (42). Trying to explain to an uncomprehending publisher why he cannot finish his current murder mystery, Plant expresses the fear of "becoming purely a technical expert" like his father, who perfected a painting technique and year after year mechanically ground out what he could do well (43). Plant's reassessment of direction, however, does not imply that Waugh intended to forsake the objective delineation of his characters. Nor did Waugh plan to engage in the kind of psychological exploration into unconscious mental processes that he deplored in the fiction of Joyce, Mansfield, Woolf, Faulkner, and Lawrence. Accordingly, Plant's reflections are conscious and do not involve the divagations of dreams or stream of consciousness to disclose arcane thoughts.

In the context of wondering how his love for Lucy and Julia's love for him can be convincingly described, Plant makes some observations on literary technique that reveal Waugh's own concerns.[3] As Plant asserts, in keeping with his previous achievement, fiction, like algebra, must "reduce its problems to symbols if they are to be soluble" (82), for he does not believe that fictional characters can be alive in the same sense that real people are. Admittedly, an author, in the fashion of a trainer controlling circus animals, can force a "Dickensian menagerie" of characters to perform their tricks before an audience, yet that does not make the characters genuinely "alive" or show them engaged in "the real business of life" (83). Since for Waugh, as for Henry James, art was not "the real thing" but rather an imaginative adaptation of reality, Plant expresses a preference for "the alternative, classical expedient" of taking "the whole man" and reducing "him to a manageable abstraction" for artistic representation. Furthermore, Waugh's new richness of style, which enhances the reflective and even the philosophical observations in the novel, is endorsed by Plant's elaborate architectural metaphor acknowledging his inclinations toward decorative and artistically wrought literature rather than the "purely functional" variety (2).[4] In both these instances the imposition of an introspective first-person narrator upon an essentially objective approach permitted Waugh to offer authorial commentary such as he had never before allowed himself in fiction. The imaginary author's examination of his own technique is a form of his creator's self-criticism.

In deviating from earlier practice, Waugh by no means renounced the polished craftsmanship for which he was well known but rather proclaimed a desire to widen his artistic horizons. What he accomplished in *Work Suspended* is convincing proof of his continued growth as an artist and serves as a response to unsympathetic critics who accused him of being a skilled technician more concerned with surface than substance. The novel's composition also indicates Waugh's awareness of the changes that had altered his own life when, as a loving husband, devoted father, and settled property owner, he became more serious toward the obligations of maturity and less amused by the hedonism of vagrant youth. Having uttered what he had to say in the old vein, he required a new approach—or, as Plant perceived his situation: "I have got as good as I ever can be at this particular sort of writing. I need new worlds to conquer" (43). But it would have been folly for Waugh—as for his fictional spokesman, who ruminates freely in the novel on his own aesthetic cul-de-sac and his aspirations to psychic and literary rebirth—to completely abandon, in favor of an untried method, the technical virtuosity, symbolic representation of abstractions, or detached attitude that had worked superbly in past writing.

In his determination to unite the seemingly incompatible approaches of irony and sentiment, however, Waugh erected for himself an extraordinary hurdle; and the difficulties involved may have had more to do with his decision not to proceed beyond the second chapter than his own explanation, in the 1942 dedicatory letter, that "the world in which and for which it was designed, has ceased to exist." Whether or not he realized it, *Work Suspended* signals a diminution in his ironic perspective and methodologies, since the emotional involvement of the central character inevitably reduces the possibilities of detachment and consequently the opportunities for ambivalence, objectivity, and indeterminacy. Even so, these hindrances did not deter Waugh from enlivening the fragmentary novel with various ironies—some in the style of his customary techniques, others in more daring applications. He incorporated many verbal and situational incongruities of the easily recognizable sort, although these do not approach the hilarious or sinister heights attained in his earlier fiction; and he ventured to introduce bizarre linkages of thought and action, intellectually stimulating if not so readily grasped, that effect a deepening of characterization greater than he had hitherto achieved.

Ironies of the simpler, more direct kind are prevalent in Plant's account of his father and the family servants, the Jellabys. The elder Plant is recalled as a mass of contradictions and yet, paradoxically, as a man who throve on them. Sometimes he was a typical *alazon* or victim of ironic circumstances; at other times he became an *eiron* or ironist himself, who knowingly collaborated in the perpetration of frauds. When a loathsome development of modern flats encroached upon his property, which at that time he could have sold for a good price, he defiantly remained, delighting in the gradual deterioration of the project even as the value of his own house declined accordingly. He also espoused unpopular social and religious causes only to reverse his position if they became popular. Although a successful enough painter in his own style to achieve membership in the Royal Academy, the elder Plant secretly produced imitations of "old masters" for dealers who passed them off as originals; but for his part in the fraud—euphemistically labeled "restoration"—he assumed no responsibility: "What they do with them afterwards is their own business" (19). His annual "Academy" tea parties for art connoisseurs were deliberate travesties of gracious entertaining, and he enjoyed them as "his own private joke" (20). He even made light of his son's literary efforts through a devastating juxtaposition of ill-matched statements: "My son John took a second in Mods and a first in Greats. He writes penny dreadfuls for a living" (12).

Relations between the elder Plant and his longtime domestics were certainly the opposite of what one might assume. He paid the Jellabys meagerly yet condoned their regular stealing from the household accounts with the dubious logic that "servants prefer it that way" because "it preserves their independence and self-respect" (9). That as a staunch atheist he should be given a Christian burial largely to satisfy the religious beliefs of such servants seems highly incongruous, especially since they dashed off eagerly after the funeral to take over a business they had set up years before with their ill-gotten gains.

John Plant's sudden return to England is precipitated not, as one would expect, by the death of his father but by his own arrest at the brothel he frequents in Fez—where the prostitutes take their profession so seriously that they consider having to perform a "native dance" for tourists to be "unseemly." What raises the irony of Plant's brief encounter with the police to dramatic status is that the means he has taken to ensure his cherished privacy—in the sense of revealing little of himself to anyone—is the very means by which it is lost on this occasion. Having purposely left not only most of his money but also his passport in the hotel, he is unable to prove his identity or to bribe the police and must seek aid from the British consul, with whom he has preferred to maintain only a superficial acquaintance. As Plant explains the change in their relationship following this incident: "We had exposed the bare minimum of ourselves; now a sudden, mutually unwelcome confidence had been forced. The bitterness lay, not in the Consul knowing the fact of my private recreations, but in his knowing that I knew he knew" (33).

Contrarieties punctuate the speech and actions of Plant's London acquaintances whenever he can view them objectively. His conversation with Roger Simmonds about buying property discloses what a self-contradictory economic philosophy Roger and his wife Lucy try to practice. Although avowed communists actively working for the world revolution that will do away with all private fortunes, they enjoy Lucy's inherited wealth without guilt by rationalizing that all investments are "bound to be temporary" (50). When Plant points out the incongruity in his friend's thinking between capitalist ownership and socialist beliefs, Roger further equivocates about the pure ideal of communism as opposed to its reality. Clearly, the Simmondses' public disdain for money cloaks their desire for what it will provide.

To unmask the hidden motives of Lucy's aunt, who has also benefited from Lucy's money, Plant as narrator simply states facts in such a way that discrepancies between pretense and actuality are unmistakable. According to his incisive depiction, the aunt, having reared her orphaned niece, continued "'making a home' for her, which meant that she subsisted largely upon Lucy's income" (78). His mention of two younger nieces who needed to be launched socially in London reveals another of the aunt's unstated reasons for maintaining a base of operations there. Plant demolishes any thought that she might have been interested primarily in Lucy's welfare by explaining with a touch of sarcasm how this "lady of delicate conscience where the issues of Lucy's marriage were involved" had opposed several suitors on the pretext that Lucy would be "[throwing] herself away" (78).

Lucy herself is not of an ironic turn, but the interplay which Waugh creates between her perspective and that of her husband and his friends provides a number of enjoyable incompatibilities.

Her uncomplicated openness and sincerity are at odds with the manner in which Roger, John, and other young authors discount their own writing. Whatever they may really believe, they claim, "in public, to regard [their work] as drudgery and [their] triumphs as successful impostures on the world at large" (79). Actually, as the narrator indicates, their cynical expressions are simply an inverted way of saying that each writer is interested only in himself—an ironic disparity between public avowal and private opinion—and should be taken no more seriously than similar derogation of Roger by his friends. But Lucy, straightforward and supportive of Roger's talents, regards their saying one thing while meaning another as a kind of artificial insincerity that she cannot accept or admire.

Her feelings in this matter and her function on one occasion as an ingenue reveal not only her personality but Waugh's attitude toward her. Roger and other friends are attempting to persuade Plant that a country house of ridiculously elaborate architecture would suit his needs, though all except Lucy know that their real interest is in having social access to it themselves. Innocent of their designs, Lucy speaks the truth—"I can't think why John should want to have a house like that" (74)—cutting through pretense and hypocrisy with simple common sense, to the delight of both Plant and the reader. That she has the author's approval as well, both in this instance and generally throughout the novel, indicates a turning point in the evolution of Waugh's fiction, for she is the first major nonironic character to be sympathetically portrayed. While Waugh clearly considered the ability to appreciate irony as a measure of a character's complexity, his positive representation of Lucy as intelligent and lovable signifies a definite pulling back from his ironic stance. The altered tone of his depiction may also reflect a change in his own perspective brought about by happy domesticity with his second wife, Laura.

In the case of Sister Kemp, however, imperceptiveness to irony indicates a lack of mental acuity, especially when her failure to grasp ironic humor is played off against Roger's subtle use of it with regard to the extravagant assortment of nursery supplies she has ordered for the baby. Asked by Lucy whether "*everyone* [has] to have all these things" (125), the class-conscious nurse replies, "Everyone who can afford them"—an unwitting revelation not only that the items are largely unnecessary but that her own snobbishness requires them as status symbols. Nor can Sister Kemp possibly comprehend Roger's retort, which so exalts the trivial to anthropological heights as to deflate her pretensions: "All this purely ceremonial accumulation of rubbish—like turtle doves brought to the gates of a temple. Everyone according to his means sacrificing to the racial god of hygiene" (125-26). Soon after Lucy gives birth, the novel breaks off on a note of ironic parody. Lucy has sunk into an uncharacteristic sentimental euphoria that Plant finds inconceivable and disgusting. She is interested only in her son, the flowers she has received, and the nurse, with whom she has formed such a bond of familiarity that they now address one another by informal names. Sister Kemp refers to her as "my Lucy" and speaks of the baby as "something very precious"; Lucy calls the nurse "Kempy" and refers to everyone and everything as "sweet." Hence when Sister Kemp shows Plant the baby, he mocks their saccharine manner by responding: "Magnificent . . . and very sweet . . . Kempy" (150).

Several conversations involving the central character and another person in the novel show off Waugh's ability to convey underlying thoughts that, as in much of Firbank, are never literally stated. The laconic exchange between Plant and the zoo attendant is an exercise in misinterpretation: since neither man grasps what is in the other's mind, they talk at cross-purposes. The attendant, having repeatedly seen Plant with the very pregnant Lucy, draws logical but erroneous conclusions about the couple's relationship and the child's paternity; his comments based on these conclusions mystify Plant, who at least temporarily reads unintended meaning into the words. As Plant narrates the incident, the zoo attendant remarks:

> "Your lady not with you to-day, sir?"
> "No, not to-day."
> "I've got five myself," he said.
> I did not understand him and repeated foolishly, "Five?"
> "Being a married man," he added. (130)

The omniscient reader of course deduces both trains of thought, which bypass one another without connecting, and is amused by the characters' failure to communicate.

A truly ingenious rendering of this technique is John Plant's discussion, after his father's death, with Mr. Godley, the inappropriately named art dealer who marketed the elder Plant's forged paintings.[5] Each participant in this dialogue, in contrast to the speakers in the zoo episode, knows precisely what meanings remain unspoken beneath the surface of the other's words, and the reader also has no doubt what each character is driving at in this verbal dance around a subject neither dares name. Godley, aware of the potential dangers in the situation, delicately probes to find out how much Plant knows about his father's surreptitious work or "pastiche" as it is euphemistically termed. He wants to ascertain whether any physical evidence exists and, if so, what Plant would do about it, particularly since the Jellabys have already attempted, even without evidence, to extort money from his firm. At the same time Godley is unwilling to reveal more than necessary about the firm's involvement. Plant, equally cagey, takes sadistic delight in making Godley squirm; he answers evasively, divulging just enough information to tantalize the dealer. Such parrying of each other's thrusts turns the conversation into a kind of fencing match, from which both men eventually emerge satisfactorily. Godley's trump card is the suggestion that Plant would not want his father's public reputation tarnished; and their agreement on how to deal with the mutual knowledge of forgery is ratified succinctly when both men utter the same esoteric phrase—"trade secrets."

The superb quality of this technical achievement in irony—one of Waugh's finest—may be seen in the following condensation:

"Your father used to do a certain amount of work for us, you know."

"I know."

"Restorations mostly. Occasionally he used to make a facsimile for a client. . . . That kind of work."

"Often they were his own compositions."

"Well, yes, I believe a few of them were. . . ."

"I saw some of them," I said.

"He was wonderfully gifted."

"Wonderfully. . . . "

"His work with us was highly confidential."

"Of course."

" . . . did he keep any records of his work or anything of the kind?"

"I'm afraid I haven't been through his things yet. I should think it quite likely. . . ."

"If anything . . . was to turn up, we could rely on your discretion. . . . it would do no one any good . . . I mean you would want your father to be remembered by his exhibited work."

"You need not worry," I said.

"Splendid. . . . We had a spot of unpleasantness with his man. . . . They both came to see us, husband and wife. . . . You might almost say they tried to blackmail us. . . . I don't think we shall be worried by them again."

"Nor by me. Blackmail is not quite in my line."

"No, no, my dear fellow . . . I didn't for a moment mean to suggest. . . . But if anything should turn up. . . ."

"Anything incriminating," I said.

"Trade secrets," said Mr. Godley.

"Trade secrets," I repeated.

This gem of "irony for irony's sake" invites many pleasurable re-readings, but it does not appear to contribute much, if anything, toward the development of either plot or characterization in the fragment that exists. Its deletion from the 1948 version may in fact reflect Waugh's orientation away from artistry that is primarily technical.

The essence of Waugh's new kind of fiction is the humanizing of its character portrayal, and what sets *Work Suspended* apart from the preceding novels is its extensive reliance on irony to deal with subjective elements—intimate feelings which characters may be too shy to express, or their own personality traits of which they may not even be aware. Irony that is capable of functioning on the psychological plane, however, must be relatively oblique, complex, and sophisticated; and Waugh created a number of unexpected, often unlikely, analogies through which the reader may understand what could not otherwise be communicated. Some of them are sustained or recurrent, their components moving roughly side by side through a series of episodes—Atwater and Plant; or Lucy's baby, the gibbon, and Plant. Others may be only momentary correlations, touching at the one point of similarity—the contemplations of Lucy and her mother during their pregnancies, or the elder Plant's Victorian home and the house in Chinese taste. In any case, each indicates a hidden truth; and the more profound or complicated the truth, the more indirect the analogy tends to be.

The intrusive Arthur Atwater represents a negative image of John Plant; and to some extent both characters are projections of their creator's personality—Plant, the Apollonian, as the reclusive and cerebral conformist; Atwater, the Dionysian, as the brash and often paranoid rebel. Indeed Waugh's use of Atwater to reveal the submerged aspects in Plant's nature bears a resemblance to the functioning of the "doubles" in Joseph Conrad's *Lord Jim* and "The Secret Sharer." As Plant's suppressed subconscious, Atwater rises to challenge the conscious into self-realization, so that the whole man is brought into view.[6] Although the two characters are very different externally, they are alike psychologically in their desire for a new start in life; and their interaction propels them toward that mutual goal.

Atwater is introduced as the agent of death for Plant's father, whose elimination must be interpreted as the requisite first step toward the son's independence and rather belated maturation. Atwater's presumptuous request for £50 must also be taken symbolically as the claiming of a reward for performing the fatal deed, and Plant's reimbursement of 10 shillings for Atwater's funeral wreath makes him an accessory after the fact. The father's demise and the subsequent destruction of the parental home effect the desired break with the past but ultimately produce a besetting loneliness, which is assuaged only for a time by Lucy's companionship.

The void left in Plant's life by Lucy's withdrawal from the scene to give birth to her baby is filled by Atwater's reappearance, and the analogous characters are drawn closer together out of necessity. At first Atwater astutely perceives that he is being used, since Plant, in order to be distracted from thoughts of Lucy's suffering, encourages his companion's incessant talk with a pound note. In a strangely accurate parallel alluding to Plant's earlier assertion that zoo animals are "paid for their entertainment value," Atwater resentfully complains, "You think I'm a kind of monkey" (140). But when Plant subsidizes an excursion to Atwater's old club, thereby entering into his counterpart's rather shady world, Atwater becomes overfamiliar, calling Plant "an old pal" and remarking on presumed affinities between them—"I know you'll like the place. . . . I expect it's the same at your club" (141). Plant's subsequent invitation to Atwater to live with him in the country can be seen as the artist's ironic acknowledgment of his present need for an integrated personality; but his final words—"Die there" (146)—take on an ominous cast that may foreshadow his future need to rid himself of less desirable characteristics.

Whereas Atwater is instrumental in the understanding of Plant's psychological makeup, Roger Simmonds is essential to the comprehension of Plant's aesthetic stance. The description of the two writers' literary achievements, with particular emphasis on the limitations Plant hopes to transcend after his career crisis, is a distorted representation of Waugh's own problems. Plant is a highly skilled contriver of plots and clues in his mystery novels—teasing, tricking, and tempting his readers into solving a crime much as an ironist invites recognition of his intended meaning; but such technical skill can easily become superficial and "mechanical." How he can add profundity of thought to his writing is never stated, but it is implied negatively through comparison with what his friend has done. Simmonds, formerly a successful humorist, author of "some genuinely funny novels" (47), has, as a result of becoming a communist, turned to serious ideological drama. He too refers to the "mechanical" aspect of his present literary medium, but his meaning of the term is very different from Plant's: all the characters in his new play are parts of an automobile. Since communist literature is supposed to deal with "economic types, not individuals" (48), it would from Simmonds's point of view be "bad art" if the characters acted like human beings. His solution to this aesthetic dilemma is to eliminate the people. If a Marxist perspective is responsible for the banishment of the human element from art, then by reverse analogy, an opposite perspective would require its development to the fullest extent. For Plant, as for Waugh, any future course must include a deeper comprehension of mankind.

It is Lucy who humanizes Plant's soul and gives him new life as an artist. In the portrayal of this transformation, the objective approach is particularly important since Plant would have difficulty divulging in first-person narration any changes in himself of which he is not fully cognizant. Another factor is his habitual reticence, probably a reflection of Waugh's own feelings at the time against baring oneself about delicate, intimate matters; as Plant phrases the problem: "To write of someone loved, of oneself loving, above all of oneself being loved—how can these things be done with propriety? How can they be done at all?" (81). In *Work Suspended* such abstruse human experiences are indirectly disclosed through the unlikely agency of a subhuman character, Humboldt's Gibbon, which Lucy and Plant watch intently on their frequent trips to the zoo.

The complex of analogies built around this creature begins with a simple juxtaposition in Lucy's thoughts; as she looks at the ape while the fetus grows in her womb, she is reminded that her own mother while pregnant would gaze upon a neoclassical sculpture in order to make her child beautiful. The reader must deduce what

Lucy herself does not understand—a subconscious desire to endow her baby with some quality she admires in the ape, perhaps its primeval masculinity since she suggests naming a male child Humboldt. The fulfillment of her unstated wish is later acknowledged by the nurse, who pronounces the newborn infant "a fine big man" (150). The gibbon also serves to mirror Lucy's negative feelings toward her unborn child during the most uncomfortable days of her pregnancy. Just as the ugly and uningratiating beast—described by Plant as "less like a man than any of his kind" (132)—is unpopular with most visitors to the zoo, the immature fetus is disliked by Lucy, who does not yet regard it as completely human.

A more crucial parallel links the ape and the child to Plant. While Lucy is nourishing the fetus with her body and carrying fruit to Humboldt's Gibbon, she is also sustaining Plant with her pure and unreserved friendship, metaphorically compared to a "rich estate" through which he might "wander at will" (112). His gradual maturation is recapitulated in the ontogeny of her child, who changes from something disagreeable into a dependent creature, like the caged monkeys in the zoo, and finally into a real human being, lovable and independently whole. Just as the baby becomes, in Lucy's words, "such a *person*" (149), so Plant becomes a more admirable man. Lucy has contributed to his personal and artistic development, since the experience of love has expanded the boundaries of his understanding. He is able to realize with some satisfaction, even though she no longer needs him, that his companionship during her pregnancy has benefited both her and the child: "Humboldt's Gibbon and I," he acknowledges, "[have] done our part" (149).

Martin Stannard has postulated that Waugh never completed the novel, even after much reworking for both the 1942 and 1948 editions, because he had failed, despite stylistic improvements, to resolve the aesthetic problems of including the "dimension of 'supernatural' reality."[7] Although it is a temptation to read as criticism of the pre-*Brideshead* novels Waugh's assertion in "Fan-Fare" that "you can only leave God out by making your characters pure abstractions,"[8] there is no indication that Waugh ever intended a spiritual dimension for *Work Suspended*. Nor is there any hint that the irreligious Plants or communist Simmondses would have future inclinations toward Christianity. It seems more likely that Plant's aesthetic problem had been solved satisfactorily but that other problems in this novel were beyond resolution. It might have been awkward, even impossible, with this set of characters to develop narratively what Laura's love had actually achieved for Waugh; and the ironical method, though challenged to an imaginative height, might still have been incompatible with the author's involvement in the subject. *Work Suspended* may have convinced Waugh that the subjective and objective approaches would not readily congeal and that ultimately one or the other would have to yield. A fresh start with different characters and situations would be necessary to portray the dilemma of an artist in need of spiritual, as well as aesthetic, regeneration.

Waugh was obliged to postpone the resolution of this problem because his entry into military service in December 1939 interrupted the progress of serious writing. As he himself conceded, he "dashed off" his next novel, *Put Out More Flags* (1942), as a diversion to relieve the tedium of a long troopship voyage in 1940, and he called it only "a minor work" compared to the "major" endeavor that he left unfinished but would later publish as *Work Suspended*.[9] *Put Out More Flags* does carry forward some of the advances of its predecessor—a more elaborate prose style and, in the affirmation of the patriotic principles for which Waugh was fighting, a more positive outlook. Its characters, however, are a reversion to the superficial Bright Young People Waugh had popularized a decade earlier—now verging on middle age and no longer considered so clever or amusing as they seemed in sparkling youth. The artists portrayed in *Put Out More Flags* exist in an entirely different context and for a radically different purpose than do those in *Work Suspended*, where the author attempts to delve sympathetically into their inward lives. In the later novel Waugh is concerned not with exploring the complex psychological development of individual artists but with presenting a somewhat ridiculous collection of effete leftist eccentrics. The character whose career crisis and readaptation to an altered world dominate the novel is Basil Seal, that unprincipled master of survival. His willingness to dispose of an old Oxford friend, Ambrose Silk, and to denounce assorted poets and painters suggests that there is no longer room for decadent aesthetes in a warrior society.

Although *Put Out More Flags* does employ touches of irony, particularly in unexpected events, in the unresolved chaos at the Ministry of Information, and in Basil's tricking of Ambrose, Waugh's previously playful attitude toward dandies and rogues turns somber under the impact of total war. The hedonists, phony artists, and muddled thinkers depicted in the novel have to be dealt the coup de grace, since a nation fighting for its life is compelled to discard the excess baggage of degenerate art and social parasitism as well as bureaucratic bungling. In such extreme circumstances civilization itself, in order to survive, must resort to primitive, even barbaric, values. It is precisely this wartime expediency that permits Basil's outrageous intrigues, deemed reprehensible in peacetime, to be admired as ingenious, since thoroughly dishonorable behavior may be necessary to save Britain from the overwhelming might of an unscrupulous enemy. *Put Out More Flags* shows Waugh to be painfully aware of the irony in these ethical inversions and ambivalent toward both the triumph of Basil's ruthless strategems and the injustice perpetrated against Ambrose. Yet the approach in the novel is generally direct rather than ironic, for in real life Waugh was too dedicated to his country's ultimate victory to treat his material in the airy, detached manner of his early fiction.

Not until *Brideshead Revisited* did he strive for a satisfactory solution to the impasse that inhibited *Work Suspended*. Reaching beyond the humanity of his characters, he turned toward the supernatural and created—through ornate style, subjectivity, and preoccupation with the spiritual element—a more comprehensive representation of his new artistic and philosophical intentions. But that novel might not have succeeded so well without the trial run of *Work Suspended* and John Plant as the antecedent of Charles Ryder.

Brideshead Revisited

*B*rideshead Revisited, though obviously a re-shaping of seminal material from *Work Suspended*, is markedly superior to its forerunner. The subject of artistic regeneration, forecast but not realized in *Work Suspended*, is redirected and expanded from a merely humanistic plane to a spiritual one, so that Waugh, by integrating an artist's romance into a religious matrix, has solved the spiritual problem and more extensively explored the aesthetic dimension. Especially well suited to this transformation is Waugh's new set of major figures, who are amenable to religious awakening and are subject to a sequence of events designed to propel them toward that end. But the characters in *Brideshead* do not serve merely as means to facilitate the author's underlying purpose. They are impressive creations in themselves—more richly portrayed and sharply individualized than the less distinct inhabitants of John Plant's artsy world. Clothing these enhanced structural elements is a language admirably adapted to the complexity, subjectivity, and philosophical depth of this modified *Künstlerroman*. Its modes of expression—sometimes brisk, often graceful, even poetically elaborate—are capable of revealing through the beauty and intensity of the diction more of Waugh's own feelings than is the rather flat style of its unfinished predecessor.

Among the aspects of *Brideshead* that differ substantially from Waugh's previous work, the novel's radically altered world view produces the greatest impact on his use of irony, since a theological stance precludes the objective suspension of judgment necessary for an ironic approach to human dilemmas. Although the ironic perspective held by Charles Ryder and other principal figures runs throughout much of the story, the opposing providential view becomes increasingly significant until the conflict is ultimately resolved through religious faith. The uncertainties of an ironic world, governed by caprice, are not simply replaced, however, by the certainties of divine guidance; they are assimilated in such a way that what may have temporarily appeared to be the ironies of fate in the lives of the unenlightened turn out to be only misunderstood providence. Admittedly Waugh's amalgamation of the two views, though boldly asserted, is not always convincingly achieved; but the tension between the phenomenal and the noumenal gives rise to some of the most interesting situations in the novel as recalcitrant characters rebel against the faith into which they are eventually drawn. With each conversion, as a character submits to the will of God and acknowledges the obligation to fulfill the purpose for which he or she was created, chaos gives way to control and ironic perception is subsumed into the concept of a divinely ordered universe.

Substantiating Waugh's intentions for *Brideshead* are a number of his own assertions about the primacy of the spiritual dimension in human life. Although he rejected the notion of literature as religious propaganda, he declared in the essay "Fan-Fare" that man's "relation to God" would be a major concern in his future work, and he pointedly criticized many "modern novelists since and including James Joyce" for their mistaken attempt "to represent the whole human mind and soul and yet omit its determining character—that of being God's creature with a defined purpose."[1] In a 1947 memorandum for prospective MGM scriptwriters, Waugh unequivocally stated that the novel's "theme is theological" and that it deals with "the operation of Grace," which he defined as "the unmerited and unilateral act of love by which God continually calls souls to Himself."[2] Like St. Augustine, he believed that only through Grace, and not man's will, is humanity able to renounce sin. In the dustjacket "Warning" for the book's first English commercial edition (1945), Waugh further described the novel as "an attempt to trace the workings of the divine purpose in a pagan world, in the lives of an English Catholic family, half-paganized themselves."[3] By no means did he postulate bliss, either earthly or heavenly, for the spiritually regenerated; rather, he asserted with wartime catastrophes in close view, "that the human spirit, redeemed, can survive all disasters."[4] The principal focus of the novel, therefore, is not Charles Ryder. As Waugh explained to Nancy Mitford, Charles "is telling the story [but] it is not his story. . . . the book is about God."[5] Since it would be difficult for a modern realistic novelist to depict God as one of the characters, as graphic and literary artists of earlier ages had done, Waugh was obliged to show His presence and operations indirectly through their impact on men's lives. Critics unwilling to accept that postulate have pounced on what they consider the novel's disunity and incompatible mixture of religion with "romantic fantasy."[6] Yet its thematic unity—the conflict between the material and spiritual realms—is repeatedly illustrated. Even an intellectual lightweight such as Sebastian voices an understanding of warring impulses when he confesses to Charles how hard it is to be a practicing Catholic. In the resolution of this problem, Lady Marchmain plays a pivotal role. The first book, "Et in Arcadia Ego," ends with her death and failure to bring her wayward children under spiritual rein; but the second book, "A Twitch upon the Thread," concludes with the fulfillment of her aspirations as the errant souls of Sebastian, Lord Marchmain, Julia, and even Charles are pulled to God like hooked fish on an angler's line.

Further curtailing the irony in *Brideshead* is its participating narrator, through whom Waugh has fashioned a complex web of subjectivity. Charles not only functions as spokesman for the author's deeply felt ideas about art, love, and providence; but he in turn creates, by reminiscence, another persona out of his former self. Although Charles's sensitivity, introspection, and eagerness to reflect upon both the past and the present make him a more highly developed character than Waugh had hitherto devised, Charles's intense emotional involvement makes him an unreliable evaluator of his own and others' experiences. One cannot even be sure whether his recollections as a thirty-nine-year-old army captain authentically portray the people and events of his earlier life or whether these mental images are merely imperfect reconstructions based on what he prefers to remember. In any event, the possibilities for detachment are greatly reduced by such a first-person narrator, and in some instances there is no attempt at all to see the story from an objective, outside perspective.

Several examples can be cited to show how Waugh, through techniques antithetic to irony, probes the characters' minds for arcane, repressed thoughts. Charles, recalling an American woman who claimed to know him "through and through," wonders how she presumed to see into the "dark places" of his consciousness that he was unable to explore.[7] Was it possible, he asks himself, for her to delve beneath the superficial level of their conversation and explain why at a deeper level his mind was consumed with unspoken thoughts of Julia? On another occasion, remembering Lady Marchmain's implication that she could deal with Sebastian's alcoholism because of prior experience with her husband, Charles looks back upon his own unexpressed rebuttal like an omniscient narrator looking into the mind of a character. An even bolder departure from the ironic stance appears in Julia's outpouring to Charles of chaotic thoughts prompted by her tormented conscience, for her revelation, though presented as an exterior monologue, is actually close to a controlled stream of consciousness such as Waugh deplored in modernist fiction.[8]

In view of this major shift in philosophic perspective and narrative technique, one may be surprised to discover that Waugh's highly developed ironic sense makes a vital contribution to the novel's artistic achievement. While irony is neither predominant, as in most of the earlier fiction, nor contrived and superimposed, as sometimes seems the case in *Work Suspended*, in *Brideshead* it is so appropriately incorporated into events and personalities that its naturalness in the human condition enhances rather than detracts from the theological significance. By delighting and informing through a variety of indirections, it functions superbly in the service of a basically didactic, nonironic work, which would be a very different creation without its leavening action. In essence, the infusion of ironic elements sophisticates what might otherwise be too direct or dogmatic an approach. Character delineation, including that of devout but fallible Catholics such as Bridey and Lady Marchmain, becomes more profound. The romance of human love and the glamor of an opulent environment, glorified in nostalgic remembrance of the past, are brought back to reality by a gentle undercutting of extravagant sentiments.[9] Even the treatment of religion is tempered, though its seriousness remains undiluted, by being brought into line with man's actual experience of it in a flawed world.

Although Waugh's new narrative style precludes some forms of irony, his framing of the novel with a prologue and an epilogue, both in present time while the bulk of the action occurs in past time, creates an irony of dual perspective, a photographic double exposure showing the discrepancy between now and then.[10] Charles's wartime encampment at Brideshead, when it is overrun by military barbarians, is contrasted with his glorious recollections of his earlier visits and residence there. But, as in many modernist novels, time in *Brideshead* is handled imaginatively; instead of being a linear progression, the past becomes discrete material to be conjured up when needed, in Proustian fashion, by association with present thoughts in Ryder's mind. His youthful experiences— first centering on Sebastian, then revolving around Julia—become more vivid than the immediate present against which they are measured; and his involuntary memory of *temps perdu* reconstructs them not exactly as they were but as his subjective mind wants to reorder and even transmute them. In a many-layered example of such an alteration, Charles in his role as narrator recounts how, during his relationship with Julia, he not only pieced together information about her earlier life partly from her own "dreamy monologues of reminiscences" but even felt that he had been "part of it, directing it by devious ways, towards" himself (183). In a less complicated but more profound instance of transformation, Charles describes his first sight of Brideshead Castle as occurring on a cloudless day in June when all nature seemed "to proclaim the glory of God" (21), thereby superimposing upon the past moment a present awareness of divinity that he, in his agnostic youth, would not have had. By resurrecting and restoring such episodes in the larger context of his life, he turns chaotic events into a parable of human salvation.

Other ironies of serious import that arise from the novel's situational matrix depend upon paradoxes or unforeseen turns of events. In the Prologue and Epilogue the war provides the most conspicuous paradox in the sense that destruction should be the means of preserving worthy ideals. Although the real battlefields are only glancingly mentioned, what happens at Brideshead is a microcosm of the wider conflict. The soldiers bivouacked there vandalize both the house and grounds with no respect for its exquisite beauty, and even the officer who shows Charles around disdainfully compares the Chinese drawing room to a brothel decorated in Japanese style. Yet it is also the war that causes the chapel, closed and stripped of its sacred objects after Lady Marchmain's death, to be restored to its proper use. In the interior story drawn from Charles's remembrances, the most fundamental ironies involve the Roman Catholic faith. It is both unexpected and illogical that Julia, having had difficulty finding a suitable English husband because of her Catholicism, should marry a man totally devoid of any spirituality, and that Charles, who has bitterly denounced religious beliefs even in the face of the Flytes' concern for Lord Marchmain's salvation, should kneel in prayer for the dying man's soul and be converted himself. It seems even more implausible that a family clearly seeking escape from orthodoxy and often in violation of its tenets should be the instrumentality of leading Charles to the Church.

Although Waugh's commitment to a religious message decreased the possibilities for detachment and comedy, there remained many opportunities to employ irony in the dialogue of his characters. The conversation between Charles and his wife Celia, when they meet in New York after a two-year separation, reveals far more than is actually uttered. By replying, "No. I'm not in love" (231), in response to Celia's questions about whether he has fallen in love with someone else, Charles is telling the truth but not the whole truth; and she, evidently understanding his evasiveness, does not press the crucial subject of his love for her. His subsequent observation that his "wife seemed content with this answer" (231) discloses not only his awareness of her insight but his understanding of her reluctance to force the issue.

More amusing are a series of double entendres that escape Celia because she does not know of her husband's shipboard adultery. After Charles has first made love to Julia and tells his wife, quite truthfully but not so innocently as it sounds, that he "spent most of the time with Julia," Celia replies: "She's one of my friends I knew you'd like. I expect you were a godsend to her" (262). Celia's comments in this instance are intended simply at face value, but Charles and the reader see an unintended meaning. In a comparable situation, Celia, still ignorant of what has occurred, remarks to Julia: "I hear you've been looking after my husband for me." Julia's response, "Yes, we've become very matey" (262), daringly puns on a cockneyism to drive the ironic nail home, although Celia cannot comprehend its real significance. Had Charles's wife been depicted previously as a sympathetic innocent instead of an opportunist and an adulteress, the reader might have regarded this deception as regrettable. But since Waugh, through careful manipulation of tone, has already created antagonism toward her, the reader can enjoy Julia's private joke at Celia's expense.

Subtler irony is at work when Charles, as an army captain, first discovers that the encampment to which his battalion has been moved during the night is at Brideshead. Without mentioning its name to the reader, he shows through mental images that ecstatically revive the past what an enduring impact the place had upon him. But to Hooper's assertion that Charles had never seen "such a thing" as the castle and the fountain, he replies with extraordinary understatement: "Yes, Hooper, I did. I've been here before" (17). This remark and Hooper's rejoinder, "Oh well, you know all about it," are reiterated in Charles's thoughts as the Prologue concludes: "I had been there before; I knew all about it" (17). Only in retrospect does the reader comprehend the disparity between this casual acknowledgment of an earlier acquaintance with Brideshead and the ebullient recollections it evokes. Whereas Hooper's flat statement reveals only indifference to what he regards as an odd monstrosity, the same words, as repeated several times by Charles, take on vastly changed meaning by conjuring up the most poignant experiences of a lifetime.

In some dialogue the most important ideas are implicitly understood by both interlocutors without ever being verbalized. In response to Charles's recommendation that it might not be best to relax the domestic restrictions on alcohol the night following the fox hunt, Samgrass pointedly replies: "You specifically advise against it *to-night*. I wonder why" (161). Evidently he deduces that Charles knows of Sebastian's plans to drink rather than hunt but dares not voice his suspicion. Samgrass is much bolder in ironically asserting that Sebastian can come to no harm because he has no money—"as long as no one is so wicked as to give him any" (161). Consequently Charles must surmise that he is already suspected of doing the forbidden deed, but of course he cannot possibly admit to comprehending the indirect accusation. Lady Marchmain and Charles reach a similar impasse when she insinuates that she is better at dealing with dipsomaniacs than he. By saying, "You see, I've been through all this before" (163), she expects to convey that *she* can handle Sebastian. What is actually revealed is Lady Marchmain's painful awareness, silently shared by Charles, that she drove her husband away and will also drive Sebastian away. Because the speakers dare not allow their perceptions to surface, the conversation gets nowhere—not, as Charles later explains to himself, "because we failed to understand one another, but because we understood too well" (163).

Waugh's well-honed technique of ironic presentation through collage or counterpoint is adroitly used to show diverse perspectives on the news of Charles's divorce and intended marriage to a divorced Julia. The elder Ryder, oblivious to Charles's failed marriage, considers it strange that his son should divorce Celia after seeming "happy" with her for years and unreasonable that he should want to assume another wife. Celia persuades her friends that her behavior merits praise while Charles's infidelity deserves condemnation. Rex Mottram cannot understand why Julia should want a divorce from him when their *ménage à trois ou quatre* has been so satisfactory. Cousin Jasper, always the utilitarian, wonders why Charles and Julia should bother to marry at all. Bridey's fiancée, having referred to Julia's "divorcing one divorced man and marrying another," tries to palliate her tactlessness with the condescending remark that "every Catholic family has one lapsed member, and it's often the nicest" (297). Nanny Hawkins resigns herself to Julia's possible remarriage with the hope that it may be "all for the best" (301). In this collection of comments two sets of discrepancies exist. On the surface the conflicting views can be read as irreconcilable differences of opinion among the speakers. But subtler irony operates within the mental processes of each speaker, and the reader who takes into account the mindset of a particular character can deduce the submerged thoughts of which the spoken words are only an incomplete, distorted version.

A somewhat different arrangement in juxtapositioning is used to counterbalance three subjective viewpoints on Charles's friendships at Oxford. Jasper's disapproval of his younger cousin's decadent lifestyle includes the conviction that Charles has fallen in with "the *very worst set in the University*" (41). While expressing some uncertainty about Sebastian's character, Jasper unequivocally brands the flamboyant Anthony Blanche as "a man there's absolutely no excuse for" (42). Immediately following this censure is Charles's spirited defense of his university life—a romanticized version focusing on the joys of his association with Sebastian, who is largely responsible for Charles's deviation from middle-class virtues. This self-exoneration is succeeded by Blanche's jaundiced exposé of the Flytes, which damns most of the family and characterizes Sebastian as charming but intellectually dim. Each of these perspectives is argued by its proponent as the only tenable "truth," though it may be diametrically opposed to the perceptions of another character. Since the conflict is unresolvable, the reader, who suspects some validity to each view, is left (for the moment, at least) in a state of suspended judgment.

Although the overall decline of irony in Waugh's writing is partly indicated by an increased number of characters in *Brideshead* who view the world and themselves in a straightforward, non-ironic manner—Cordelia, Cara, Nanny Hawkins, the priests, and the local doctor—there is ample room within the author's doctrinal stance for ironic elements to enrich the delineation of most of the major characters. Charles Ryder may not in himself be a highly.intriguing or complex personality; but he serves as an important means of unifying the book, and the ironies associated with him are essential to both the thematic and artistic concerns of the novel. As its central character, whom Waugh loosely termed "my hero" in the aforementioned dustjacket "Warning," Charles, like John Plant, reveals through his pursuits of art and human love the ironies of his own life. As narrator, recounting and interpreting all the events of the story, Charles is able, like his creator, to sense and depict the ironies in other people.

The glamorous environment to which the Flytes introduce him provides a set of contradictory values that invite ironic exploitation. His first acquaintance with the splendor of their palatial home so excites his passion for its architectural style that he feels "a whole new system of nerves alive within" him and looks upon its fountain as "a life-giving spring" (82). But even while sensing the architect's desire to embody the vitality, variety, and grandeur of divinity in "that high and insolent dome . . . those tricky ceilings . . . those arches and broken pediments" (82), Charles is totally unaware that his "conversion to the baroque" is a prelude to his religious conversion.[11] In his unbelieving youth, he cannot consciously realize that man may reach the sacred through the profane or that God may work His will through man's aesthetic sense.

Nor can Charles foresee that this stimulating ambiance will subsequently prove to be a limitation on his vocation as an artist. By surrounding him with physical beauty, it encourages him to exalt the worldly, as he unconsciously acknowledges at the end of Book I in identifying himself with Browning's Renaissance painters. He does not fulfill the promise of his *"exquisite"* early sketches because "charm . . . the great English blight," which according to Anthony Blanche can be fatal to an artist (273), leads him astray. He cannot be what Blanche defines as a true artist, "solid, purposeful, observant—and, beneath it all, p-p-passionate" (52), because mundane distractions prevent the single-minded concentration necessary to the development of a unique talent. Instead of converting the inspiration of Brideshead into something original, Charles prostitutes his abilities in the service of the aristocracy by painting their decaying mansions, while his materialistic wife Celia promotes the commercialization of his work to the point of suggesting that he design Hollywood scenery.[12] Even his attempt to revive his flagging imagination among the ruins of a lost American civilization leaves him "unchanged, still a small part of [himself] pretending to be whole" (229).

Ironically it is the Catholic Flyte family who, having first attracted him and then distracted him with their charm, are finally instrumental in bringing him to wholeness, though Charles could never have imagined the nature of that wholeness or anticipated the way in which it would come about. His love for Sebastian and later for Julia becomes, like the quickening of his aesthetic sense, a step toward spiritual awakening; but, as in the case of art, the periods of his happiness with them temporarily divert him toward the mundane. Only after the relationships fall apart, only after Julia and Lord Marchmain return to their religious faith, does Charles's acquaintance with Brideshead enable him to progress beyond mortal passions to a love of God. Although Waugh is not explicit about Charles's conversion, Hooper's remark to him in the Prologue about the "R.C." service—"More in your line than mine" (17)— suggests that by the time of the revisit he is already a Catholic or has at least become serious about religion.[13] Whether the spiritual dimension will ever make him a first-rate artist is not substantiated in the novel; but unlike Tony Last and John Plant, Charles has acquired a positive frame of reference and a definite set of values on which to rely. His cheerfulness at the end of the Epilogue indicates the renewal of an inner strength capable of influencing all aspects of his life.

As narrator of his own experiences, Charles himself employs irony. While he is not objective in the usual sense of being unconcernedly detached, he is nevertheless capable of detecting contradictions and ambiguities in his acquaintances. In one of the rare instances in which a Waugh narrator actually calls attention to an inherent irony, Charles points directly to Lady Marchmain's undercutting of her "faith" in the fox hunt as a means of correcting Sebastian's drinking problem. His comment that she "mocked herself . . . with that delicate irony for which she was famous" (162) alerts the reader to the discrepancies in her assertions. First declaring that she had "always detested hunting" because it turns even "the nicest people" into "boastful . . . self-opinionated, monomaniac louts," she then states: "And yet . . . my heart is quite light today to think of Sebastian out with them. 'There's nothing wrong with him really,' I say, 'he's gone hunting'—as though it were an answer to prayer" (162). Compounding the logical inconsistency in her feelings about the sport is her underlying knowledge that Sebastian's hunting is neither a panacea nor "an answer to prayer." What Lady Marchmain mocks by uttering thoughts that she does not believe is her own pious optimism. What the reader sees in this ironic presentation is a more complex and realistic personality than could be achieved otherwise. Since all the characters in *Brideshead* are seen through Charles's perceptive eyes, a great many of them are ironically portrayed; and, in general, the more ironic the depiction, the more fascinating the character.

Charles describes his own father not only as a man of ironic contradictions but as an ironist who evidently enjoys making other people the victims of his jests. A humorous eccentric beyond rational explanation, he is a literary descendant of Col. Blount and John Plant's father, though Cousin Jasper's evaluation of him as a dotty old man not "really in touch with things" (41) ignores his conniving powers. While he seems to want his son's company during vacations—as evidenced by the many verbal declarations about doing the right things for Charles—his erratic and seemingly perverse behavior nullifies his noble protestations. Advising Charles to go on sketching excursions or attend the theater, he ignores his son's complaints of poverty as though the pecuniary problem could be solved merely by refusing to acknowledge it. His intentions become even more unfathomable when he repeatedly refers to a cousin who escaped financial disgrace by emigrating to Australia, and when he gloats over his success in getting rid of a sister who was upsetting his way of life. One cannot be sure whether he wants to drive his son away, teach him fiscal responsibility, or play a combative game with him.

The social diversions he provides for Charles also seem to cancel out his professions of good will. Having urged his son to seek younger companions, he discomfits the acquaintance whom Charles brings to dinner by keeping up an extended fancy that the guest is an American until, with a gleeful reference to cricket as the young man's "national game," he throws his little joke into reverse.

A subsequent dinner and musicale are planned ostensibly to relieve the boredom of Charles's long vacation, but the tedious guests seem to have been chosen not for conviviality but in the spirit of mockery, the menu selected not to achieve gustatory delight but to carry out a color scheme. Yet Charles's father, even while conceding that his entertainment was a fiasco, nevertheless declares: "The obligations of hospitality must be observed. As long as you are here, you shall not be dull" (72). By such means, he so destroys his own credibility that neither Charles nor the reader can determine precisely what the old man is up to.

A very different kind of confrontational relationship exists between Charles and one of his wartime subalterns, Lt. Hooper, who represents the antithesis of all that Charles esteems. Their uncomfortable connection—much like the linkage of Plant and Atwater in *Work Suspended* (though without the psychological undertones) or of Guy Crouchback and Apthorpe in *Men at Arms*—stimulates, in a negative way, many of Charles's positive thoughts. Waugh evidently realized that by creating Hooper as a foil he had hit upon a shrewd technique for enabling his first-person narrator to define himself obliquely. Hooper is what Waugh denigrates as the common man of the twentieth century. The product of egalitarian, utilitarian education, he uses substandard speech, has no sense of the traditional or heroic values with which Charles will soon align himself, and has no romantic or idealistic aspirations. His philistine comments on Brideshead particularly set him at odds with Charles. Unapologetic about his lower-class outlook, Hooper tolerates the army as he would the measles, lacks respect for authority, and, because he cannot manage inferiors, is hopeless as a leader. His incompetence occasions an irony pointed out by Charles—that Hooper, while totally unreliable and inefficient himself, should express the highest regard for business efficiency and deplore its absence in military procedures. Charles also seems to sense irony in the fact that for someone as obnoxious as his lieutenant he should have "a feeling which almost [amounts] to affection" (8).

While Charles's relationship to Hooper is oppositional despite a measure of compassion, his attachment to Sebastian is emotionally positive despite some rational misgivings. Although Blanche slyly casts aspersions on Sebastian's character and mental capacity, thereby putting an ironic twist on the way the reader and possibly Charles see him, neither this detractive appraisal nor Cousin Jasper's warning that Sebastian "looks odd" and "gets himself talked about" (41) succeeds in disrupting the friendship. Charles's retrospective view of what he learned from this close relationship—"that to know and love one other human being is the root of all wisdom" (45)—not only epitomizes the great value he places upon it but hints at its lasting impact. Its beneficial consequences are perhaps surprising since Sebastian's corruptive influence might logically have led Charles toward hedonistic destruction. Instead, Sebastian, by also being the entrée to art, love, and religion, unforeseeably alters his friend's destiny for the better. Charles's love for Sebastian, whom he designates as "the forerunner" (303), becomes the prelude to his love for Julia, which in turn leads to his love for God.

Sebastian's worldly degradation, brought about by escapes into drunkenness, stems primarily from unresolved self-contradictions that are conspicuous from his first appearance in the novel. The "strange jumble of objects" in his Oxford rooms (31) and the incongruous mixture of guests at his luncheon party reflect an inner chaos, which he recognizes as the battle between natural inclinations and moral demands. Other tensions arise from his desire to remain a child rather than assume adult responsibilities, as evidenced by his teddy bear, his devotion to Nanny, and Cara's observation that he "is in love with his own childhood" (103). The bear further serves as his ironic double, upon whom he can project his own bad features, thereby shifting the blame for misbehavior. His good characteristics he identifies with Julia, whom he claims to love, in an unconscious admission of narcissism, because she so resembles him—at least in appearance and manner. His glib remark that he could never love anyone with a character similar to his own is also more self-revealing than he realizes, for it is an expression of truth not intended to be taken seriously (much like Brenda's apparent jest about carrying on with young men, though without her deceitful intent). Sebastian's inner conflicts account for some of the most dramatic turns of events in his life. Glaringly ironic is his irrational withdrawal from his only devoted friend on the false assumption that Charles has become one of the enemy aligned against him. That his spiritual resuscitation should be accomplished through the instrumentality of someone as repulsive as Kurt seems even more unlikely; but once Sebastian has put another's need and suffering before his own, he becomes the good Samaritan. The struggle within him between the world and the spirit is largely resolved, despite periodic lapses into drunkenness, by his return to the faith in the humble role of underporter at a Tunisian monastery.

That failed instrumentality of maternal authority over Sebastian, a young Oxford don named Samgrass, is inevitably at odds with Charles and is therefore presented with reductive irony. Employed to help Lady Marchmain edit a memorial volume honoring her eldest brother, Samgrass is obviously a clever, unscrupulous "intellectual-on-the-make" (110). Sebastian first describes him as "someone of Mummy's," but Charles comes to realize that he is "someone of almost everyone's who [possesses] anything to attract him" (109)—the sort of academic who substantiates the elder Plant's contention in *Work Suspended* that "anyone can buy a don" (12). Whether Lady Marchmain sees through him or whether she overlooks his faults in order to use him, as he indeed uses her, is left to the reader's speculation. To achieve his own advancement, Samgrass twists the truth without compunction, and the irony about him lies primarily in the fact that everything he says or does is undercut by the implication of an ulterior motive. When he perjures himself to save Sebastian from harsh legal punishment, his real intention is to ingratiate himself with the Flytes. When he lies concerning Sebastian's whereabouts after his charge has eluded him in Greece, he evidently does so to continue the first-class accommodations Lady Marchmain provides for her son's traveling companion. Charles, after hearing Sebastian's own explanation of his absence from the Levantine photographs and his late arrival at Brideshead, senses that Samgrass is "not only bluffing but cheating" (151). That Samgrass unwittingly exposes even more of his propensities is suggested through an ironic Proustian allusion in his remark about "spending a cosy afternoon . . . with the incomparable Charlus" (124).[14]

To some extent the extraordinary Anthony Blanche may be seen as a cross between the intelligent, untrustworthy Samgrass and the attractive, hedonistic Sebastian. A lineal descendant of Ambrose Silk in *Put Out More Flags*, Blanche epitomizes the sybaritic aesthete. But he is not merely an eccentric: Charles's description of him—"ageless as a lizard . . . foreign as a Martian" (32)—suggests both the repellent and fascinating characteristics of a truly exotic personality. Brilliant, witty, decadent, and slightly reptilian, he is locked in a love-hate conflict with mindless "hearties" such as Boy Mulcaster; and largely to shock bourgeois sensibilities, he delights in flaunting his unconventionality and cosmopolitan liberation.

Among more tolerant acquaintances, whom he amuses with histrionic flair and acid tongue, he inspires both admiration and fear. Even Charles, who does not especially like him, holds "him in considerable awe" (46).

Blanche's most important contribution to the novel's irony lies in his startling, often highly critical, remarks about other characters, for his negative opinions tend to qualify Charles's sentimental, romanticized perspective. Complicating this irony of contrary views is the problem of Blanche's reliability, since his habit of embroidering the truth with exaggeration and his strong biases call his judgments into question. Cast in the role of oracle by his recitation of Tiresias's lines from Eliot's *Waste Land*, he surprises both Charles and the reader with the accuracy of many of his predictions. His insights about Sebastian and the teddy bear, like his observations on the destructive impact of "charm" and Charles's artistic failure, show Blanche to be a shrewd psychoanalyst. But his malicious gossip about Sebastian at Eton and the "*very sinister*" Flyte family (53) must be regarded with distrust, since his suspicions that Sebastian once tattled on him and that the Flytes' Venetian relatives snubbed his family could indicate a vengeful motive. Yet his comments cannot be dismissed as blithely as Sebastian does by attributing Blanche's "great charm" to a lack of veracity. As manuscript revisions prove, Waugh, in presenting Blanche to the reader, took extraordinary pains to make his character's pronouncements both plausible and, wherever personal animus is involved, highly suspect.[15] Inevitably some of Blanche's evaluations must remain in that tantalizing gray area between truth and falsehood. What makes them doubly fascinating is that they are first seen by the reader as probably false, because of Charles's initial unwillingness to believe them, but later as more than slightly true in the light of subsequent developments. Through skillful manipulation of the ironic indeterminacy resulting from Blanche's cynical wisdom, Waugh greatly enriched his character portrayals and counterbalanced some of the novel's excesses.

The most ironically depicted character in *Brideshead* is Lady Marchmain, whom Waugh himself designated as "an enigma."[16] She is first introduced through Blanche's jaundiced account, which emphasizes the discrepancy between what he considers her real character and what he interprets as only a deceptive mask. In extravagant metaphors depicting her fraudulence, Blanche casts her as a would-be Madame Récamier sucking the blood of an enslaved coterie, a nun parading her piety before a theatrical audience, and an avenging fury using her advertised virtue to hound her unfaithful husband "out of society" (55). In questioning how she can convince most people of her goodness while being so vindictive, Blanche implies that behind the façade of serene and saintly beauty lies a demonic power.

Charles's presentation of Lady Marchmain diminishes her alleged saintliness more subtly and gradually as he recounts not only her conspiratorial ventures with Samgrass but also his own private conversations with her. He perceives in her a tendency to twist ideas to suit herself, for she speaks of riches being sanctified by Grace and defends that idea with her own unorthodox interpretation of scripture: "Of *course* . . . it's very unexpected for a camel to go through the eye of a needle, but the gospel is simply a catalogue of unexpected things. . . . It's all part of the poetry, the Alice-in-Wonderland side, of religion" (127). Her deviousness is especially apparent when she attempts to manipulate Charles during one of her carefully orchestrated "little talks" with him. Analyzing in retrospect the way her mind maneuvered him toward certain topics, he recalls: "She took hold of her subject in a feminine, flirtatious way, circling, approaching, retreating, feinting; she hovered over it like a butterfly; she played 'grandmother's steps' with it, getting nearer the real point imperceptibly while one's back was turned" (137).

The central irony about Lady Marchmain, however, involves her genuinely good intentions. There is no doubt of her unwavering loyalty to the Catholic faith, of the very real pain she suffers for her family's sins, or of her rather naive desire to persuade others, including Charles, to accept what she believes. Yet the greatest discrepancy lies not between what she considers to be a worthy purpose and the underhanded methods she sometimes employs to effect it but rather in the fact that her efforts usually misfire. Her inclination to make a mess of things is revealed in Sebastian's explanation of her failure at painting: "Someone told her that you could only appreciate the beauty of the world by trying to paint it. . . . She couldn't draw at all, and however bright the colours were in the tubes, by the time Mummy had mixed them up, they came out a kind of khaki" (82). When Charles uses her paints, "muddy smears on the palette" corroborate Sebastian's parable, though neither of them seems to understand, as does the reader, its larger implications.

In dealing with deviant members of her family, Lady
Marchmain employs tactics so unsound psychologically that they
produce extreme unhappiness, in effect blighting and alienating
those she loves most. Her treatment of Sebastian as a little boy
rather than as an adult may have contributed to his inability to
grow up, and her insistence that he live with Monsignor Bell at Oxford inadvertently incites him to open rebellion and confirms his
dipsomania. While she is right in declaring Rex "unsuitable" for
Julia, her proscription against him leads directly to Julia's foolish
marriage and rejection of religion. Sebastian, upon learning that
his mother is about to die, sums up the tragic contradiction in her
character by observing: "Poor Mummy. She really was a *femme fa-
tale*. . . . She killed at a touch" (214). From a theological point of
view the temporal misery Lady Marchmain caused must be
weighed against her motive of steering her family toward eternal
salvation. Waugh did not lessen the ambivalence with which she is
portrayed when he responded to Nancy Mitford's inquiry: "Are
you or are you not on Lady Marchmain's side? I couldn't make
out."[17] "No I am not on her side," he explained, "but God is, who
suffers fools gladly."[18] Yet the unanswerable question is whether
she serves as the indirect means through which God effects the
"twitch upon the thread" or whether He achieves the desired goal
in spite of her well-meant bungling.

The uncertainties surrounding Lord Marchmain derive from the
fact that he is presented largely through other characters' conflicting opinions—all tenable, according to different criteria of judgment. Lady Marchmain recalls his distressing bouts of heavy
drinking, Julia refers to him as a "family skeleton" (161), and
Sebastian implies that no respectable person would admit knowing
such "a social leper" (23). From Blanche's liberated perspective
Lord Marchmain is "*very* handsome, a *magnifico*, a voluptuary, Byronic" (54); far from deserving social ostracism, he should be
praised for being magnanimous to his wife. Charles, upon first
meeting him in Venice, a city long famous for its liberal views on
marriage and religion, finds him outwardly charming, learned, and
well adjusted to the local ambiance. But Lord Marchmain's mistress, Cara, speaks of the intense hatred that he harbors, beneath
that calm exterior, for his wife and everything associated with her,
including "all the illusions of boyhood—innocence, God, hope"
(103). There is little direct access, however, to his attitudes and
emotions. Although Charles offers insights into the minds of many

other characters, with Lord Marchmain he plays the ironic, withdrawn narrator. Hence the reader can never be sure exactly how the paterfamilias feels about wife, mistress, family, or religion. Only once does he talk about Lady Marchmain and her religion, about his own freedom and conscience: "What became of the chapel? . . . I built it for her. . . . Then I went away—left her in the chapel praying. . . . It was the place for her. I never came back to disturb her prayers. They said we were fighting for freedom; I had my own victory. Was it a crime? . . . Crying to heaven for vengeance?" (334). This brief surfacing of submerged thoughts, while more tantalizing than informative, does suggest mental reflections that pave the way for one of the novel's most unforeseen turns of events—Lord Marchmain's deathbed repentance and return to the Catholic fold.

The Earl of Brideshead represents the paradox, not uncommon in Waugh's Catholic novels, of being a success in the eyes of God but a failure in the ways of man. Having been prevented from becoming a priest by his father's insistence that he carry on the Marchmain title, he is adrift in the secular world without any sense of purpose. Wasting his time on trivia, such as collecting matchboxes, and belatedly marrying a woman who cannot produce an heir, he neglects the very obligations for which he gave up his spiritual vocation. As Sebastian explains Bridey's unhappiness, "He's all twisted inside" (88). Blanche's assessment of him as "a learned bigot, a ceremonious barbarian, a snowbound lama" (54) becomes more meaningful in the context of Bridey's pronouncements on religious matters. While he remains firmly anchored in the Catholic faith, his attempts to enunciate church doctrine, though accurate, are marred by his pompous ineptitude, which more often offends than enlightens. He particularly annoys Charles by bringing God into everything, by being inconsiderate of others' feelings, and by displaying a conviction of absolute rectitude. It is Bridey's strict Catholic principles, not his fiancée's, that prevent him from bringing her to Brideshead, where, as he phrases it, Julia lives "in sin with Rex or Charles or both" (285). But ironically it is this tactless utterance that awakens Julia's conscience and prompts her regeneration.

That the beautiful and gracious Julia should be attracted, in her search for a husband, to a shady power broker like Rex Mottram may at first seem highly improbable, especially after her brilliant debut in London. But Julia's gravitation toward Rex is not so implausible in the context of her ambitions and social circumstances. Blanche, who describes her hyperbolically as "Renaissance tragedy . . . acquisitive, intriguing, ruthless" (54), accurately diagnoses her desire for power; and her speech to the Conservative Women's meeting, when she first appears in the novel, suggests politics as a means to that end. Even so, she is obliged to tailor her aspirations to the possible. Aware that her religion may bar her from a desirable aristocratic alliance in a country where the state is linked to a Protestant faith, she drifts into a disastrous marriage with a rising member of Parliament. Having reached the fringes of power, she might accomplish for the Brideshead set (as Rex's associates are known) what Lady Astor did for the Cliveden set; but the vulgar opportunism of her husband's political allies so repels Julia that she withdraws in disillusionment from what she had apparently desired. There is even more poignant irony in her relationship with Charles: having found a man with whom she is much more compatible than Rex, and with whom she has shared much happiness, she must reject him in order to return to her faith.[19]

As the only significant character totally impervious to religion, Rex exists as a relic of Waugh's earlier ironic world and as such is vulnerable to satiric reduction. On the surface he has all the attributes of a successful politician—confidence, ambition, wealth, and skill in wielding influence. But as Charles and the reader learn to know him, the veneer slips away, revealing a hollow man. Rex displays incredibly vulgar tastes, crassly idolizes money, snobbishly seeks an aristocratic marriage, duplicitously conceals his first marriage, and amorally retains his mistress. His willingness to become a Catholic, as though doing so required nothing more than his signature, unwittingly exposes his own shallowness, for conversion signifies nothing more to him than a means to his marital goal. His conversations with the priest who tries vainly to instruct him disclose a total lack of interest in prayer, theology, and anything else religious. As Julia later deduces, Rex has no spiritual dimension and is not "a complete human being at all" (200). Assuming that money and power can obtain whatever he desires in the Catholic Church, as they already have for him in the political arena, he envisions an ostentatious wedding uniting him with an old aristocratic family. But a providence that he cannot comprehend renders ironic justice on him. When the discovery that he has a divorced wife makes a Catholic wedding impossible, he and Julia are married in a grubby Prostestant ceremony, shunned by her prestigious connections; and he discovers, to his disgust, that he has "married an outcast" (200).

Rex's unsavory cohorts are shown in action through some of Waugh's perennial ironic techniques. An incongruous, almost grotesque, mélange of political elements seeking Parliamentary power, they are represented by a few faceless characters who gather at Brideshead:

> "young conservatives" in the early forties, with sparse hair and high blood-pressure; a socialist from the coal mines . . . whose cigars came to pieces in his lips . . . ; a lovesick columnist . . . gloating sombrely on the only woman of the party; a financier older than the rest, and, one might guess from the way they treated him, richer; a woman they called "Grizel," a knowing rake whom . . . they all feared a little. (274-75)

Their conversation, presented as a collage in which the speakers are not identified, deals with the burning issues of the day in a superficial, gossipy, unprincipled fashion, while their insistence on all talking at once defeats the purpose of verbal exchange. Although they are dismissed by Charles and Julia as inconsequential, a subsequent, more frenzied, pastiche of conversation demonstrates their growing involvement in the government on the eve of war. Indeed because of the war, Rex and his political allies are elevated to unprecedented eminence, contrary to justifiable expectations. As Nanny Hawkins candidly observes, "Who would have thought of Mr. Mottram doing so well?" (349).

Even while barbarism flourishes in various forms, Christianity endures; and Charles finds its blessings on his final return to the place where he had so often rejected it. The house and grounds not only remind him of past joys and sorrows; they resurrect as well religious overtones that had originally struck him as meaningless. By reevaluating the events in his life and in the lives of his friends as the operation of divine grace, Charles grasps their significance in a logical progression leading toward acceptance of God's will. Sensing his spiritual identification with the Flytes in their championing of Christian civilization,[20] he understands his own place in the providential plan. Like the Crusaders of old, like the generations of artists and architects who built Brideshead, like Bridey, Cordelia, and Julia now in the Holy Land, he too has an opportunity to help preserve the traditions in which he has come to believe. Faith triumphs in the Epilogue as Charles's quiet discovery of hope in the chapel dispels the disillusionment and malaise occasioned by disappointments in love and in his artistic and military careers. The chaos that surrounds him becomes not only tolerable but meaningful as he views from a radically changed perspective a universe he once saw in ironic terms. Relativism, paradox, and indeterminacy give way before the conviction that an immanent, transcendent Deity is the ultimate reality.

Waugh's enunciation of this positive credo marks a conscious turning away from philosophical irony—with its essentially skeptical vision—as the underlying world view for his fiction. Although his later serious novels may contribute to his stature as a literary artist, critic of society, and Catholic apologist, they do little to advance his reputation as an ironist. Since their more direct approach, increasingly solemn tone, and preoccupation with religious themes diminish the possibilities even for technical irony, these works are not within the scope of this study. Evidently Waugh sensed that he had crossed a watershed when, nearing the completion of *Brideshead*, he noted in his diary: "I think perhaps it is the first of my novels rather than the last."[21] There would be sporadic attempts in subsequent writing to revive his earlier techniques, especially in the service of satire as in *The Loved One* and *Love Among the Ruins*, but irony after *Brideshead* would be reduced to ancillary status.

CHAPTER NINE

The Loved One

*T*he Loved One, the only extensively ironic novel written after *Brideshead*, appears at first glance so unlike its romantic and overtly religious predecessor as to belie Waugh's declared intention of dealing in "future books" with "man in his relation to God."[1] A parody of the artist's romance, it is a reversion to the approach of the earlier short novels. The personality of its central figure, Dennis Barlow, is an amalgam of traits associated with previous antiheroes and the caddish Basil Seal. The supporting characters are eccentric, the situations are grotesque, and the narrator views all with indifference. In one respect *The Loved One* even outdoes its early counterparts. Whereas in most of the preceding fiction an occasional bizarre death or ghastly murder functions as one element among many in an overall scheme, in *The Loved One* death itself is the ideational matrix from which implications about love, art, society, and religion arise. Partly for that reason the irony is grimmer, with little of the exuberant comedy that sparkles in the earlier works.

Waugh's handling of death in this instance is also distinguished by his altered viewpoint toward it. He is not merely amusing us with the absurdities of civilized or uncivilized barbarism that sometimes result in the extraordinary demise of a character; he is on the attack against practices of which he strongly disapproves. Consequently his writing, undergirded by unqualified conviction, becomes appropriately more satirical. Waugh had passed the point in his creative development where he could approach a subject without seeing it in a religious context; and although he may not have considered *The Loved One* as a religious book[2] in the positive sense that *Helena* and the war trilogy would be, he employs, as a Roman Catholic, a definite set of standards against which to judge. Beneath the superficial façade of his narrator's stance, he unambiguously condemns both the funeral customs and the social climate that pervert the Church's teachings about earthly life, death, and the afterlife. In its basic premises, therefore, *The Loved One* expresses negatively the same perspective on the world as does *Brideshead*, while its irony is better subsumed into both satire and religion. It may look backward for much of its style, but its underlying message is definitely in keeping with Waugh's new resolve.

The impetus for this Januslike volume was Waugh's visit to Los Angeles in February–March 1947 to discuss a proposed filming of *Brideshead* by Metro-Goldwyn-Mayer. Although he was generally disgusted by the falseness and pervasive theatricality of the Hollywood milieu, he became fascinated, as well as appalled, by the beautiful fantasy world of Forest Lawn Memorial Park in Glendale. What he regarded as extreme contradictions in the southern California environment, especially as epitomized by this incredible burial place, apparently stimulated his creative imagination just as scenes of wild disorder in Oxford, London, and Africa had inspired his earliest fiction. But whereas in youth he had delighted in portraying a chaotic world and its incohesive society, the changes that had come over him rendered such an attitude impossible in 1947. Los Angeles appeared to be not merely a Godless city in the simply negative sense but one that had substituted the idolatry of materialism for true Christianity.

Having long been fascinated by the subject of death, Waugh had become interested in what archeologists, historians, and comparative religionists could deduce about extinct cultures on the basis of their burials. Evidently he believed that the way people respond to death serves as an index to the dominant philosophy with which they confront life. According to Sykes, Waugh often pointed out, in conversations about Forest Lawn, that the ancient Egyptians' obsession "with funerary celebration" provides us with much of our knowledge about their beliefs; and he also wondered what future theoreticians would deduce about modern Western culture from "our burial customs and monuments to the dead."[3] Even before journeying to California, Waugh had toyed with these thoughts in *Brideshead*. Early in the Prologue Charles Ryder imagines the logical but fallacious deductions later archeologists might make from excavations of a twentieth-century army camp superimposed on the roads and drainage system of a planned suburb. They would likely conclude, Charles surmises, that low-level barbarians had overrun an advanced civilization, since the invaders must have buried their dead far from their primitive settlement and since their women seem to have worn no adornment.[4]

In California Waugh discerned a real-life parallel in the overturning of the old Spanish culture by waves of recent immigrants. In his essay "Half in Love with Easeful Death" (1947), he predicts that fatuous archeologists of the year 2947 may well come to the wrong conclusions in trying to reconstruct the civilization that gave rise to Forest Lawn, especially since the sepulchral customs of the newcomers, who built that phenomenal necropolis, are difficult to understand even with firsthand knowledge of their mindset. Beneath this tongue-in-cheek humor, however, lies a serious concern, for early in the essay he asserts that historical scholars a thousand years hence may correctly agree "that the great cultural decline of the twentieth century was first evident in the graveyard."[5] Dramatizing this view in *The Loved One*, Waugh turns the obvious excesses and incongruities of the Los Angeles scene into a wild fantasy, which, by indirectly involving readers in the judgmental process, becomes a more effective vehicle for censure than direct denunciation. Crucial to the literary interaction between author and audience is Waugh's return to a detached narrator, who can provoke subjective reactions by being completely objective, prick consciences by being callous toward matters that few can ignore, expose moral problems without being preachy, and encourage readers to draw conclusions because he does not do so.

Some of the choicest comedy arises from the narrator's deadpan humor. By recounting in a sober fashion behavior that characters themselves take seriously but readers regard as essentially funny, he increases the discrepancy and therefore the irony's impact. In the passage describing Aimée's preparations for a romantic evening, he uses such inappropriate and exaggerated diction that her ritual is expanded to ridiculous heights, and his terming of her anticipated fate as "manifest destiny" applies that phrase as it was never meant by American historians.

> With a steady hand Aimée fulfilled the prescribed rites of an American girl preparing to meet her lover—dabbed herself under the

arms with a preparation designed to seal the sweatglands, gargled another to sweeten the breath, and brushed into her hair some odorous drops from a bottle labelled: "Jungle Venom"— [advertised as coming] *"From the depth of the fever-ridden swamp . . . with the remorseless stealth of the hunting cannibal."*

Thus fully equipped for a domestic evening . . . she was all set to accept her manifest destiny.[6]

Seen in the context of the novel, this passage reveals additional ironies—that Aimée, while taking pride in being highly "ethical," should employ a battery of drugstore products with the intention of effecting her own seduction, and that in spite of such tactics her hopes are never fulfilled.

Even the most macabre situations are turned into unforgettable absurdities by the matter-of-fact manner in which the narrator lingers over details of the undertaking business. One cannot easily banish visions of Joyboy pinching the thigh of a corpse as merrily as if it were a living friend, or of Dennis firing up the furnace at the pet mortuary to cremate his fiancée as nonchalantly as if she were a dead dog. Nor can one resist a wry smile at the peculiar similarities between Aimée's suitors when in a single chapter the narrator juxtaposes, without comment, descriptions of them at work—the one embalming corpses that convey by their facial expressions his sentiments toward her, the other cremating animals while cribbing poetry to send her.

Among the numerous examples of verbal wrenching in conversation, perhaps most delightful is the complex of misunderstandings, double entendres, and false deductions involving Joyboy, Dennis, and the new apprentice at the pet mortuary. When Joyboy arrives unexpectedly in tears, Dennis, having recently arranged the last rites for Mrs. Joyboy's parrot, asks in jest if there is another parrot to be disposed of. When Joyboy indicates that his distress is about Aimée, Dennis, unaware of her suicide, inquires facetiously—and according to the narrator, "with high irony" (152)—whether he must also take care of *her* funeral. Inadvertently Dennis has hit upon the truth and thereby foreshadowed his own future actions. But Joyboy, taking his rival's repartee seriously, jumps to the wrong conclusion that Dennis must know of their beloved's death and therefore must have killed her. To alleviate the apprentice's embarrassment at the sight of Joyboy's weeping, Dennis ambiguously explains, "We have here a client who has just lost a little pet" (154). Thus with sardonic humor he teases the apprentice into a literal but erroneous interpretation of "little pet" while taunting Joyboy with the epithet's metaphorical insinuations. The reader, however, soon discovers that Joyboy is less perturbed by the loss of his "loved one" than by fears of professional ruin should her poisoned body be found in his refrigerator.

In the sharply ironic plot structure, the ultimate fates of the three main characters are in extreme contrast to what they might have expected. Joyboy and Aimée could never have anticipated any permanent involvement with the pet cemetery, which they scorn as an inferior imitation of their noble mortuary. Certainly Aimée could never have conceived of her own demeaning end in its crematorium. Joyboy's destiny is a complex of several ironies. His distinguished career in embalming corpses is threatened by the unforeseen appearance of an unwanted corpse; his need to dispose of it secretly puts him at the mercy of his rival in love; and the unending consequence of using the facilities at the Happier Hunting Ground will be annual postcards reading—in the vein of those sent to pet owners—"Your little Aimée is wagging her tail in heaven tonight, thinking of you" (163). Although from the reader's point of view some degree of poetic justice makes the fates of these funereal characters not unsuitable, it is the very lack of justice in Dennis's case that seems inappropriate. What happens to him may be quite different from his expectations, but if he is indeed the fraud and scoundrel that many critics see, then being set free from the phoniness and amorality of Los Angeles is better than he deserves.

The ironic character of *The Loved One* is far more profound, however, than the amusing or shocking disparities provided by the author's technical expertise. Waugh's underlying theme—the falseness of California culture—is inherently ironic because it is based on discrepancies between illusion and reality and because the objects of his greatest displeasure—Angeleno society, the film industry, the mortuary cult—are highly susceptible to self-contradiction. In the novel this duality is sometimes indicated by the narrator, but it is most effectively presented through the thoughts and interactions of the characters in their cultural contexts. Although they are not merely representational symbols, these fictional men and women do embody or espouse various kinds of fraudulence, often abetted by the fakery of institutions. Particularly in the undertaking business and among its patrons, Waugh believed he had found not only an inclination to prefer illusion but an absolute determination to substitute it for reality. As he postulates in "Half in Love with Easeful Death," the tendency to blur the distinction between the living and the dead is accentuated in California by an unusually large number of retirees, who welcome the "preposterous cults" that strive to make the transition from life into death imperceptibly smooth.[7] The desire to obscure painful truth raises deception to a fine art: illusionists at the mortuaries attempt to dispel the fact of corporeal decay by making the body appear more beautiful in death than it was in life and by promoting the idea that everything flawed on earth will be perfected in the next world.

To expose the sham of such unrealistic funeral practices, Waugh in *The Loved One* sets up Whispering Glades as a fictional Forest Lawn, replete with physical beauties and noble sentiments, which he then undermines through discordant juxtapositions. The two inscriptions that Dennis sees when he enters the cemetery through its golden gates to arrange Sir Francis's funeral are in high contrast, both in size and sentiment. The larger one, with foot-high letters cut in marble, describes how the founder, aptly designated The Dreamer, had translated his vision into "*a New Earth sacred to HAP-PINESS*" (39), where not only the dead buried there but also their survivors are assured of eternal bliss. Yet the insignificant wooden board nearby subverts this lofty message by directing clients to the office where costs of such "passports into heaven" may be ascertained. The most striking contrast occurs on Dennis's second visit to the mortuary, when he is shown the results of the mortician's art on Sir Francis. Whereas the embalmer (Joyboy) and the cosmetician (Aimée) are extraordinarily pleased with their handiwork, especially the joyful smile created on the dead man's face, Dennis finds this "painted and smirking" mask of life more gruesome in its unreality than was his friend's hanged and facially disfigured appearance at the time of his suicide (75).

Incongruity characterizes Dennis's initial dealings with the "mortuary hostess," as she shows him coffins and explains burial procedures to the piped-in accompaniment of the "Hindu Love-song" and sounds of nightingales, those immortal birds "not born for death." Her canned speeches are filled with euphemisms that gloss over the real aspects of death: corpses are called "loved ones," dying becomes "passing over," the bereaved survivors are "the waiting ones," and the place for viewing embalmed bodies is "the slumber room." But an occasional slip from what the narrator terms her "high diction"—

such as the inadvertent reference to a "stiff"—betrays her true sentiment beneath the veneered sales pitch. Her attempt to sell Dennis "Before Need Arrangements" is an odd mixture of overblown generalizations, advertising rhetoric, and trite catch phrases—"death is not a private tragedy . . . but the general lot of man. . . . Choose now . . . pay . . . while you are best able . . . shed all anxiety. Pass the buck . . . Whispering Glades can take it" (53).

Through Dennis's acquaintance with the necropolis, Waugh obliquely indicates what he believes to be the essential similarity between the mortuary dream and the products of filmdom. The special resting place reserved for members of the motion-picture colony suggests by its very name—Shadowland—a close philosophical connection with the Hollywood of the moviemakers, which is also portrayed as a dream factory where mere shadows of reality are passed off as the genuine article. At Waugh's fictional studio, Megalopolitan Pictures, illusory fabrications are as prevalent as they are in Whispering Glades. The insubstantiality of the film industry is brought home to Dennis when he discovers that the ostensibly solid structures on movie sets are only propped-up façades. Yet the deception is not just in their flimsiness but in their pretense to be something they are not. That Dennis sees the same element of make-believe in the well-constructed edifices of the memorial park is implied by the juxtaposition of his thoughts on the two industries as he reads Whispering Glades's claim of being *forever* impervious to destruction.

Human concerns in Hollywood are also distorted in the service of mammon. Even the ideas of life, death, and existence have acquired their own peculiar interpretations among members of the film colony who, instead of clouding their meaning as do morticians, define them sharply and narrowly. That span "between the signature of the contract and its expiration" (33) is considered life. What follows may be professional extinction, which for those whose lives have been dedicated to their work is tantamount to death. When Sir Francis hears himself spoken of as "some old Britisher who's just kicked off" (29), he must realize, as does the reader, that from the studio's point of view he has abruptly ceased to exist. Another kind of obliteration may affect performing artists, for the studio does not hesitate to counterfeit the identities of the living, just as the mortuary changes the appearances of the dead. Megalo actress Juanita del Pablo, originally Jewish Baby Aaronson, had earlier been transformed by a nose bob and flamenco singing lessons into a scowling Spanish refugee. She is again being re-born—through dentures, dyed hair, and instruction in the Irish brogue—as a winsome colleen. But during the metamorphosis her agent questions whether she legally exists at all. That the former Juanita is suffering an identity crisis is evident when, at Sir Francis's funeral, she sings "The Wearing of the Green." Not only are the song's anti-British lyrics unsuitable for English mourners; her rendition of the Celtic tune is strangely flamenco.

The narrator's satiric description of the society in which Megalopolitan Pictures and Whispering Glades flourish contains a hodgepodge of incomprehensible illogicalities: stoneless peaches that taste unappetizingly like "damp, sweet cotton-wool" (86); ciga-rettes "prepared by doctors" to protect the respiratory system (118); men's evening wear in such absurd combinations as Mr. Heinkel's "Donegal tweeds, sandals, [and] a grass-green silk shirt" (18); and women so standardized in mien and dress that Dennis considers them nondescript articles "off the assembly-lines ready for imme-diate home-service" (87). Angelenos' disjointed education is repre-sented by Aimée's college curriculum of psychology, beauty culture, art, and Chinese; and their cultural illiteracy is indicated by her admiration for the atrocious art works at Whispering Glades. The superficiality of their social relations is revealed in Sir Francis's observations that these "decent, generous" people "talk entirely for their own pleasure" without expecting anyone to listen (5). His re-marks, though meant as praise, can be seen as inadvertent con-demnation by the reader, who realizes that much in this baffling society defeats the purpose for which it was intended.

In essence, Californians, like the people of Waugh's imaginary Azania, are portrayed as members of a chaotic, heterogeneous soci-ety devoid of meaningful values. Having no history, no roots, and no culture they can call their own, they are, like birds of passage, constantly looking back toward their true homes elsewhere. Even the provision of distinctive burial facilities at Whispering Glades for Americans of Irish, Scottish, and English descent is based on the assumption that each of these groups will be attracted to its an-cestral heritage. Although Americans, in spite of this multinational splintering, seem confident of a national identity, the narrator un-dercuts the validity of their belief when Aimée, whose spirit is definitely *not* Americanized, questions whether Dennis will "*ever make a real American home*" (128) since "*he is British and therefore in many ways quite Un-American*" (102). Waugh was apparently struck by the lack of cohesion and native tradition in the United States, for in a letter to Cyril Connolly explaining what ideas prompted him to write *The Loved One*, he maintained: "There is no such thing as an American. They are all exiles uprooted, transplanted & doomed to sterility."[8] He further declared, in an oblique commentary on his own situation, that European exploiters of America were fortunate if they succeeded in getting their spoils and themselves back home. Though Waugh himself had failed to reach agreement with MGM, he had gained the inchoate materials for another novel. In this context Dennis ultimately realizes that he is "singularly privileged" to get out of Los Angeles with his "artist's load" of experience (163).

Would-be raiders who fail to escape, like Sir Francis Hinsley, are trapped in California's false paradise and become enslaved to it. In his essay "The Man Hollywood Hates" (1947), Waugh similarly asserted that no European could "live in that place of exile and retain the standards of civilization quite unpolluted."[9] To illustrate the corruptive aspects of Hollywood, the narrator in the opening scene of *The Loved One* deceptively presents what initially seems to be an outpost of empire in equatorial Africa. Intense heat, frog voices, palm trees, a "dry water-hole," and "the ever present pulse of music from the neighbouring native huts" set the scene for Englishmen who have been "exiled in the barbarous regions of the world" and at the end of a blistering day relax over drinks for "brief illusory rehabilitation" (3-4). Only gradually does the reader discover, as the narrator relaxes his irony, that the location is not the bush but Sir Francis's bungalow in a once fashionable, now shabby, area of Hollywood. "The dry water-hole" (3), at one time his swimming pool frequented by film beauties, is now "cracked and over-grown with weed" (7)—its deterioration emblematic of its owner's decline. Formerly chief script writer at Megalo and social leader of Hollywood's English community, Sir Francis has been reduced to an almost forgotten employee. His life in America can be seen as classic irony in that the profession to which he devoted all his efforts has largely abandoned him. Even with his career in shambles, however, he tries to convince himself that he does not regret sacrificing his literary potential to Hollywood, but he undercuts his own credibility by strongly advising Dennis to flee from a society inimical to both art and the artist.

Whereas Sir Francis has gambled and lost on Hollywood's acceptance of his talents, Sir Ambrose Abercrombie has succeeded by adapting to the phoniness expected by the film community. His long career in "acrobatic heroic historic" roles has established him as the most distinguished English actor in Hollywood, and in life he directs all his efforts toward maintaining filmland's stereotypical image of the English gentleman. Having unwittingly burlesqued that part on the screen, he now unknowingly caricatures it in reality. Never without his monocle, he dresses in gray flannels, Eton Rambler tie, and boater hat for California's hot weather, and in tweeds, deerstalker cap, and Inverness cape for cooler temperatures. In his relations with other people Sir Ambrose is often self-deluded, especially in assuming that he has successfully deceived or manipulated them. He is not aware that Sir Francis sees through his pretenses of paying a purely social visit to a long-neglected friend; nor does he realize that his attempt to steer Dennis away from a job demeaning to the image of a proper Englishman will have no influence on the free-spirited young poet.

In dealing with Sir Francis's suicide and funeral, Sir Ambrose hypocritically sets out to restore the deceased's damaged reputation not for the sake of his former colleague but in order to keep up the status of the English colony "in the eyes of the industry" (36). Twisting the truth about the cause of Sir Francis's death, he redirects the blame away from the studio and toward Dennis through guilt-by-association reasoning: "Frank lost face," Sir Ambrose explains, "sharing a house with a fellow who worked in the pets' cemetery" (35). Nevertheless, to produce an impressive ceremony he calls on Dennis to write a flattering ode for graveside delivery and to locate (or, if necessary, invent) something from Sir Francis's works. Sir Ambrose himself composes the service, which members of the Cricket Club recite, since, according to the narrator's acerbic observation, "Liturgy in Hollywood is the concern of the Stage rather than of the Clergy" (62). But in trying to manage the press, he is tripped up by Dennis, who, in the process of assigning seats in the church, adds his own touch of irony to the obsequies by giving the private, curtained pew, ordinarily reserved for the deceased's family, to the gossip columnists.

Aimée Thanatogenos, whom Dennis meets while making arrangements for Sir Francis's funeral, is constituted of so many paradoxes that she virtually cancels herself out before she actually does so. Her name, which suggests a loved one born of death, indicates opposing forces in her personality; and her appearance is presented in contradictory terms. The narrator describes a profile that is "pure and classical" but eyes that are "remote, with a rich glint of lunacy" (55), while Dennis's reference to her "exquisite dim head" (142) adds the inference of limited intellect beneath exterior beauty. Strangest of all is what goes on in Aimée's mind, for she has developed an extreme fascination with the concept of poetry and transferred it incongruously to her job as a mortuary cosmetician. Actually knowing little about poetry and having no acquaintance with live poets before meeting Dennis, Aimée nevertheless claims to have learned "soul" from studying the corpse of a poetess, and she believes her own work to be "poetic." Her delusions about poetry and its connection with death make her highly susceptible to Dennis's amorous, melancholy verses until she is scandalized by the discovery that they are plagiarized. But her absorption in the mortuary dream prevents her from seeing that Joyboy's messages of love are also based on deception, for she cannot comprehend the contradiction in making the dead assume the emotions of the living.

Though virtually making a cult of Whispering Glades, Aimée is not fully aware of the divinity she worships or the end to which such devotion may lead. Her morbid "religion" proves so deficient, however, in offering spiritual strength for the problems of life that at the time of her amatory dilemma she turns for advice to the fraudulent Guru Brahmin. But neither her dizzying oscillation between lovers nor the Guru's final suggestion to jump off a tall building is by itself the determining factor in her suicide. Her cosmetic work on the dead, accompanied by depression over its ephemerality, has already oriented her toward death; and as the appeal of Eros diminishes, the call of Thanatos proves so irresistible that she rejects both suitors in favor of "the deity she [serves]" (150). In presenting Aimée's last thoughts as a communion with the spirits of Hellenic forebears, the narrator not only emphasizes her essentially Greek soul, alien and adrift in southern California despite her assumption of being American, but sets up an oblique analogy between Aimée and heroines of antiquity who chose death as the best possible solution to their earthly problems. The clinching irony in this comparison is that, unlike Iphigenia, Alcestis, and Antigone, Aimée does not martyr herself in behalf of some noble cause; rather, as a burlesque of the tragic heroine, she ends her life because it is empty and purposeless.

The comedy engendered by Joyboy arises primarily from the irreconcilable differences between his lofty importance as an embalmer and the reader's revulsion toward both the man and his ghoulish achievements. His extraordinary abilities are corroborated, if somewhat questionably, from four points of view—the narrator's mock encomiums of his genius, Aimée's worshipful admiration, his international reputation among morticians, and his own inflated self-concept. At Whispering Glades, as he moves smoothly between the quick and the dead, he is considered "a figure of romance" among the female cosmeticians (99). On the worldwide scene Joyboy is so distinguished that his engagement to Aimée receives extensive coverage in the best professional journals. His expertise is so phenomenal that he can restore even mutilated corpses to living beauty, but the specialty he enjoys most is creating "the Radiant Childhood smile" on the faces of dead children (68). His skill in molding expressions that reflect the deceased's personality goes awry, however, when he substitutes his own feelings of joy or sadness about his romance with Aimée on the "loved ones" destined for her cosmetic finishing. In a scene that parodies the meeting of Shelley's Urania and Death over the body of Adonais, Joyboy first appears in the novel delivering to Aimée the body of a radiantly smiling Sir Francis.

Joyboy's prestige is partly undermined by the narrator, who often subverts his own praise with detracting images or jarring words. He casts a shadow over the senior mortician's superiority merely by showing him "sucking a digestive lozenge" after lunch in the mortuary canteen (107). In stating that Joyboy's "photograph . . . had appeared in *Time* magazine," the narrator slyly diminishes the fame he pretends to substantiate by interjecting a reference to the picture's "ribald caption" (67). While he extols Joyboy as an embodiment of "moral earnestness" and "the perfection of high professional manners," his insistence on the unimportance of the man's "physical defects" tends rather to emphasize them (66-67). In likening the embalmer's debonair work on a corpse to the finesse of a sentimental Victorian hero, he uses such an inappropriate tone of high seriousness that the analogy collapses under its own weight.

Joyboy is discredited with less obliquity through unfolding events. The wide discrepancy between his public glamor and private drabness is revealed by Aimée's visit to his shabby bungalow in a run-down neighborhood. While she expects his domestic life to reflect his exalted professional status, as do his clothes and car, she learns that he spends money only where it can enhance his success. Most disillusioning is her discovery that Joyboy is dominated by a rude, vulgar mother, who has psychologically castrated him. At the end of the novel he is thoroughly debased by his willingness to conceal Aimée's death in order to save his reputation *and* his "Mom."

Like Aimée and Joyboy, Dennis is torn by the rival claims of death and love only to discover that in his case the two are working in tandem. Whereas in Henry James's classic situations the ingenuous American leaves home to acquire European sophistication, Dennis, a cynical Englishman, comes to the land of childlike innocence to acquire experience that will make him a better poet. His muse, whose melancholy promptings have already directed him to Keats and Shelley, now leads him through work on a film life of Shelley to a pet cemetery and ultimately to Whispering Glades, which, like Keats's "belle Dame," holds "him in thrall" (79). Although Dennis's love for a priestess in this temple of the dead might seem to divert him from the muse's objective—the understanding of death itself—the exact opposite occurs. The tragedy of Aimée's unexpected demise contributes ironically to the deepening of his knowledge and even liberates him from artistic doom.

Dennis's journey to the Lake Island of Innisfree serves as a burlesque allegory of his quest for inspiration in a habitat where death and love are deliciously confused, where the dead become the "loved ones." The boatman, a Charon figure who ferries Dennis across the water into this sepulchral realm, undercuts its enchantment with his realistic observations. He shatters the picturesque associations with Yeats's poem by revealing that mechanical devices have replaced real bees and beehives; and he disturbingly links poetry with price in calling this most expensive area in Whispering Glades "the poeticest place in the whole darn park" (82). His most depreciatory remarks concern the popular use of the island not by the wealthy dead for whom it was intended but by the amorous living—"Paolos and Francescas" looking for a secluded spot to consummate their lust. Further diminishing the romantic vision, he likens the lecherous couples to cemetery cats seeking privacy to accomplish their business. In this haven for lovers, Dennis seems strangely out of place, for he goes there alone to find an appropriate place to compose his elegiac poem on Sir Francis. There love quite unexpectedly appears to him in the guise of Aimée, whose endorsement of the death-wish passage in "Ode to a Nightingale" confirms the association of love and death in poetic art.

Because Waugh portrays Dennis with a whimsical humor that diminishes his faults as well as his virtues, it is possible to interpret his character in different ways. Dennis can be considered a callous adventurer bent on his own welfare, a "comic rogue," or "another hollow man" incapable of genuine feeling.[10] His seeming lack of concern for Sir Francis, his sudden interest in marriage when Aimée's income appears sufficient to support him, his plagiarizing, his reasons for becoming a nonsectarian minister, his extortion of money from Joyboy, and his cavalier incineration of his fiancée while reciting verses that identify her as the means of first-class passage to England—all suggest a person of dubious ethics. However, Dennis can also be viewed as a serious literary artist, who, in order to fulfill the poet's quest, must remain somewhat detached from the painful experiences necessary to his maturation.[11] His rational acceptance of Sir Francis's death, his imperturbability in storing his supper among the cadavers in the mortuary refrigerator and eating it while on duty, his shrewd manipulation of Aimée, Joyboy, and Sir Ambrose, and his decisively efficient handling of the crisis brought on by Aimée's death—all indicate a sensible temperament well suited to the preeminent demands of the muse. Whether a man with such contradictory qualities, even after personal acquaintance with tragedy, will ever create literature of enduring value is problematic. But in any case this mock-heroic depiction of Dennis suggests that he is meant to be a burlesque of the true poet and that his quest is a parody of the traditional one.

While Waugh allowed his narrator to present with detached amusement the black humor of a graveyard poet, the elegant vulgarities of a necropolis, and the absurdities of Hollywood, the author could not lightheartedly accept the various travesties of religion that he encountered in southern California. At these he strikes with the directness and sharpness of satire, which leaves no doubt concerning the response that is expected from the reader. In order to discredit that superficial, pseudo-exotic brand of eastern philosophy popular among those lacking serious religious affiliation, Waugh presents the Guru Brahmin, who serves as "spiritual director" (100) for readers of his daily newspaper column although he is himself as phony as the "solace and solution" he dispenses. Unmasked, he is revealed to be not the bearded, half-naked sage of the accompanying photograph but rather a composite of three collaborators—a man who writes the column, another who replies to readers' correspondence, and a secretary. The letter-answering component, far from providing Aimée with sympathetic counseling, offers her platitudinous pieties or inappropriate congratulations in a standard form letter. At the time of her greatest need, when he himself is depressed as well as drunk, his flippant recommendation of suicide affords her the worst possible guidance.

Coming under Waugh's fire are also some basically Christian organizations that from his point of view promote unorthodox beliefs. Briefly mentioned, only to be demolished, is the New Thought movement, which originated in New England during the nineteenth century and influenced such notables as Mary Baker Eddy, Ralph Waldo Emerson, and other transcendentalists with its emphasis on the power of mind over matter. Waugh carries its tenets to a ridiculous extreme when Aimée says that her mother "took to New Thought" and refused to believe "there was such a thing as death" (93). Another specific organization—the Los Angeles-based Church of the Four Square Gospel founded by evangelist Aimée Semple McPherson—is introduced and disparaged as the investment scheme through which Aimée Thanatogenos's father lost all his money. The nonsectarian ministry is glaringly derided in the obsequies for an Alsatian dog at the Happier Hunting Ground, where animals are assured of passage into heaven. As the coffin is lowered into a flower-lined grave, the Rev. Bartholomew debases a familiar passage from Job by adapting it to the canine species: "Dog that is born of bitch hath but a short time to live" (122). The profession stands even more condemned when Bartholomew unlocks for Dennis the knowledge of how to become a minister himself and thereby elevate his status in a materialistic society. Initially one needs only "the Call," correspondence courses, and a bank loan; then will come buildings, a radio congregation, wealth, and prestige. While advising Dennis where the most money is to be made, Bartholomew paradoxically laments that some recent nonsectarians are so competitive as to engage in practices for which there is no "scriptural authority" (123).

For the mortuary cult Waugh reserved his most devastating satirical irony, portraying his fictional cemetery as a full-blown religious institution, complete with its own theology, scripture, hierarchy, aesthetic appeal, and the capability of granting eternal bliss to its occupants. Even the terminology used by the narrator and the characters in connection with this extraordinary place is drawn from the ethos of religion. Aimée, who believes that Whispering Glades exists to make death painless and beautiful, as in

Keats's "Ode to a Nightingale," considers her job there to be "a work of consolation" (94), which she is said to perform "like a nun, intently, serenely" (69). Mr. Joyboy, whom she regards as "the sole sun of the mortuary" (111) and describes as "kinda holy" (95), claims to be "inspired" by "something higher" (71-72). And the artfully restored corpses they prepare are said to be "transfigured" (93, 95). Certainly Joyboy seems convinced of the holiness of their calling when he pompously informs Aimée that, through his intercession with the founder of the memorial park, she will become its first female embalmer.

Dennis, who shares their vocation at an institution of lesser repute, is aware that the professional language used at the pet cemetery is derived from the "high pure source" of the "great necropolis" (38); and when he first drives through its golden gates, the narrator ironically likens him to "a missionary priest making his first pilgrimage to the Vatican" (38). Dennis also realizes that Aimée—who looks upon Whispering Glades as "the most wonderful thing outside heaven" (142) and on the Happier Hunting Ground's attempts to emulate it as "kinda blasphemous" (95)—has made a surrogate church of her own place of employment. By reminding her that at the Lovers' Nook she swore to love him "with the most sacred oath in the religion of Whispering Glades" (143), he takes advantage of her belief in its sanctity. By calling her "the nautch girl and vestal virgin of the place," while dubbing Joyboy "the incarnate spirit" and the "mediating logos" between the founder-creator and "common humanity" (143), he expands the religious analogy to such an extreme of metaphorical praise that the whole institution is reduced to blasphemy.

Of all the illusions that Waugh subjected to satiric irony in *The Loved One*, the distortions and pretensions he found at Forest Lawn seem to have disturbed him the most. Because the mortuary cult in the United States had wrapped itself in religious trappings, especially those of Christianity, but had ignored genuine Christian precepts, he saw it as a serious heretical threat to what he believed. By glorifying and preserving the body, it glossed over the fact of mortal decay. By disguising death as an entrance into immediate happiness, it obliterated the possibility of purgatory and hell. By suggesting that the departed dwell perpetually in an Eden of innocent childhood, it sanctified the American cult of youth, which, in shielding the young from the reality of evil, eliminated their need to assume moral responsibility.[12] This deliberate confusion of life and death, good and evil, salvation and damnation could so negate the consequences of ethical choice that those deluded by the mortuary dream would be unable to lead truly Christian lives.

However bizarre such "tribal" beliefs and customs may have seemed to Waugh, he could not toss them off lightly as the idiosyncrasies of some remote, inconsequential people, as he might have done in earlier travel accounts, because the United States had recently established itself as the dominant international power. At a time when western Europe was obliged to look toward the United States with a mixture of gratitude, hope, and resentment, many aspects of American popular culture, nowhere more flagrantly exemplified than in southern California, filled traditionalists with consternation. European intellectuals were more than a little apprehensive of American leadership and quite fearful lest the whole world become Americanized. The extraordinary interest accorded Geoffrey Gorer's book *American People: A Study in National Character* (1948) testifies to the desire of Englishmen to understand the peculiarities of American society from a cultural anthropologist's perspective, even though English readers were dismayed to think that American mores might shape their future. Waugh, in his essay "The American Epoch in the Catholic Church" (1949), cites Gorer's account not only because he is interested in the transatlantic impact on European cultural traditions but because he is concerned with what American hegemony will mean for Roman Catholicism as a universal church.[13] The prospect that a whole culture might succumb to the deceptive lure of a mortuary cult must not have seemed impossible to Waugh since he found himself so strangely fascinated by the "great necropolis" in Los Angeles that he repeatedly visited it, confessed to being "entirely obsessed" by it, and later gave as the first reason for writing *The Loved One* "quite predominantly over-excitement with the scene of Forest Lawn."[14] If he, a devout, thoughtful Catholic, could be temporarily seduced while clearly perceiving that the art and doctrine beneath its neo-Christian façade were directed not toward God but toward pagan materialism, it should not be surprising that he had grave fears for the rest of humanity.

Afterword

EVELYN WAUGH ATTRACTS such a diversity of admirers—from those
who regard him as a brilliant entertainer to those who read him for
religious enlightenment—that his appeal cannot be accounted for
on the basis of any single attribute in his writing. Evidently there
are many qualities in his carefully wrought works that have the
power to engage a wide audience. Surely a major reason for the
continuing popularity of his novels is his ironic approach, which
enabled him to represent the instabilities he had encountered in a
manner highly congenial to twentieth-century readers. His fictional presentation of a world not static but in a constant state of
flux reflects the disorder, ambiguities, dualities, and contradictions
familiar to modern men and women; and even those with strong
religious convictions, finding it difficult to "justify the ways of God
to men" amid the chaos and unpredictability of their environment,
can relate to an ironic depiction. Having been seriously shaken by
the aftermaths of two world wars and a severe depression, present-
day society tends to question, as did Waugh, many of the assumptions held inviolable in the nineteenth century.

Since modern readers, in dealing with the confusions of their
age, are more open than their predecessors to the coexistence of
conflicting ideas, they are likely to find Waugh's irony compatible
with their own modes of thinking. Their belief in tolerance encourages the expression of all viewpoints, including those contrary to
their own; and Freudian acknowledgment of the unconscious as
well as the conscious further conditions them to hold contradictory

truths in suspension without necessarily labeling any as false. Instead of espousing a single norm as correct for a fragmented society, modern readers can more readily countenance a multiplicity of values, recognizing that no one panacea for the plight of humanity can be acceptable to everyone. Therefore, in trying to cope with increasingly complex social problems, they frequently reject facile or dogmatic solutions in favor of tentative remedies, realizing that no corrective measure, however efficacious at the moment, will be applicable indefinitely. In attempting to sway opinion or effect change, they often find irony's indirect approach more persuasive than satire's frontal attack, which presupposes unrealistically fixed standards of judgment and is more easily brushed aside as irrelevant or offensive by those against whom it is aimed. In all these respects, their acceptance of practical realism—which encourages objectivity rather than subjectivity and emphasizes concrete thought rather than abstractions—is definitely in tune with an ironic perspective.

In the literary realm, the use of irony, which is more prevalent in the writings of the twentieth century than in those of earlier, more stable times, has distinct advantages for both authors and readers, for it infuses a sophistication that allows works to be read on more than one level. Waugh's novels, like *Gulliver's Travels*, can simply be enjoyed on a superficial plane for their intriguing characters, bizarre situations, and fast-moving style. But on a deeper level Waugh's ability, like Swift's, to convey enlightening ideas without explicitly stating them brings additional gratification to those who, by rereading and reflecting on what may lie beneath the surface, discover nuances and artistry undetected on first acquaintance. The subtleties of irony, in fact, lead inquisitive readers to participate, through the free play of their mental acuity, in decoding the author's latent or obliquely presented thoughts.

In several respects, therefore, Waugh's ironic stance is a significant factor in creating the unique and enduring character of his much-read novels. By enabling him to combine extraordinary humor with philosophical insight—uniting the *dulce* with the *utile* in a seemingly incompatible but very effective mixture—irony functions as leavening for these lively twentieth-century masterworks.

Notes

Introduction

1. Wayne C. Booth, *A Rhetoric of Irony* (Chicago: Univ. of Chicago Pr., 1974), ix.

2. Douglas C. Muecke, *The Compass of Irony* (London: Methuen, 1969), 5.

3. Muecke, *Compass of Irony*, 115.

Chapter 1: Irony as Waugh's Perspective and Method

1. Hayden White has argued that Foucault was working within the tradition of the four rhetorical tropes and that "for Foucault, the human sciences of the twentieth century are characterizable precisely by the *Ironic* relationship which they sustain with their objects" ("Foucault Decoded: Notes from Underground," in *Tropics of Discourse: Essays in Cultural Criticism* [Baltimore: Johns Hopkins Univ. Pr., 1978], 255).

2. Christopher Sykes, *Evelyn Waugh: A Biography* (Boston: Little, 1975), 43.

3. Nancy Mitford's letter of 18 June 1969 to Jeffrey Heath, *Evelyn Waugh Newsletter* 7 (Spring 1973): 9.

4. Anthony Powell, *Messengers of Day* (London: Heinemann, 1978), 131.

5. Waugh to Cyril Connolly, 11 Dec. 1947, *The Letters of Evelyn Waugh*, ed. Mark Amory (New Haven: Ticknor, 1980), 262; hereafter cited as *Letters*.

6. Evelyn Waugh, *A Little Learning* (London: Methuen, 1964), 122.

7. Waugh, *Little Learning*, 129.

8. Christopher Hollis, *The Oxford Union* (London: Evans, 1965), 165.

9. Hollis, *Oxford Union*, 166.

10. Waugh, *Little Learning*, 186.

11. Waugh, *Little Learning*, 182.

12. *Conversion* has been published in *Evelyn Waugh, Apprentice: The Early Writings, 1910-1927*, ed. Robert Murray Davis (Norman, Okla.: Pilgrim, 1985), 94-115.

13. *The Balance* has been reprinted in *Evelyn Waugh, Apprentice,* 155-85.

14. Robert Murray Davis, "Evelyn Waugh's Early Work: The Formation of a Method," *Texas Studies in Literature and Language* 7 (1965): 97-108. For additional commentary on the impact of film techniques on Waugh's fiction, see George McCartney, *Confused Roaring: Evelyn Waugh and the Modernist Tradition* (Bloomington: Indiana Univ. Pr., 1987), 99-135.

15. A critic for the *Daily Express* (13 Feb. 1929, 19) pronounced Firbank to be Waugh's "most direct literary ancestor." Late in life Waugh conceded that he "began under the brief influence of Ronald Firbank but struck out for" himself (preface to the second uniform edition of *Vile Bodies* [London: Chapman, 1965], 7).

16. See Waugh, "Ronald Firbank," *Life and Letters,* Mar. 1929; repr. in *The Essays, Articles and Reviews of Evelyn Waugh,* ed. Donat Gallagher (London: Methuen, 1983), 56-59, hereafter cited as *Essays*; Robert Murray Davis, "Evelyn Waugh on the Art of Fiction," *Papers on Language and Literature* 2 (1966): 243-52; and James F. Carens, *The Satiric Art of Evelyn Waugh* (Seattle: Univ. of Washington Pr., 1966), 5-10.

17. Waugh, "Ronald Firbank," in *Essays,* 57.

18. Ronald Firbank, *Cardinal Pirelli,* in *The Complete Ronald Firbank* (London: Duckworth, 1961), 688.

19. Waugh to Anthony Powell, 7 Apr. 1928, *Letters,* 27. The original manuscript title was "Picaresque: or the Making of an Englishman." See Martin Stannard, *Evelyn Waugh: The Early Years 1903-1939* (London: Dent, 1986), 148.

20. See Robert Byron, *The Byzantine Achievement* (London: Routledge, 1929), 19. Waugh's library, now at the University of Texas, contains a copy of Gibbon's *Decline and Fall.*

21. Waugh, "Felo de Se," *Spectator,* 15 Apr. 1938; repr. in *Essays,* 224.

22. Waugh, *Helena* (London: Chapman, 1950), 122. Waugh again stressed the impressiveness of Gibbon's prose, despite his erroneous judgments, in "Literary Style in England and America," *Books on Trial,* Oct. 1955; repr. in *Essays,* 477-81.

23. *The Autobiographies of Edward Gibbon,* ed. John Murray (London: Murray, 1896), 143.

24. Waugh, *Tourist in Africa* (Boston: Little, 1960), 12.

25. For a view of Waugh's travel books as "moral entertainments," see Paul Fussell, *Abroad: British Literary Traveling Between the Wars* (New York: Oxford Univ. Pr., 1980), 171-202.

26. Waugh, *Remote People* (London: Duckworth, 1931), 51.

27. Waugh diary entry, 29 Aug. 1943, *The Diaries of Evelyn Waugh,* ed. Michael Davie (Boston: Little, 1976), 548; hereafter cited as *Diaries.*

28. On Waugh's role-playing, see Powell, *Messengers of Day*, 20; Dudley Carew, *A Fragment of Friendship* (London: Everest, 1974), 15; Harold Acton, *More Memoirs of an Aesthete* (London: Methuen, 1970), 318.

29. Waugh, *The Ordeal of Gilbert Pinfold* (Boston: Little, 1957), 13.

30. Jeffrey Heath, *The Picturesque Prison: Evelyn Waugh and His Writing* (Kingston: McGill-Queen's Univ. Pr., 1982), 54.

31. Alan Pryce-Jones, "Escape from Golders Green," in *Evelyn Waugh and His World*, ed. David Pryce-Jones (Boston: Little, 1973), 13-14.

32. Waugh, "What to Do with the Upper Classes: A Modest Proposal," *Town and Country*, Sept. 1946; repr. in *Essays*, 312-16. For Waugh's straightforward, nonironic attack on socialist theory, see his "Palinurus in Never-Never Land; or, the *Horizon* Blue-Print of Chaos," *Tablet*, 27 July 1946; repr. in *Essays*, 309-12.

33. Waugh, "What to Do with the Upper Classes," in *Essays*, 315. Subsequent quotations from this essay are cited parenthetically in the text.

34. Waugh, *Love Among the Ruins: A Romance of the Near Future* (London: Chapman, 1953), 8, 10, 4. Subsequent quotations from this edition of the novel are cited parenthetically in the text.

35. This review was first published as "The Heart's Own Reasons," *Commonweal*, 17 Aug. 1951; as "The Point of Departure," *Month*, 6 Sept. 1951; repr. in *Essays*, 404-6.

36. Waugh, "Scenes of Clerical Life," *Commonweal* 63 (30 Mar. 1956): 667.

37. Waugh, "Fan-Fare," *Life*, 8 Apr. 1946; repr. in *Essays*, 303-4.

38. Waugh, "Ronald Firbank," in *Essays*, 59.

39. Waugh gave his father a copy of Knox's *Essays in Satire* in 1935; the inscribed copy later reverted to Waugh and is now at the University of Texas. In his biography of Knox (1959) he alludes to the *Essays* several times.

40. Ronald A. Knox, *Essays in Satire* (London: Sheed, 1928), 31, 37.

41. R. A. Knox, *Essays*, 31.

42. R. A. Knox, *Essays*, 31.

43. Waugh, "Turning over New Leaves," *Vogue* (London), 17 Oct. 1928; repr. in *Essays*, 41.

44. Waugh, "Satire and Fiction," *Graphic*, 25 Oct. 1930; repr. in *Essays*, 102.

45. Waugh's introduction to *The Unbearable Bassington*, by H. H. Munro (London: Eyre, 1947); repr. in *Essays*, 324.

46. Frederick J. Stopp, *Evelyn Waugh: Portrait of an Artist* (London: Chapman, 1958), 190.

47. Stopp, *Evelyn Waugh*, 195.

48. Malcolm Bradbury, *Evelyn Waugh* (Edinburgh: Oliver, 1964), 5.

49. Bradbury, *Evelyn Waugh*, 15.

50. McCartney, *Confused Roaring*, 2.

51. Carens, *Satiric Art*, xi-xii, 57-67.

52. Heath, *Picturesque Prison*, 56-58.

53. A number of critics have claimed that Waugh's essentially Catholic morality can be detected from the beginning of his career. See especially A. A. De Vitis, *Roman Holiday: The Catholic Novels of Evelyn Waugh* (New York: Bookman, 1956), 19-39.

54. James W. Nichols, "Romantic *and* Realistic: The Tone of Evelyn Waugh's Early Novels," *College English* 24 (1962-63): 46-56.

55. William J. Cook, Jr., *Masks, Modes, and Morals: The Art of Evelyn Waugh* (Rutherford, N.J.: Fairleigh Dickinson Univ. Pr., 1971), 45-46.

56. Daniel James Machon, "The Failure of the Ironic Mask: Irony as Vision and Technique in the Early Novels of Evelyn Waugh," Ph.D. diss., Temple University, 1975.

57. Ian Littlewood, *The Writings of Evelyn Waugh* (Totowa, N.J.: Barnes, 1983).

58. Robert R. Garnett, *From Grimes to Brideshead: The Early Novels of Evelyn Waugh* (Lewisburg, Pa.: Bucknell Univ. Pr., 1990).

59. Garnett, *From Grimes to Brideshead*, 24-26.

60. Northrop Frye, *Anatomy of Criticism: Four Essays* (Princeton: Princeton Univ. Pr., 1957), 223.

61. Frye, *Anatomy*, 40.

62. Morton L. Gurewitch, "European Romantic Irony," Ph.D. diss., University of Michigan, 1957, 13; quoted in Muecke's *Compass of Irony*, 27; and in Booth's *Rhetoric of Irony*, 92.

63. Booth, *Rhetoric of Irony*, ix.

64. *The Letters of John Keats, 1814-1821*, ed. Hyder E. Rollins, 2 vols. (Cambridge: Harvard Univ. Pr., 1958), 1:387.

65. For Ernest Oldmeadow's misreading of *Black Mischief*, see the *Tablet*, 21 Jan. 1933, 85; repr. in *Evelyn Waugh: The Critical Heritage*, ed. Martin Stannard (London: Routledge, 1984), 133. See also Stannard, *Evelyn Waugh: Early Years*, 336, 342, 382.

Chapter 2: *Decline and Fall*

1. Jerome Meckier considers the novel to be an attack on the Bildungsroman. See his "Cycle, Symbol, and Parody in Evelyn Waugh's *Decline and Fall*," *Contemporary Literature*, 20 (1979): 51-75.

2. Muecke identifies romantic irony primarily with the contradictions of art and relates it to general irony—awareness of the ineluctable contradictions of life. See *Compass of Irony*, 159-215. The breaking and remaking of artistic illusion is especially associated with the German writers Ludwig Tieck and Jean Paul Richter, as well as the English poets Coleridge and Byron.

3. Philosophical discussion about reality versus illusion or appearance, stimulated by the writings of F. H. Bradley, continued to be in vogue at the time *Decline and Fall* was composed.

4. Waugh, *Decline and Fall* (1928; reprint, Boston: Little, 1977), 164. Subsequent quotations from this edition of the novel are cited parenthetically in the text.

5. W. B. Yeats, "The Second Coming," lines 3-4.

6. Waugh, *Little Learning*, 169, 171.

7. Muecke, *Compass of Irony*, 102.

8. Henri Bergson, *Laughter*, trans. Cloudesley Brereton and Fred Rothwell (New York: Macmillan, 1914), 29. Waugh's *Letters* (3) and *Diaries* (215, 218) establish his reading of Bergson, which he began at Lancing. Stannard (*Evelyn Waugh: Early Years*) and McCartney (*Confused Roaring*) have discussed Bergsonian philosophy in Waugh's writing but have not mentioned the essay *Laughter*.

Chapter 3: *Vile Bodies*

1. Waugh, *Vile Bodies* (1930; reprint, Boston: Little, 1977), 284. Subsequent quotations from this edition of the novel are cited parenthetically in the text.

2. As Waugh told Christopher Sykes, the frequent rain was "one of the technical devices he had used to give the book its dark character." See Sykes, *Evelyn Waugh*, 99.

3. In Norman D. Knox's analysis, the basic kinds of irony vary according to three aspects: the observers' concept of reality, their attitude toward the victim, and the fate of the victim. In ironies where reality reflects the values of author and/or reader, the *comic* variety results in the *triumph* of a *sympathetic* victim while the *satiric* results in the *defeat* of an *unsympathetic* victim. Where reality is hostile to human values and defeat is inevitable, *sympathy* with the *tragic* victim predominates while in *nihilistic* irony *detachment* dominates sympathy. Between these two main categories Knox places the *paradoxical* variety in which the values are relative and the norms shift. See N. D. Knox, "Irony," in *Dictionary of the History of Ideas*, ed. Philip P. Wiener (New York: Scribner, 1973-74), 2:627.

4. Waugh, "The War and the Younger Generation," *Spectator*, 13 Apr. 1929; repr. in *Essays*, 61-63.

5. Waugh, "Too Young at Forty," *Evening Standard*, 22 Jan. 1929; repr. in *Essays*, 46.

6. Stannard dates the turning point in Waugh's attitude about mid-April 1929, after the Mediterranean cruise, when his first wife became increasingly involved in that social set while he withdrew to write *Vile Bodies* (*Evelyn Waugh: Early Years*, 177-85).

7. In his preface to the second uniform edition (1965), Waugh acknowledged: "The composition of *Vile Bodies* was interrupted by a sharp disturbance in my private life and was finished in a very different mood from that in which it was begun. The reader may . . . notice the transition from gaiety to bitterness" (7).

8. Waugh, "Max Beerbohm," *Sunday Times*, 27 May 1956; *Atlantic*, Sept. 1956; repr. in *Essays*, 517-18.

9. See Davis, "Evelyn Waugh's Early Work," 104.

10. The name Rothschild might in itself be considered paradoxical for a Jesuit priest.

11. Sykes challenged Waugh concerning the logic of this passage and records the author's concession that it is "very silly" (*Evelyn Waugh*, 99).

12. Waugh knew that Rosa Lewis, Lottie's prototype, provided even more services than he dared include in *Vile Bodies*. See his two interesting missives of July-Aug. 1962 to Daphne Fielding, who was then writing *The Duchess of Jermyn Street* (*Letters*, 589-90).

13. Booth, *Rhetoric of Irony*, 240-50. See also Muecke, *Compass of Irony*, 119-33 on "general irony," a state in which all life is beset by inexplicable contradictions; and N. D. Knox, "Irony," in *Dictionary of the History of Ideas* 2:627 on "nihilistic irony."

Chapter 4: *Black Mischief*

1. See Waugh, *Ninety-Two Days* (London: Duckworth, 1934), 13.

2. See Ernest Oldmeadow's editorials in the *Tablet* for 7 Jan., 21 Jan., and 18 Feb. 1933; repr. in Stannard, *Evelyn Waugh: Critical Heritage*, 132-40.

3. Waugh, *Black Mischief* (1932; reprint, Boston: Little, 1977), 155. Subsequent quotations from this edition of the novel are cited parenthetically in the text.

4. Waugh to the Cardinal of Westminster, May 1933, *Letters*, 77.

5. Waugh, *Robbery Under Law: The Mexican Object-Lesson* (London: Chapman, 1939), 279.

6. For the peculiar affinity between rogue and dandy, especially as it applies to Basil Seal and Ambrose Silk in *Put Out More Flags*, see Martin B. Green, *Children of the Sun: A Narrative of "Decadence" in England after 1918* (New York: Basic, 1976), 12-13.

7. Muecke, *Compass of Irony*, 113.

8. For a different slant on the conclusion, which asserts that *Black Mischief* and *Scoop* are "based largely on a sly appeal to the white man's sense of racial superiority," see Conor Cruise O'Brien [Donat O'Donnell], "The Pieties of Evelyn Waugh," in *Maria Cross* (New York: Oxford Univ. Pr., 1952), 122.

Chapter 5: *A Handful of Dust*

1. Waugh to Katharine Asquith, Jan. 1934, *Letters*, 84.
2. Waugh to Henry Yorke, Sept. 1934, *Letters*, 88.
3. For Waugh's early attempt to be cavalier about Teresa's refusal, see his letter of October 1933 (?) to Lady Mary Lygon (*Letters*, 81). See also Stannard, *Evelyn Waugh: Early Years*, 298-300, 353, 356.
4. Waugh to Henry Yorke, Sept. 1934, *Letters*, 88.
5. Robert Murray Davis, *Evelyn Waugh, Writer* (Norman, Okla.: Pilgrim, 1981), 69-86.
6. Waugh diary entries, 27 Feb. 1933, 4 Mar. 1933, 29-31 Mar. 1933, 16 Aug. 1936, *Diaries*, 374-75, 383, 398. After reading *Dombey and Son* in Dubrovnik, Waugh pronounced it "the worst book in the world" (Waugh to Laura Waugh, 23 Jan. 1945, *Letters*, 198).
7. Waugh diary entry, 24 Aug. 1920, *Diaries*, 97-98.
8. For an interpretation of *A Handful of Dust* as an attack on Victorian society, architecture, literature, and religion, see Richard Wasson, "*A Handful of Dust*: Critique of Victorianism," *Modern Fiction Studies* 7 (1961-62): 327-37. Jerome Meckier, emphasizing Dickens as a satiric symbol, argues that *A Handful of Dust* satirizes "the idea that one can make a substitute religion out of Dickens" ("Why the Man Who Liked Dickens Reads Dickens Instead of Conrad: Waugh's *A Handful of Dust*," *Novel*, 13 [1979-80]: 172). Robert Garnett claims that "Waugh's attitude toward Dickens" was "ambivalent in a filial way, both admiring and occasionally rebellious" (*From Grimes to Brideshead*, 171).
9. Waugh, "Fan-Fare," in *Essays*, 303.
10. Frye, *Anatomy*, 48.
11. Carens, *Satiric Art*, 81-86.
12. See Waugh's preface to the new uniform edition of *A Handful of Dust* (London: Chapman, 1964), 7.
13. Sykes, *Evelyn Waugh*, 139.
14. "Alternative Ending" in the new uniform edition of *A Handful of Dust* (1964), 261. Subsequent quotations from this edition of the novel are cited parenthetically in the text.
15. Waugh was evidently proud of this superbly ironic conclusion, for he chose to reprint it as "By Special Request" in *Mr. Loveday's Little Outing and Other Sad Stories* (1936), as well as to append it to the 1964 edition of *A Handful of Dust*.
16. Several critics have commented on Waugh's interest in Spengler, which Stannard believes began at Oxford. See Robert Murray Davis, "The Mind and Art of Evelyn Waugh," *Papers on Language and Literature* 3 (1967): 272; Stannard, *Evelyn Waugh: Early Years*, 167, 170, 201, 211; and McCartney, *Confused Roaring*, 17-20.
17. Waugh's preface to the new uniform edition of *A Handful of Dust* (1964), 7.

18. Waugh, *Rossetti: His Life and Works* (London: Duckworth, 1928), 52.

19. Waugh, *Rossetti*, 28-29.

20. Waugh to Tom Driberg, Sept. 1934, *Letters*, 88.

21. Waugh, *A Handful of Dust* (1934; reprint, Boston: Little, 1977), 209. Subsequent quotations from this edition of the novel are cited parenthetically in the text.

22. Waugh, "Fan-Fare," in *Essays*, 304.

23. For similar apprehensions about secular humanism, see T. S. Eliot, "The Humanism of Irving Babbitt" (1927) and "Second Thoughts about Humanism" (1928), in *Selected Essays 1917-1932* (New York: Harcourt, 1932), 383-402. T. E. Hulme regarded romanticism as one of the worst heresies of the humanist tradition.

24. Alec Waugh, *My Brother Evelyn & Other Profiles* (London: Cassell, 1967), 191-92. For John Henry Cardinal Newman's commentary on the dangers of religious liberalism, see Note A, "Liberalism," in *Apologia Pro Vita Sua*.

25. For incisive comments on Waugh's practice of characterizing people through objects associated with them, see Peter Green, "Du Côté de Chez Waugh," *Review of English Literature* 2 (Apr. 1961): 89-100.

26. Sykes, *Evelyn Waugh*, 138.

27. For an interpretation of Tony's and Messinger's search for the City as a burlesque of Percivale's and Galahad's quest for the Grail in Tennyson's *Idylls*, see Wasson, "A Handful of Dust," 331-36.

Chapter 6: *Scoop*

1. Waugh, *Remote People*, 29.

2. For an exaggeration of the fairy-tale element, see Alain Blayac, "Technique and Meaning in *Scoop*: Is *Scoop* a Modern Fairy-Tale?" *Evelyn Waugh Newsletter* 6 (Winter 1972): 1-8.

3. Waugh, "An Act of Homage and Reparation to P. G. Wodehouse," *Sunday Times*, 16 July 1961; repr. in *Essays*, 567.

4. For other comments on the Wodehouse influence, see Stopp, *Evelyn Waugh*, 64, 65, 74, 187, 188, 212; and Davis, *Evelyn Waugh, Writer*, 90, 97-98, 104.

5. Waugh, "Act of Homage," in *Essays*, 567.

6. Davis records that in the first draft Waugh attributed to the prime minister's private secretary the blunder of awarding a knighthood to the wrong Boot (*Evelyn Waugh, Writer*, 98-99). The prime minister, who was "nuts on rural England," must have been Stanley Baldwin, whose private secretary, Sir Geoffrey Fry, was Evelyn Gardner's brother-in-law. But in revision Waugh removed that personal dig and laid the blame on the "third and fourth secretaries." For Fry's treatment of Waugh, see Frederick

L. Beaty, "Evelyn Waugh and Lance Sieveking: New Light on Waugh's Relations with the BBC," *Papers on Language and Literature* 25 (1989): 186-200.

7. Eleanor N. Hutchens, *Irony in "Tom Jones"* (University: Univ. of Alabama Pr., 1965), 46-47.

8. Waugh, *Scoop* (1938; reprint, Boston: Little, 1977), 18. Subsequent quotations from this edition of the novel are cited parenthetically in the text.

9. Both Heath and Garnett comment on John and William Boot as embodiments of diverse aspects of Waugh's personality. See Heath, *Picturesque Prison*, 135-36, and Garnett, *From Grimes to Brideshead*, 122-23.

10. For commentary on self-irony, see Muecke, *Compass of Irony*, 20, 87-91.

11. Heath asserts that *Scoop* has two fortune figures—Julia Stitch and Mr. Baldwin (*Picturesque Prison*, 134).

12. In the manuscript version Mrs. Stitch, doubting her success with Copper, advises John Boot to take holy orders because she has influence with the archbishop. See Jeffrey Heath, "Waugh's *Scoop* in Manuscript," *Evelyn Waugh Newsletter* 11 (Autumn 1977): 9-11.

13. Quoted by Heath, *Picturesque Prison*, 126.

14. Hutchens defines connotative irony as "the use of a word with its literal meaning intact but its connotations . . . stripped away" (*Irony in "Tom Jones"*, 104).

15. Julian Jebb, "Evelyn Waugh: An Interview," *Paris Review* 8 (Summer-Fall 1963): 79. For an illuminating analysis of how Waugh used style to convey meaning, see D. Paul Farr, "The Novelist's Coup: Style as Satiric Norm in *Scoop*," *Connecticut Review* 8 (Apr. 1975): 42-54.

16. See Heath, "Waugh's *Scoop* in Manuscript," 10.

17. N. D. Knox, "Irony," in *Dictionary of the History of Ideas* 2:627; cited in Muecke, *Irony and the Ironic* (London: Methuen, 1982), 51.

Chapter 7: *Work Suspended*

1. Waugh, *Work Suspended: Two Chapters of an Unfinished Novel* (London: Chapman, 1942), 5. Subsequent quotations from this edition of the novel are cited parenthetically in the text.

2. Stannard has asserted that "the paradox at the heart of [Waugh's] 'climacteric'" was "the problem of describing the subjective objectively" ("*Work Suspended*: Waugh's Climacteric," *Essays in Criticism* 28 [1978]: 313). That problem appears to have been with Waugh from the start, for Davis has maintained that *The Balance* "shows Waugh attempting . . . to discover a technique by which he could present as objectively as possible his own subjective reactions and thus transmute autobiography into fiction" ("Evelyn Waugh's Early Work," 97).

3. Davis has interpreted Plant's views on objective characterization as an endorsement of Waugh's practice not only in the early novels but in his later critical observations on "flat" characters ("Evelyn Waugh on the Art of Fiction," 244-45; "Textual Problems in the Novels of Evelyn Waugh," *Papers of the Bibliographical Society of America* 62 [1968]: 261-62). Heath believes, to the contrary, that Waugh is attacking Plant's views (*Picturesque Prison*, 141-42).

4. Waugh deleted the foregoing critical comments on style and technique from the 1948 revision.

5. Waugh, *Work Suspended* (1942), 61-63. Waugh deleted this conversation when he revised the fragmentary novel for 1948 publication.

6. Stopp has elaborated on the peculiar relationship between Plant and Atwater, as well as the parallels between Plant and the ape (*Evelyn Waugh*, 101-7). See also Heath, *Picturesque Prison*, 144-46.

7. Stannard, "Work Suspended," 319.

8. Waugh, "Fan-Fare," in *Essays*, 302.

9. Evelyn Waugh to Arthur Waugh, 5 Dec. 1941, *Letters*, 158.

Chapter 8: *Brideshead Revisited*

1. Waugh, "Fan-Fare," in *Essays*, 302.

2. Typescript dated 18 Feb. 1947 in Waugh manuscripts, University of Texas Humanities Research Center. Waugh's preface to the revised 1960 edition of *Brideshead* also defines the novel's principal theme as "the operation of divine grace." See Evelyn Waugh, *Brideshead Revisited* (London: Chapman, 1960), 9.

3. Repr. in Stannard, *Evelyn Waugh: Critical Heritage*, 236.

4. Dustjacket "Warning," 1945; repr. in Stannard, *Evelyn Waugh: Critical Heritage*, 236.

5. In a letter of 7 Jan. 1945 to Nancy Mitford, Waugh called Charles "dim" and "a bad painter" (*Letters*, 196). Although Waugh was averse to permitting Little, Brown to change the novel's title for American publication, his suggested alternative, "A Household of the Faith," is further evidence of the book's orientation. See Waugh's letter of 30 Sept. 1944 to A. D. Peters (*Letters*, 188-89).

6. For Edmund Wilson's scathing attack on *Brideshead*, see "Splendors and Miseries of Evelyn Waugh," *New Yorker* 21 (5 Jan. 1946): 71-74.

7. Waugh, *Brideshead Revisited: The Sacred and Profane Memories of Captain Charles Ryder* (1945; reprint, Boston: Little, 1979), 242-43. Subsequent quotations from this edition of the novel are cited parenthetically in the text. The original 1945 version rather than the 1960 revision is used in this analysis since it enunciates the ironic conflicts more distinctly.

8. For a résumé of Waugh's opinions on modernist writers, see Davis, "Evelyn Waugh on the Art of Fiction," 243-52.

9. Sykes suggests that Waugh's admiration for aristocratic society in *Brideshead* is rescued from the charge of snobbishness by being couched in irony; by encouraging us to laugh at the foibles of the "beautiful people," Waugh allegedly frees us to indulge our repressed admiration for them (*Evelyn Waugh*, 245).

10. For discussion of narrative point of view in terms of a "now I," a "then I," and an "intermediate I," see Cook, *Masks, Modes, and Morals*, 193-235.

11. Oswald Spengler pronounced baroque architecture, in its efforts to suggest the metaphysical and strive for the infinite, to be the true heir of the Gothic.

12. For Waugh's feelings on Hollywood's soulless, money-grubbing debasement of art, see his essay "Why Hollywood Is a Term of Disparagement," *Daily Telegraph and Morning Post*, 30 Apr. and 1 May 1947; repr. in *Essays*, 325-31.

13. Davis has asserted that Waugh deleted from his "manuscript the sole implication of the fact" that Charles "is already Catholic" (*Evelyn Waugh, Writer*, 185). For opinions on what can be deduced from the printed text about Ryder's conversion, see articles by John W. Osborne, Donald Greene, and John W. Mahon in the *Evelyn Waugh Newsletter* 22 (Winter 1988): 4-7; 23 (Spring 1989): 3-7; 23 (Winter 1989): 1-3; 24 (Autumn 1990): 3-4; 25 (Spring 1991): 2-3.

14. The Baron de Charlus is the degenerate uncle of Saint-Loup in Proust's *À la Recherche du Temps Perdu*.

15. See Davis, *Evelyn Waugh, Writer*, 126-35.

16. Waugh to A. D. Peters, 20 May 1944, *Letters*, 185.

17. Nancy Mitford to Waugh, *Letters*, 196.

18. Waugh to Nancy Mitford, 7 Jan. 1945, *Letters*, 196.

19. Julia's marriage to Rex, a divorced man, was not ecclesiastically valid. What makes it impossible for her to remain in the Church if she marries Charles is *his* previous marriage.

20. In his essay "Converted to Rome," Waugh asserts: "Civilization . . . has not in itself the power of survival. It came into being through Christianity, and without it has no significance or power to command allegiance" (*Daily Express*, 20 Oct. 1930; repr. in *Essays*, 104).

21. Waugh diary entry, 21 May 1944, *Diaries*, 566.

Chapter 9: *The Loved One*

1. Waugh, "Fan-Fare," in *Essays*, 302.

2. In a letter of 9 July 1947 to Peters, Waugh asserted: "[*The Loved One*] comes rather poorly after an article in *Life* in which I declared that I would only write religious books in future" (*Letters*, 255).

3. Sykes, *Evelyn Waugh*, 310.

196 · Notes to Pages 168–82

4. Waugh, *Brideshead* (1979), 7.

5. Waugh, "Half in Love with Easeful Death," *Tablet*, 18 Oct. 1947; repr. in *Essays*, 331. A modified form of this essay, entitled "Death in Hollywood," first appeared in *Life*, 29 Sept. 1947.

6. Waugh, *The Loved One: An Anglo-American Tragedy* (1948; reprint, Boston: Little, 1977), 111. Subsequent quotations from this edition of the novel are cited parenthetically in the text.

7. Waugh, "Half in Love with Easeful Death," in *Essays*, 335.

8. Waugh to Cyril Connolly, 2 Jan. 1948, *Letters*, 265-66. Connolly subsequently incorporated Waugh's comments in his introduction to *The Loved One* in the February 1948 issue of *Horizon*.

9. Waugh, "The Man Hollywood Hates," *Evening Standard*, 4 Nov. 1947; repr. in *Essays*, 338.

10. See Malcolm Bradbury, "America and the Comic Vision," in *Evelyn Waugh and His World*, ed. David Pryce-Jones (Boston: Little, 1973), 165-82; and Carens, *Satiric Art*, 20-22. Sykes calls Dennis "loathsome" (*Evelyn Waugh*, 309).

11. See Joseph F. Vogel, "Waugh's *The Loved One*: The Artist in a Phony World," *Evelyn Waugh Newsletter* 10 (Autumn 1976): 1-4; Robert Barnard, "What the Whispering Glades Whispered: Dennis Barlow's Quest in *The Loved One*," *English Studies* 60 (1979): 176-82; and Heath, *Picturesque Prison*, 188-97.

12. In his essay "Why Hollywood Is a Term of Disparagement" (1947), Waugh asserts, with respect to film censorship, that "Americans are devoted to a conception of innocence which has little relation to life" (*Essays*, 330).

13. Waugh, "The American Epoch in the Catholic Church," *Life*, 19 Sept. 1949; *Month*, Nov. 1949; repr. in *Essays*, 377-88.

14. Waugh to A. D. Peters, 6 Mar. 1947, and Waugh to Cyril Connolly, 2 Jan. 1948, *Letters*, 247, 265. See also Sykes, *Evelyn Waugh*, 306.

Selected Bibliography

Acton, Harold. *More Memoirs of an Aesthete*. London: Methuen, 1970.

Barnard, Robert. "What the Whispering Glades Whispered: Dennis Barlow's Quest in *The Loved One*." *English Studies* 60 (1979): 176-82.

Bergson, Henri. *Laughter*. Translated by Cloudesley Brereton and Fred Rothwell. New York: Macmillan, 1914.

Blayac, Alain. "Technique and Meaning in *Scoop*: Is *Scoop* a Modern Fairy-Tale?". *Evelyn Waugh Newsletter* 6 (Winter 1972): 1-8.

Booth, Wayne C. *A Rhetoric of Irony*. Chicago: Univ. of Chicago Pr., 1974.

Bradbury, Malcolm. "America and the Comic Vision." In *Evelyn Waugh and His World*, edited by David Pryce-Jones, 165-82. Boston: Little, 1973.

_____. *Evelyn Waugh*. Edinburgh: Oliver, 1964.

Carens, James F., ed. *Critical Essays on Evelyn Waugh*. Boston: Hall, 1987.

_____. *The Satiric Art of Evelyn Waugh*. Seattle: Univ. of Washington Pr., 1966.

Carew, Dudley. *A Fragment of Friendship*. London: Everest, 1974.

Carpenter, Humphrey. *The Brideshead Generation: Evelyn Waugh and His Friends*. London: Weidenfeld, 1989.

Cook, William J., Jr. *Masks, Modes, and Morals: The Art of Evelyn Waugh*. Rutherford, N.J.: Fairleigh Dickinson Univ. Pr., 1971.

Crabbe, Katharyn W. *Evelyn Waugh*. New York: Continuum, 1988.

Davis, Robert Murray, Paul A. Doyle, Donat Gallagher, Charles E. Linck, and Winnifred M. Bogaards, eds. *A Bibliography of Evelyn Waugh*. Troy, N.Y.: Whitston Pub., 1986.

Davis, Robert Murray. *Evelyn Waugh and the Forms of His Time*. Washington, D.C.: Catholic Univ. of America Pr., 1989.

_____. "Evelyn Waugh on the Art of Fiction." *Papers on Language and Literature* 2 (1966): 243-52.

_____. "Evelyn Waugh's Early Work: The Formation of a Method." *Texas Studies in Literature and Language* 7 (1965): 97-108.

_____. *Evelyn Waugh, Writer*. Norman, Okla.: Pilgrim, 1981.

_____. "The Mind and Art of Evelyn Waugh." *Papers on Language and Literature* 3 (1967): 270-87.

_____. "Textual Problems in the Novels of Evelyn Waugh." *Papers of the Bibliographical Society of America* 62 (1968): 259-63.

De Vitis, A. A. *Roman Holiday: The Catholic Novels of Evelyn Waugh.* New York: Bookman, 1956.

Doyle, Paul A. *Evelyn Waugh: A Critical Essay.* Grand Rapids, Mich.: Eerdmans, 1969.

_____. *A Reader's Companion to the Novels and Short Stories of Evelyn Waugh.* Norman, Okla.: Pilgrim, 1988.

Eliot, T. S. *Selected Essays 1917-1932.* New York: Harcourt, 1932.

Farr, D. Paul. "The Novelist's Coup: Style as Satiric Norm in *Scoop.*" *Connecticut Review* 8 (Apr. 1975): 42-54.

Firbank, Ronald. *The Complete Ronald Firbank.* London: Duckworth, 1961.

Frye, Northrop. *Anatomy of Criticism: Four Essays.* Princeton: Princeton Univ. Pr., 1957.

Furst, Lilian R. *Fictions of Romantic Irony.* Cambridge: Harvard Univ. Pr., 1984.

Fussell, Paul. *Abroad: British Literary Traveling Between the Wars.* New York: Oxford Univ. Pr., 1980.

Garnett, Robert R. *From Grimes to Brideshead: The Early Novels of Evelyn Waugh.* Lewisburg, Pa.: Bucknell Univ. Pr., 1990.

Gorra, Michael. *The English Novel at Mid-Century.* New York: St. Martin, 1990.

Green, Martin B. *Children of the Sun: A Narrative of "Decadence" in England after 1918.* New York: Basic, 1976.

Green, Peter. "Du Côté de Chez Waugh." *Review of English Literature* 2 (Apr. 1961): 89-100.

Greene, Donald. "A Partiality for Lords: Evelyn Waugh and Snobbery." *American Scholar* 58 (1989): 444-59.

Gurewitch, Morton L. "European Romantic Irony." Ph.D. diss., University of Michigan, 1957.

Hall, James. *The Tragic Comedians: Seven Modern British Novelists.* Bloomington: Indiana Univ. Pr., 1963.

Heath, Jeffrey. *The Picturesque Prison: Evelyn Waugh and His Writing.* Kingston: McGill-Queen's Univ. Pr., 1982.

_____. "Waugh's *Scoop* in Manuscript." *Evelyn Waugh Newsletter* 11 (Autumn 1977): 9-11.

Hollis, Christopher. *Evelyn Waugh.* London: Longmans, 1954.

_____. *Oxford in the Twenties: Recollections of Five Friends.* London: Heinemann, 1976.

_____. *The Oxford Union.* London: Evans, 1965.

Hutchens, Eleanor N. *Irony in "Tom Jones".* University: Univ. of Alabama Pr., 1965.

Jebb, Julian. "Evelyn Waugh: An Interview." *Paris Review* 8 (Summer-Fall 1963): 73-85.

Kermode, Frank. "Mr. Waugh's Cities." *Encounter* 15 (Nov. 1960): 63-66, 68-70.

Kernan, Alvin B. "The Wall and the Jungle: The Early Novels of Evelyn Waugh." *Yale Review* 53 (1963-64): 199-220.

Knox, Norman D. "Irony." In *Dictionary of the History of Ideas*, edited by Philip P. Wiener, 2:626-34. New York: Scribner, 1973-74.

Knox, Ronald A. *Essays in Satire*. London: Sheed, 1928.

Lane, Calvin W. *Evelyn Waugh*. Boston: Twayne, 1981.

Linck, Charles E., Jr., and Robert M. Davis. "The Bright Young People in *Vile Bodies*." *Papers on Language and Literature* 5 (1969): 80-90.

Littlewood, Ian. *The Writings of Evelyn Waugh*. Totowa, N.J.: Barnes, 1983.

Lodge, David. *Evelyn Waugh*. New York: Columbia Univ. Pr., 1971.

Machon, Daniel James. "The Failure of the Ironic Mask: Irony as Vision and Technique in the Early Novels of Evelyn Waugh." Ph.D. diss., Temple University, 1975.

McCartney, George. *Confused Roaring: Evelyn Waugh and the Modernist Tradition*. Bloomington: Indiana Univ. Pr., 1987.

McDonnell, Jacqueline. *Evelyn Waugh*. New York: St. Martin, 1988.

_____. *Waugh on Women*. New York: St. Martin, 1985.

Meckier, Jerome. "Cycle, Symbol, and Parody in Evelyn Waugh's *Decline and Fall*." *Contemporary Literature* 20 (1979): 51-75.

_____. "Why the Man Who Liked Dickens Reads Dickens Instead of Conrad: Waugh's *A Handful of Dust*." *Novel* 13 (1979-80): 171-87.

Mellor, Anne K. *English Romantic Irony*. Cambridge: Harvard Univ. Pr., 1980.

Morris, Margaret and D. J. Dooley. *Evelyn Waugh: A Reference Guide*. Boston: Hall, 1984.

Muecke, Douglas C. *The Compass of Irony*. London: Methuen, 1969.

_____. *Irony*. London: Methuen, 1970.

_____. *Irony and the Ironic*. London: Methuen, 1982.

Nichols, James W. "Romantic *and* Realistic: The Tone of Evelyn Waugh's Early Novels." *College English* 24 (1962-63): 46-56.

O'Brien, Conor Cruise [Donat O'Donnell]. "The Pieties of Evelyn Waugh." In *Maria Cross*, 119-34. New York: Oxford Univ. Pr., 1952.

Phillips, Gene D. *Evelyn Waugh's Officers, Gentlemen, and Rogues: The Fact behind His Fiction*. Chicago: Nelson-Hall, 1975.

Powell, Anthony. *Messengers of Day*. London: Heinemann, 1978.

Pryce-Jones, Alan. "Escape from Golders Green." In *Evelyn Waugh and His World*, edited by David Pryce-Jones, 7-14. Boston: Little, 1973.

Pryce-Jones, David, ed. *Evelyn Waugh and His World*. Boston: Little, 1973.

Schlüter, Kurt. *Kuriose Welt im modernen englischen Roman*. Berlin: Schmidt, 1969.

Spengler, Oswald. *The Decline of the West*. Translated by Charles Francis Atkinson. 2 vols. New York: Knopf, 1926-29.

Sperry, Stuart M. "Toward a Definition of Romantic Irony in English Literature." In *Romantic and Modern: Revaluations of a Literary Tradition,* edited by George Bornstein, 3-28. Pittsburgh: Univ. of Pittsburgh Pr., 1977.

Stannard, Martin, ed. *Evelyn Waugh: The Critical Heritage.* London: Routledge, 1984.

⸻. *Evelyn Waugh: The Early Years 1903-1939.* London: Dent, 1986.

⸻. "*Work Suspended:* Waugh's Climacteric." *Essays in Criticism* 28 (1978): 302-20.

Stopp, Frederick J. *Evelyn Waugh: Portrait of an Artist.* London: Chapman, 1958.

Sykes, Christopher. *Evelyn Waugh: A Biography.* Boston: Little, 1975.

Vogel, Joseph F. "Waugh's *The Loved One:* The Artist in a Phony World." *Evelyn Waugh Newsletter* 10 (Autumn 1976): 1-4.

Wasson, Richard. "*A Handful of Dust:* Critique of Victorianism." *Modern Fiction Studies* 7 (1961-62): 327-37.

Waugh, Alec. *My Brother Evelyn & Other Profiles.* London: Cassell, 1967.

Waugh, Evelyn. "Alternative Ending." In *A Handful of Dust,* 255-65. London: Chapman, 1964.

⸻. *Black Mischief.* 1932. Reprint. Boston: Little, 1977.

⸻. *Brideshead Revisited: The Sacred and Profane Memories of Captain Charles Ryder.* 1945. Reprint. Boston: Little, 1979.

⸻. *Decline and Fall.* 1928. Reprint. Boston: Little, 1977.

⸻. *The Diaries of Evelyn Waugh.* Edited by Michael Davie. Boston: Little, 1976.

⸻. *The Essays, Articles and Reviews of Evelyn Waugh.* Edited by Donat Gallagher. London: Methuen, 1983.

⸻. *Evelyn Waugh, Apprentice: The Early Writings, 1910-1927.* Edited by Robert Murray Davis. Norman, Okla.: Pilgrim, 1985.

⸻. *A Handful of Dust.* 1934. Reprint. Boston: Little, 1977.

⸻. *Helena.* London: Chapman, 1950.

⸻. *The Letters of Evelyn Waugh.* Edited by Mark Amory. New Haven: Ticknor, 1980.

⸻. *A Little Learning.* London: Methuen, 1964.

⸻. *Love Among the Ruins: A Romance of the Near Future.* London: Chapman, 1953.

⸻. *The Loved One: An Anglo-American Tragedy.* 1948. Reprint. Boston: Little, 1977.

⸻. *Ninety-Two Days.* London: Duckworth, 1934.

⸻. *The Ordeal of Gilbert Pinfold.* Boston: Little, 1957.

⸻. *Put Out More Flags.* London: Chapman, 1942.

⸻. *Remote People.* London: Duckworth, 1931.

⸻. *Robbery Under Law: The Mexican Object-Lesson.* London: Chapman, 1939.

_____. *Rossetti: His Life and Works*. London: Duckworth, 1928.

_____. "Scenes of Clerical Life." *Commonweal* 63 (30 Mar. 1956): 667.

_____. *Scoop*. 1938. Reprint. Boston: Little, 1977.

_____. *Tourist in Africa*. Boston: Little, 1960.

_____. *Vile Bodies*. 1930. Reprint. Boston: Little, 1977.

_____. *Waugh in Abyssinia*. London: Longmans, 1936.

_____. *Work Suspended: Two Chapters of an Unfinished Novel*. London: Chapman, 1942.

Wilson, Edmund. "Splendors and Miseries of Evelyn Waugh." *New Yorker* 21 (5 Jan. 1946): 71-74.

Index

Proclaimed "the greatest novelist" of his generation by one of its foremost historians, Evelyn Waugh (1903-1966) portrays the intricacies of human life on a broad and colorful canvas. His many famous novels—as well as his lesser-known nonfiction writings—continue to attract readers and to challenge critics. The heart of their appeal, Beaty shows, is Waugh's rich and varied use of irony to explore the texture of society.

This study is the first detailed examination of irony in Waugh's fiction. By delving into eight novels—*Decline and Fall, Vile Bodies, Black Mischief, A Handful of Dust, Scoop, Work Suspended, Brideshead Revisited,* and *The Loved One*—Beaty reveals how irony is applied to theme, plot, and character. He further demonstrates that an understanding of irony not only enhances readers' enjoyment but also is crucial to an appreciation of Waugh's artistry.

Beaty explains that during much of Waugh's literary career the novelist's instinctive way of approaching the vicissitudes of life was predominantly ironic, though his perspective was later modified by religious conviction. Thus irony was interwoven into the fabric of Waugh's writing—both as a world view and as a methodology for presenting ideas, events, and characters. Drawing on definitions of recent ironologists, Beaty illustrates Waugh's numerous literary techniques and offers original insights into their functioning.

The Ironic World of Evelyn Waugh presents a view of Waugh primarily as